STAR WARS™

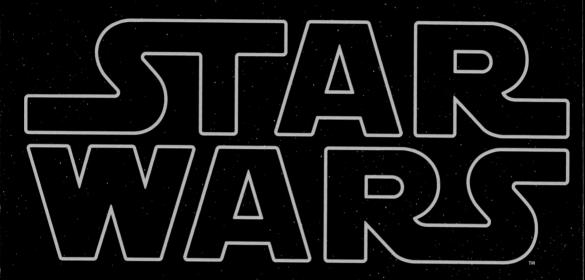

THE ESCAPE

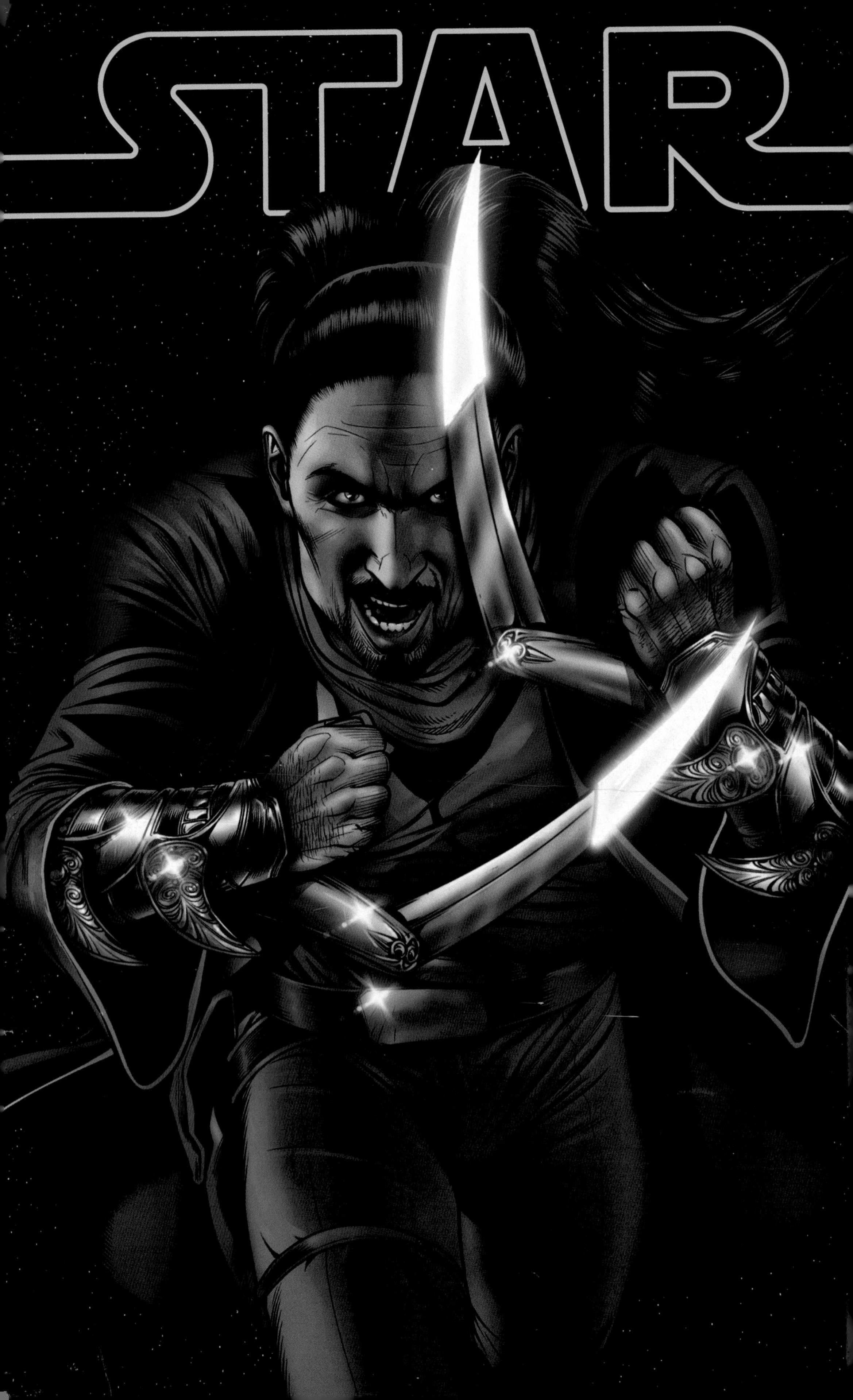
STAR

THE ESCAPE

Writer	**KIERON GILLEN**
Artists	**ANDREA BROCCARDO** (#56, #61) &
	ANGEL UNZUETA (#57-60)
Color Artist	**GURU-eFX**
Letterer	**VC's CLAYTON COWLES**
Cover Art	**JAMAL CAMPBELL**
Assistant Editor	**TOM GRONEMAN**
Editor	**MARK PANICCIA**
Editor in Chief	**C.B. CEBULSKI**
Chief Creative Officer	**JOE QUESADA**
President	**DAN BUCKLEY**

For Lucasfilm:

Senior Editor	**ROBERT SIMPSON**
Executive Editor	**JENNIFER HEDDLE**
Creative Director	**MICHAEL SIGLAIN**
Lucasfilm Story Group	**JAMES WAUGH, LELAND CHEE, MATT MARTIN**

MAY 2019

Collection Editor.	**JENNIFER GRUNWALD**	VP Production & Special Projects	**JEFF YOUNGQUIST**
Assistant Editor	**CAITLIN O'CONNELL**	SVP Print, Sales & Marketing	**DAVID GABRIEL**
Associate Managing Editor	**KATERI WOODY**	Book Designer	**ADAM DEL RE**
Editor, Special Projects	**MARK D. BEAZLEY**		

STAR WARS VOL. 10: THE ESCAPE. Contains material originally published in magazine form as STAR WARS #56-61. First printing 2019. ISBN 978-1-302-91449-3. Published by MARVEL WORLDWIDE, INC., a subsidiary of MARVEL ENTERTAINMENT, LLC. OFFICE OF PUBLICATION: 135 West 50th Street, New York, NY 10020. STAR WARS and related text and illustrations are trademarks and/or copyrights, in the United States and other countries, of Lucasfilm Ltd. and/or its affiliates. © & TM Lucasfilm Ltd. No similarity between any of the names, characters, persons, and/or institutions in this magazine with those of any living or dead person or institution is intended, and any such similarity which may exist is purely coincidental. Marvel and its logos are TM Marvel Characters, Inc. Printed in the U.S.A. DAN BUCKLEY, President, Marvel Entertainment; JOHN NEE, Publisher; JOE QUESADA, Chief Creative Officer; TOM BREVOORT, SVP of Publishing; DAVID BOGART, SVP of Business Affairs & Operations, Publishing & Partnership; DAVID GABRIEL, SVP of Sales & Marketing, Publishing; JEFF YOUNGQUIST, VP of Production & Special Projects; DAN CARR, Executive Director of Publishing Technology; ALEX MORALES, Director of Publishing Operations; DAN EDINGTON, Managing Editor; SUSAN CRESPI, Production Manager; STAN LEE, Chairman Emeritus. For information regarding advertising in Marvel Comics or on Marvel.com, please contact Vit DeBellis, Custom Solutions & Integrated Advertising Manager, at vdebellis@marvel.com. For Marvel subscription inquiries, please call 888-511-5480. **Manufactured between 2/1/2019 and 3/5/2019** by LSC COMMUNICATIONS INC., KENDALLVILLE, IN, USA.

10 9 8 7 6 5 4 3 2 1

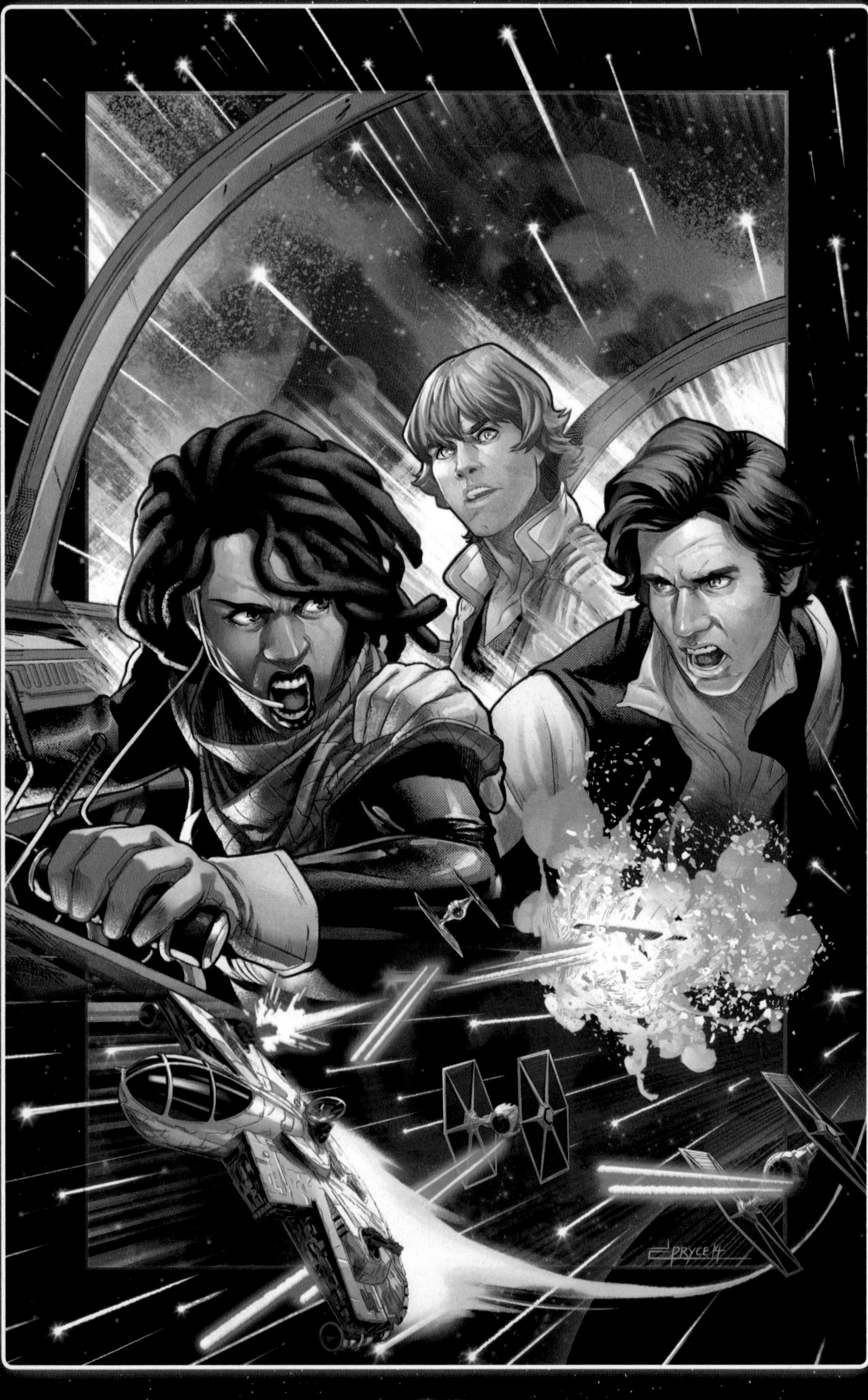

THE ESCAPE

Queen Trios of Shu-Torun's betrayal has left the heroic Rebel Alliance at the mercy of the evil Galactic Empire!

Although many rebels, including Luke Skywalker, Leia Organa and Han Solo, managed to escape Darth Vader's devastating assault, their newly assembled fleet has been all but destroyed.

Now, Mon Mothma has ordered the freedom fighters to disperse and find the right opportunity to regroup so that they can take the fight back to the enemy. But Luke, Han and Leia are now wanted criminals, and no one in the galaxy can stay hidden from the Empire for long. . . .

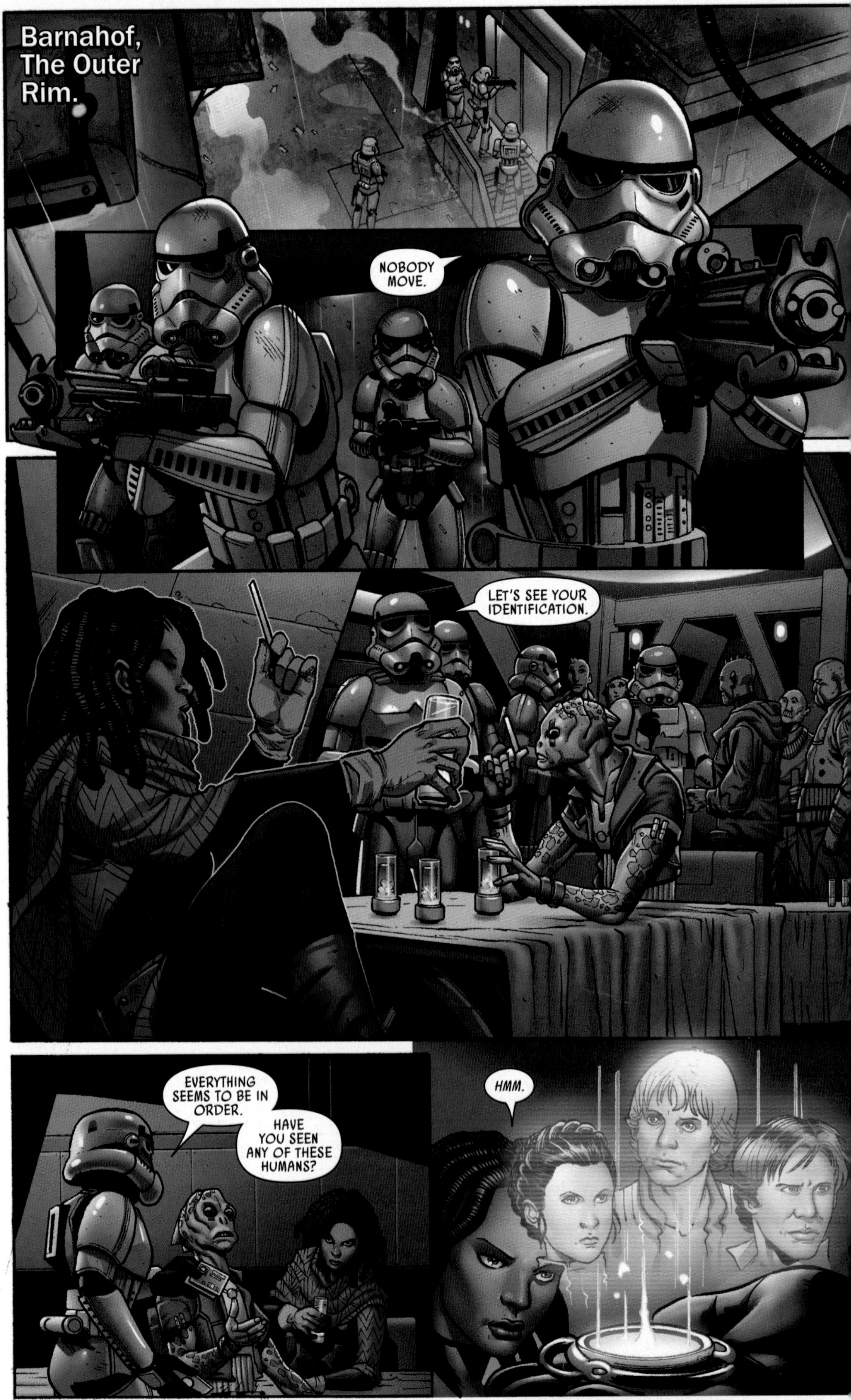
Barnahof, The Outer Rim.
NOBODY MOVE.
LET'S SEE YOUR IDENTIFICATION.
EVERYTHING SEEMS TO BE IN ORDER.
HAVE YOU SEEN ANY OF THESE HUMANS?
HMM.

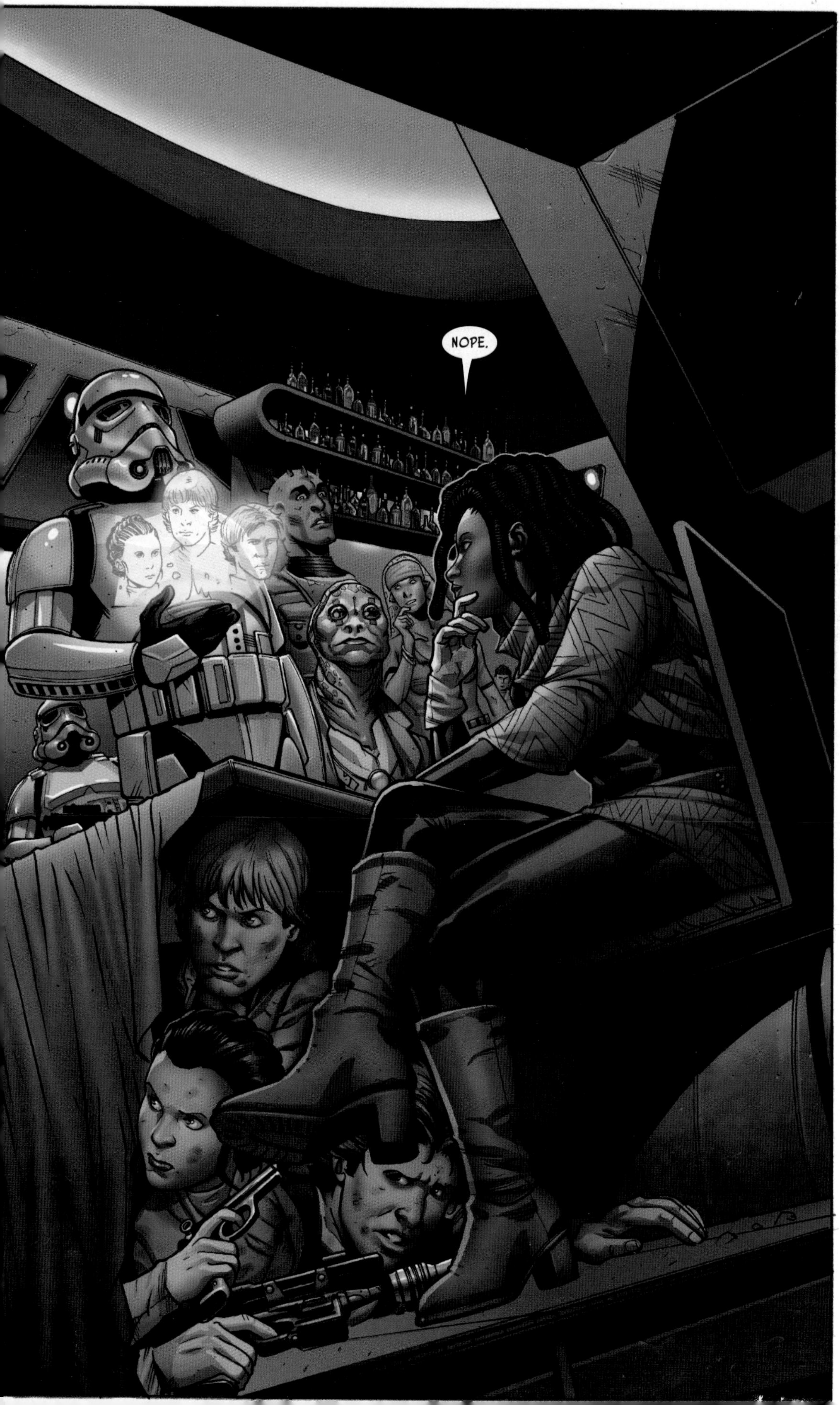
NOPE.

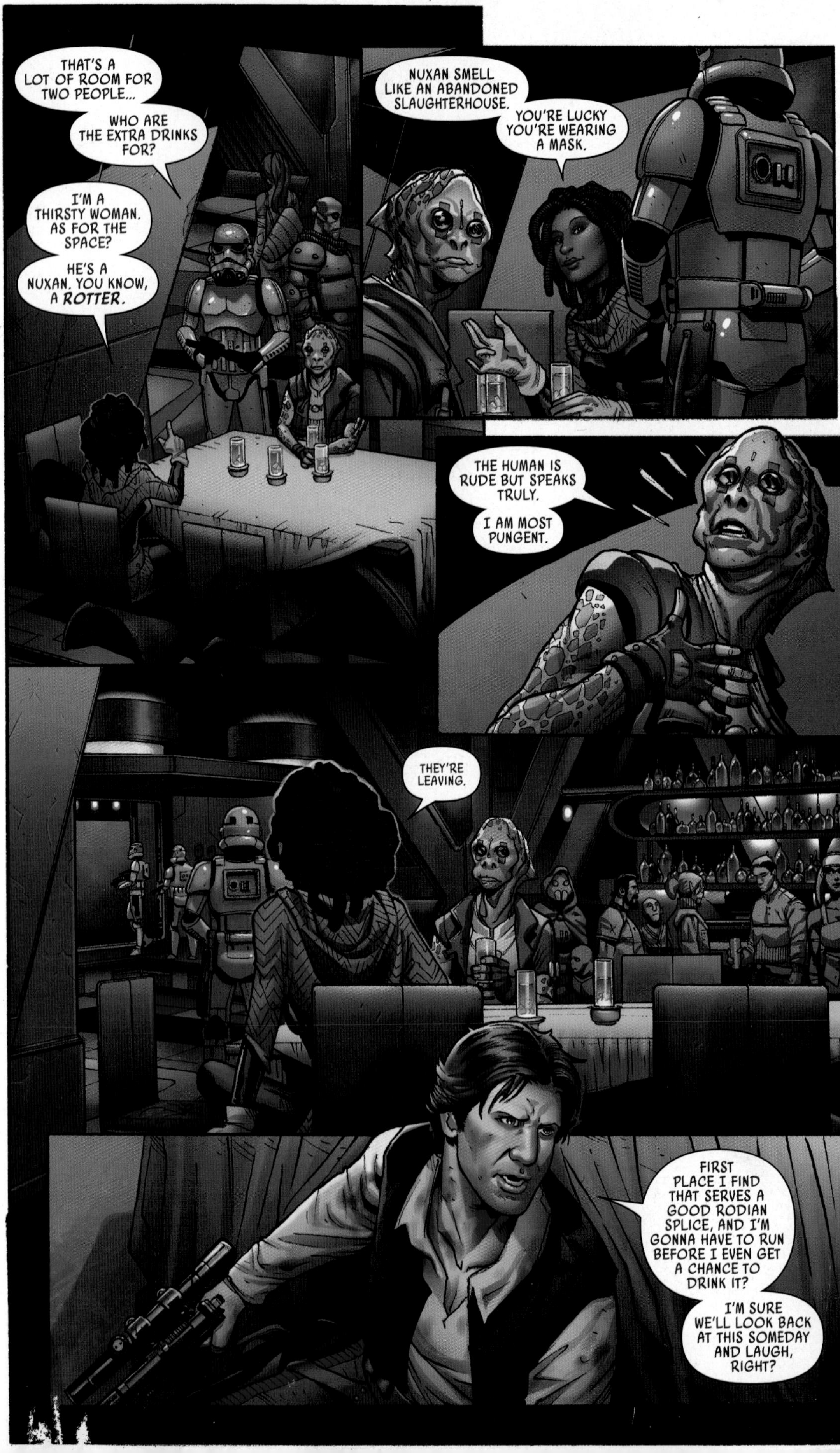
THAT'S A LOT OF ROOM FOR TWO PEOPLE...
WHO ARE THE EXTRA DRINKS FOR?
I'M A THIRSTY WOMAN. AS FOR THE SPACE?
HE'S A NUXAN. YOU KNOW, A ROTTER.
NUXAN SMELL LIKE AN ABANDONED SLAUGHTERHOUSE.
YOU'RE LUCKY YOU'RE WEARING A MASK.
THE HUMAN IS RUDE BUT SPEAKS TRULY.
I AM MOST PUNGENT.
THEY'RE LEAVING.
FIRST PLACE I FIND THAT SERVES A GOOD RODIAN SPLICE, AND I'M GONNA HAVE TO RUN BEFORE I EVEN GET A CHANCE TO DRINK IT?
I'M SURE WE'LL LOOK BACK AT THIS SOMEDAY AND LAUGH, RIGHT?

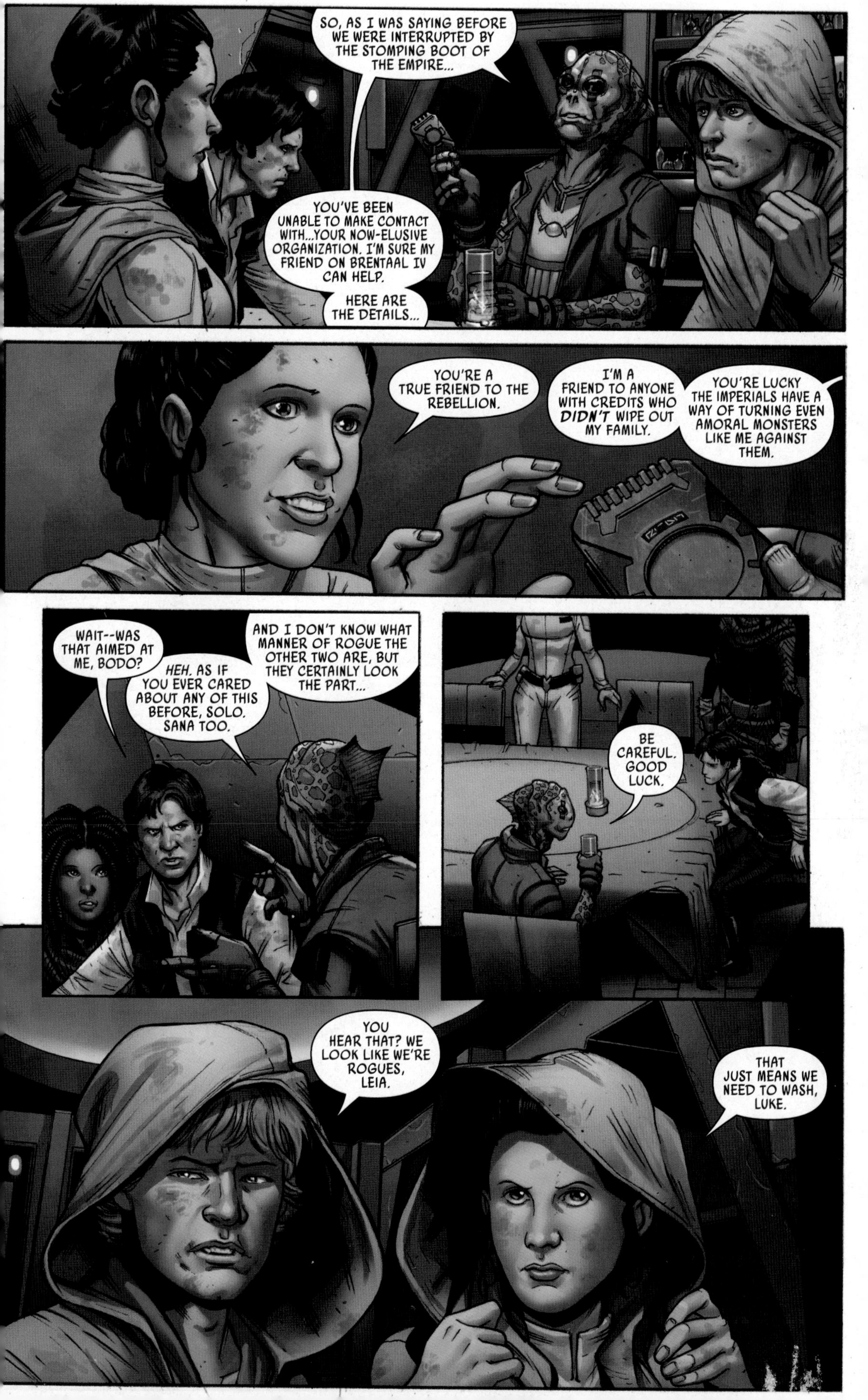
SO, AS I WAS SAYING BEFORE WE WERE INTERRUPTED BY THE STOMPING BOOT OF THE EMPIRE...
YOU'VE BEEN UNABLE TO MAKE CONTACT WITH...YOUR NOW-ELUSIVE ORGANIZATION. I'M SURE MY FRIEND ON BRENTAAL IV CAN HELP.
HERE ARE THE DETAILS...
YOU'RE A TRUE FRIEND TO THE REBELLION.
I'M A FRIEND TO ANYONE WITH CREDITS WHO *DIDN'T* WIPE OUT MY FAMILY.
YOU'RE LUCKY THE IMPERIALS HAVE A WAY OF TURNING EVEN AMORAL MONSTERS LIKE ME AGAINST THEM.
WAIT--WAS THAT AIMED AT ME, BODO?
HEH. AS IF YOU EVER CARED ABOUT ANY OF THIS BEFORE, SOLO. SANA TOO.
AND I DON'T KNOW WHAT MANNER OF ROGUE THE OTHER TWO ARE, BUT THEY CERTAINLY LOOK THE PART...
BE CAREFUL. GOOD LUCK.
YOU HEAR THAT? WE LOOK LIKE WE'RE ROGUES, LEIA.
THAT JUST MEANS WE NEED TO WASH, LUKE.

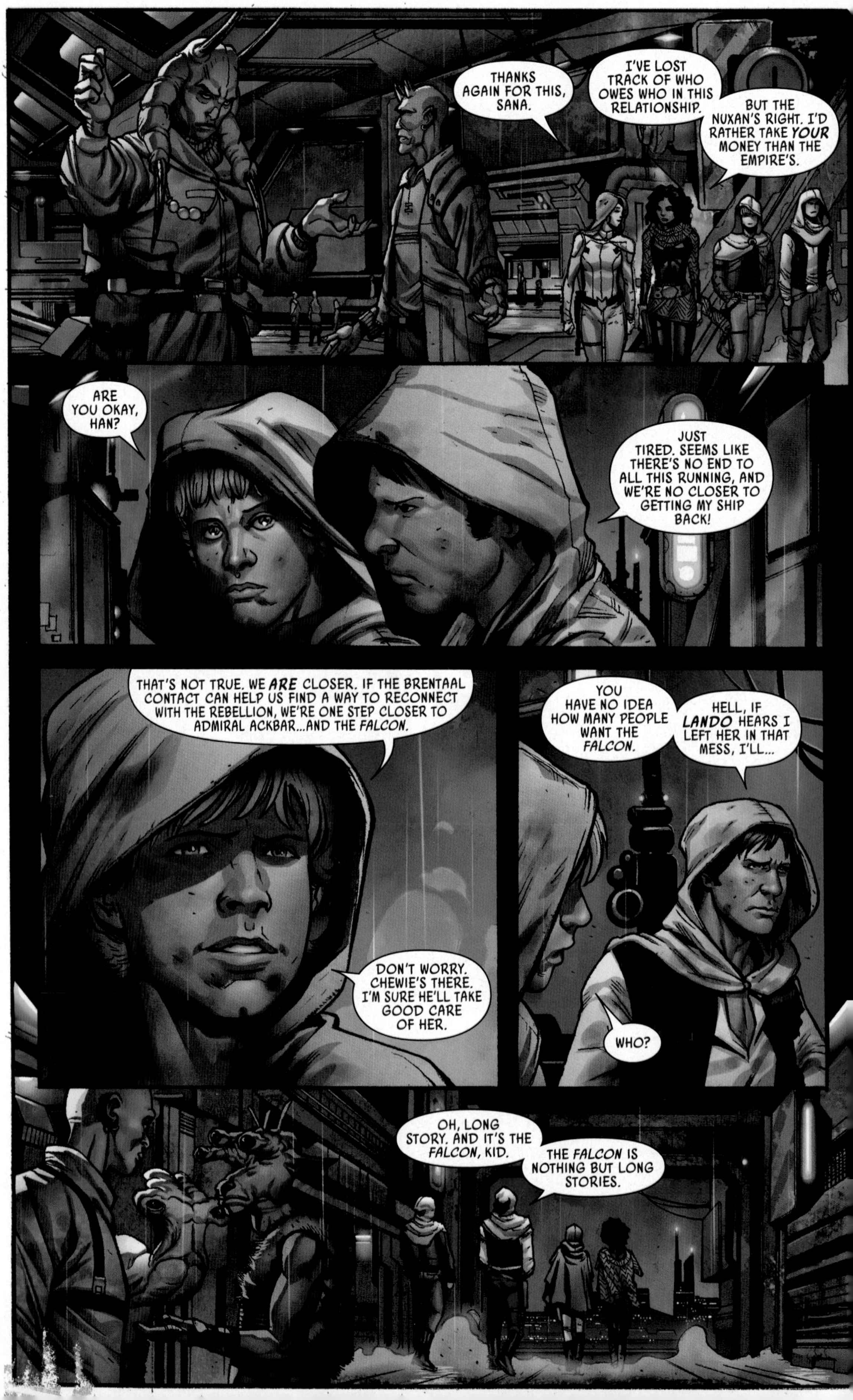
THANKS AGAIN FOR THIS, SANA.
I'VE LOST TRACK OF WHO OWES WHO IN THIS RELATIONSHIP.
BUT THE NUXAN'S RIGHT. I'D RATHER TAKE *YOUR* MONEY THAN THE EMPIRE'S.
ARE YOU OKAY, HAN?
JUST TIRED. SEEMS LIKE THERE'S NO END TO ALL THIS RUNNING, AND WE'RE NO CLOSER TO GETTING MY SHIP BACK!
THAT'S NOT TRUE. WE *ARE* CLOSER. IF THE BRENTAAL CONTACT CAN HELP US FIND A WAY TO RECONNECT WITH THE REBELLION, WE'RE ONE STEP CLOSER TO ADMIRAL ACKBAR...AND THE *FALCON*.
YOU HAVE NO IDEA HOW MANY PEOPLE WANT THE *FALCON*.
HELL, IF *LANDO* HEARS I LEFT HER IN THAT MESS, I'LL...
DON'T WORRY. CHEWIE'S THERE. I'M SURE HE'LL TAKE GOOD CARE OF HER.
WHO?
OH, LONG STORY. AND IT'S THE *FALCON*, KID.
THE *FALCON* IS NOTHING BUT LONG STORIES.

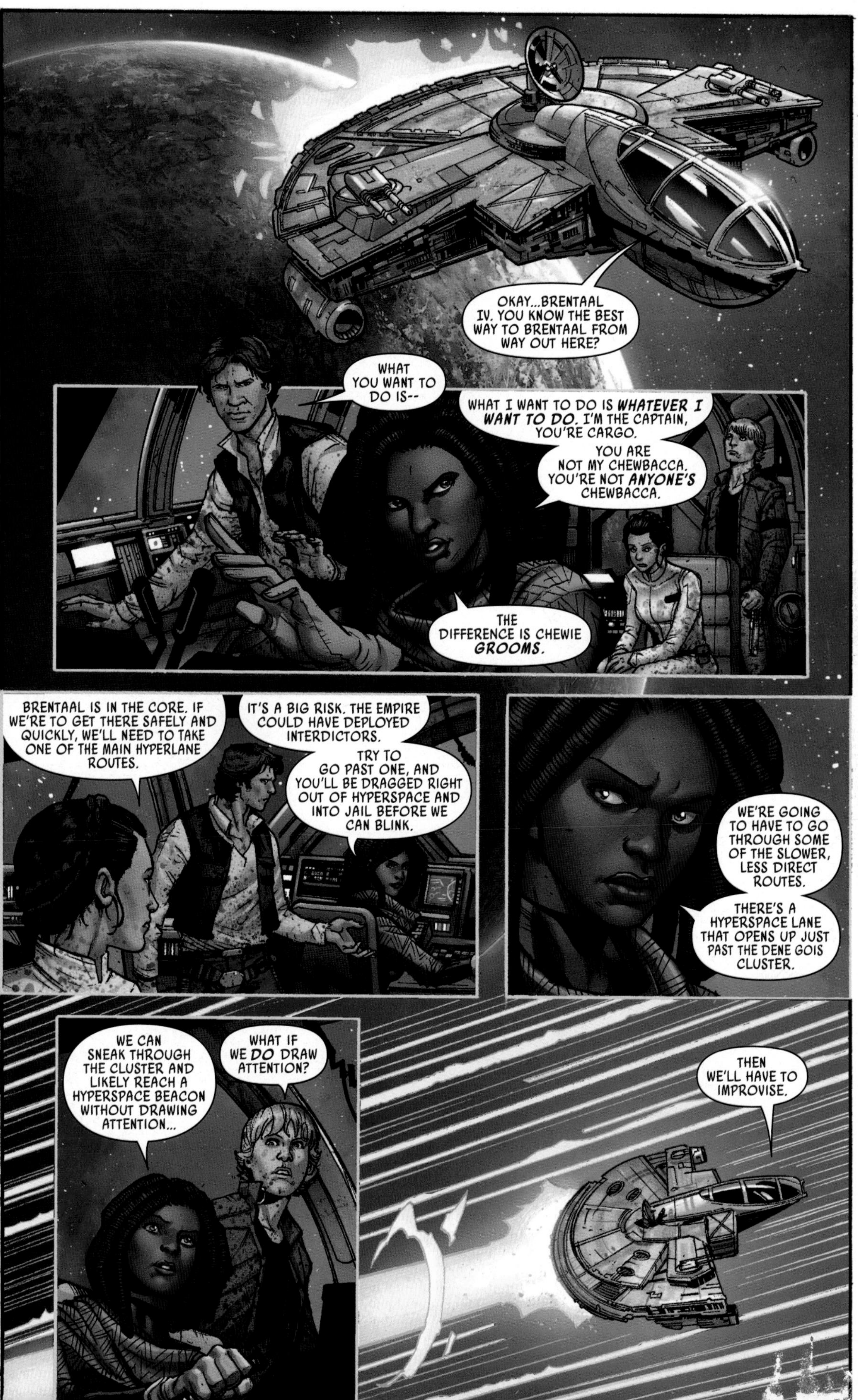
OKAY...BRENTAAL IV. YOU KNOW THE BEST WAY TO BRENTAAL FROM WAY OUT HERE?
WHAT YOU WANT TO DO IS--
WHAT I WANT TO DO IS *WHATEVER I WANT TO DO.* I'M THE CAPTAIN, YOU'RE CARGO.
YOU ARE NOT MY CHEWBACCA. YOU'RE NOT *ANYONE'S* CHEWBACCA.
THE DIFFERENCE IS CHEWIE ***GROOMS.***
BRENTAAL IS IN THE CORE. IF WE'RE TO GET THERE SAFELY AND QUICKLY, WE'LL NEED TO TAKE ONE OF THE MAIN HYPERLANE ROUTES.
IT'S A BIG RISK. THE EMPIRE COULD HAVE DEPLOYED INTERDICTORS.
TRY TO GO PAST ONE, AND YOU'LL BE DRAGGED RIGHT OUT OF HYPERSPACE AND INTO JAIL BEFORE WE CAN BLINK.
WE'RE GOING TO HAVE TO GO THROUGH SOME OF THE SLOWER, LESS DIRECT ROUTES.
THERE'S A HYPERSPACE LANE THAT OPENS UP JUST PAST THE DENE GOIS CLUSTER.
WE CAN SNEAK THROUGH THE CLUSTER AND LIKELY REACH A HYPERSPACE BEACON WITHOUT DRAWING ATTENTION...
WHAT IF WE *DO* DRAW ATTENTION?
THEN WE'LL HAVE TO IMPROVISE.

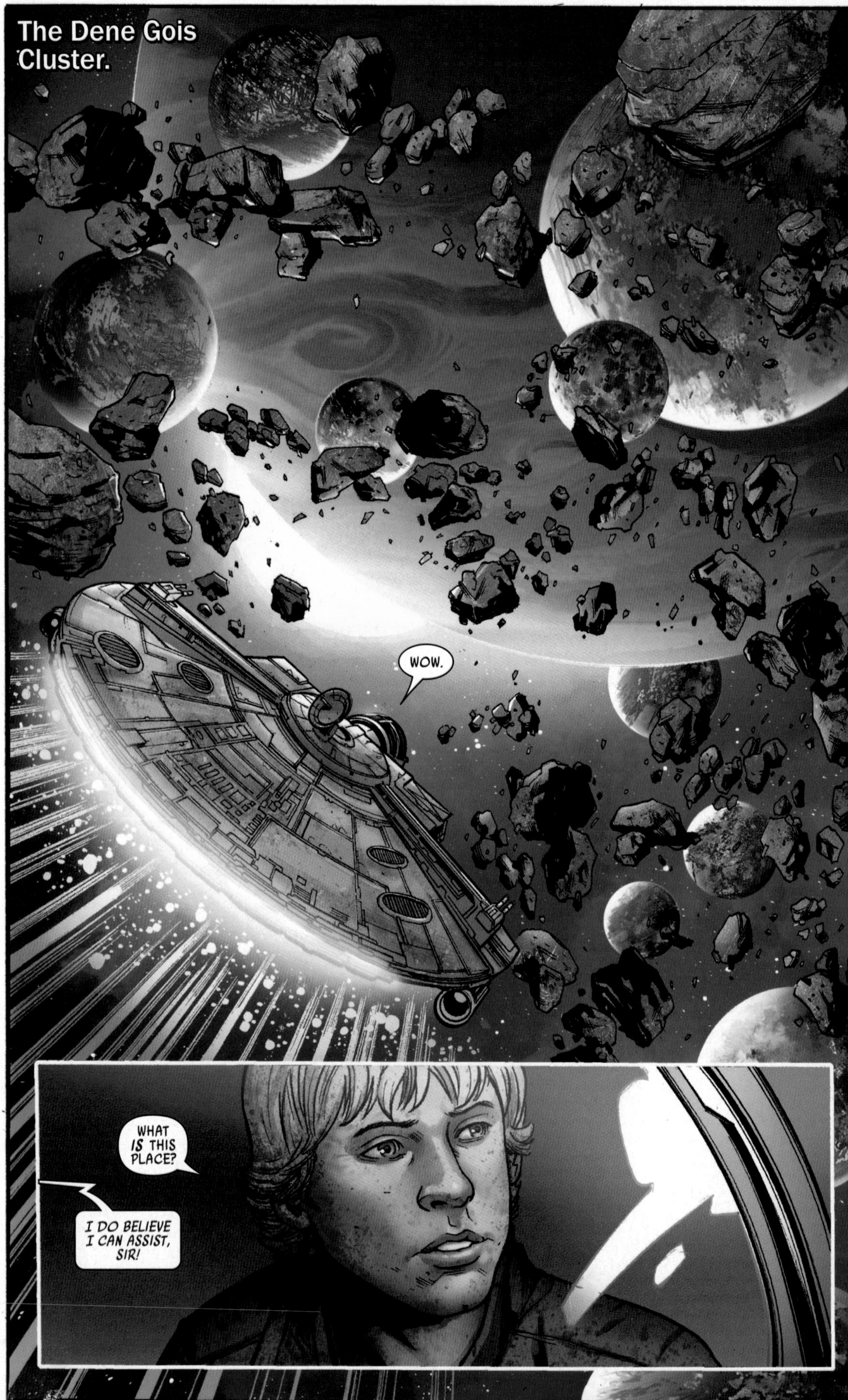
The Dene Gois Cluster.
WOW.
WHAT IS THIS PLACE?
I DO BELIEVE I CAN ASSIST, SIR!

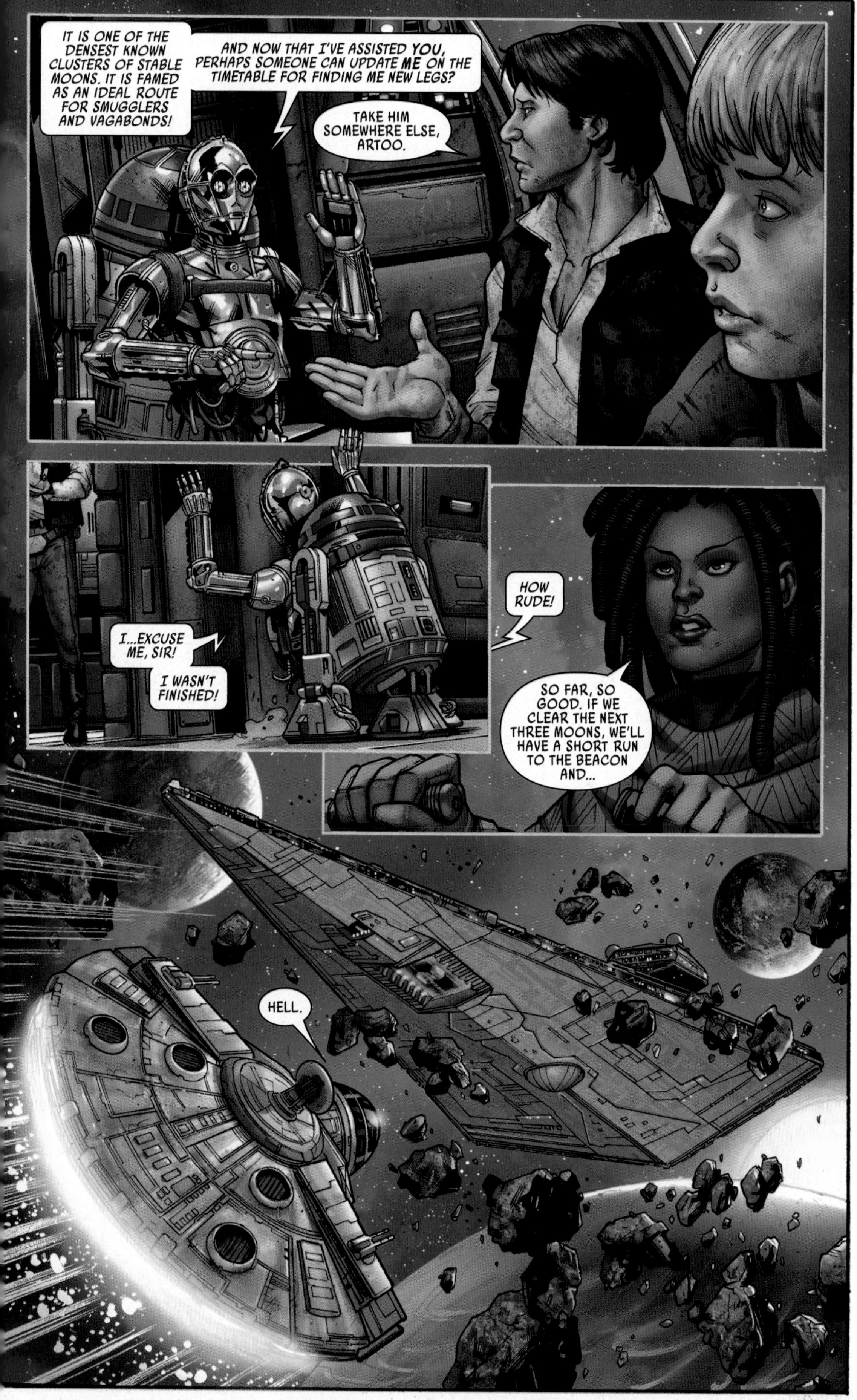
IT IS ONE OF THE DENSEST KNOWN CLUSTERS OF STABLE MOONS. IT IS FAMED AS AN IDEAL ROUTE FOR SMUGGLERS AND VAGABONDS!
AND NOW THAT I'VE ASSISTED YOU, PERHAPS SOMEONE CAN UPDATE ME ON THE TIMETABLE FOR FINDING ME NEW LEGS?
TAKE HIM SOMEWHERE ELSE, ARTOO.
I...EXCUSE ME, SIR!
I WASN'T FINISHED!
HOW RUDE!
SO FAR, SO GOOD. IF WE CLEAR THE NEXT THREE MOONS, WE'LL HAVE A SHORT RUN TO THE BEACON AND...
HELL.

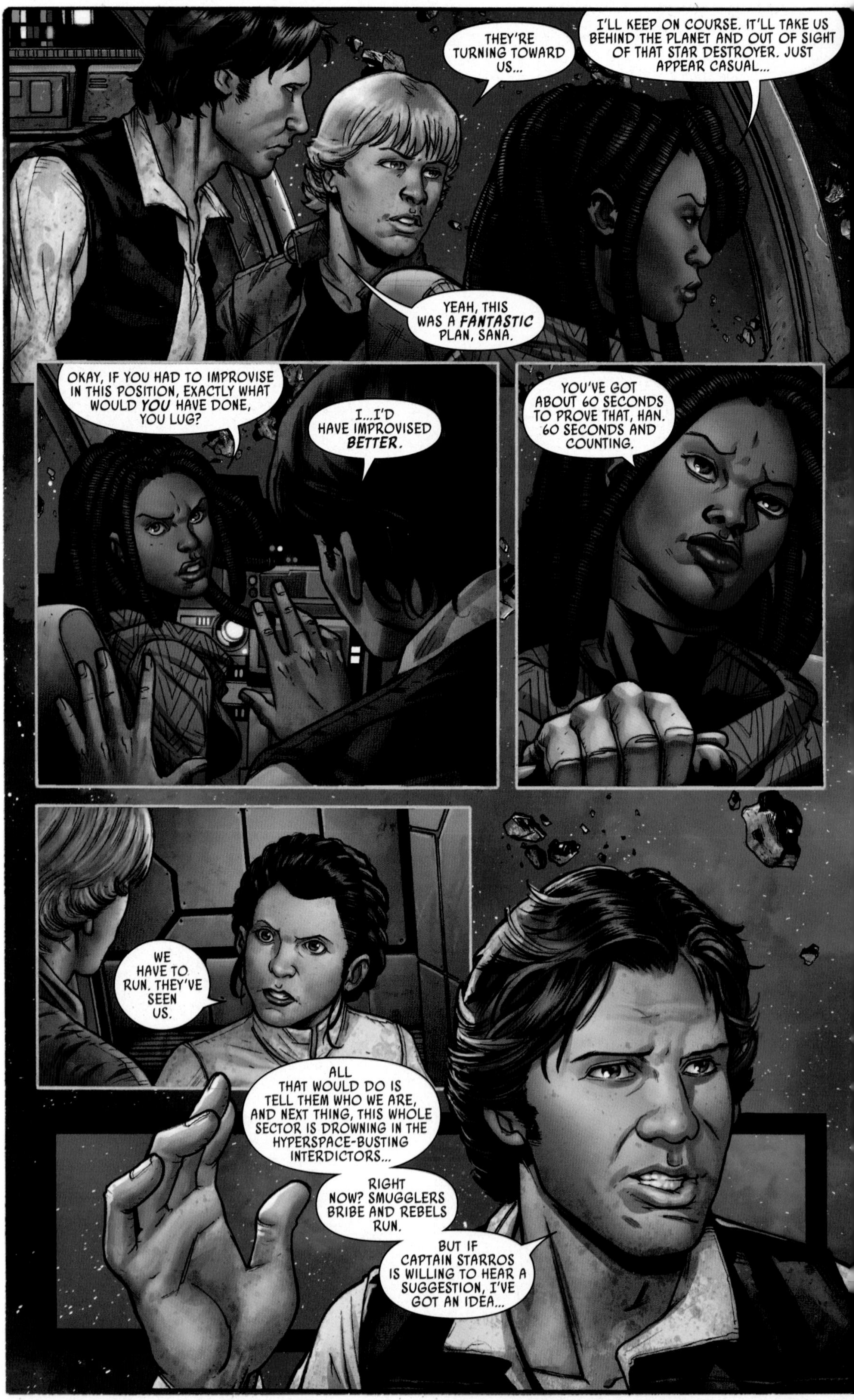
THEY'RE TURNING TOWARD US...
I'LL KEEP ON COURSE. IT'LL TAKE US BEHIND THE PLANET AND OUT OF SIGHT OF THAT STAR DESTROYER. JUST APPEAR CASUAL...
YEAH, THIS WAS A FANTASTIC PLAN, SANA.
OKAY, IF YOU HAD TO IMPROVISE IN THIS POSITION, EXACTLY WHAT WOULD YOU HAVE DONE, YOU LUG?
I...I'D HAVE IMPROVISED BETTER.
YOU'VE GOT ABOUT 60 SECONDS TO PROVE THAT, HAN. 60 SECONDS AND COUNTING.
WE HAVE TO RUN. THEY'VE SEEN US.
ALL THAT WOULD DO IS TELL THEM WHO WE ARE, AND NEXT THING, THIS WHOLE SECTOR IS DROWNING IN THE HYPERSPACE-BUSTING INTERDICTORS...
RIGHT NOW? SMUGGLERS BRIBE AND REBELS RUN.
BUT IF CAPTAIN STARROS IS WILLING TO HEAR A SUGGESTION, I'VE GOT AN IDEA...

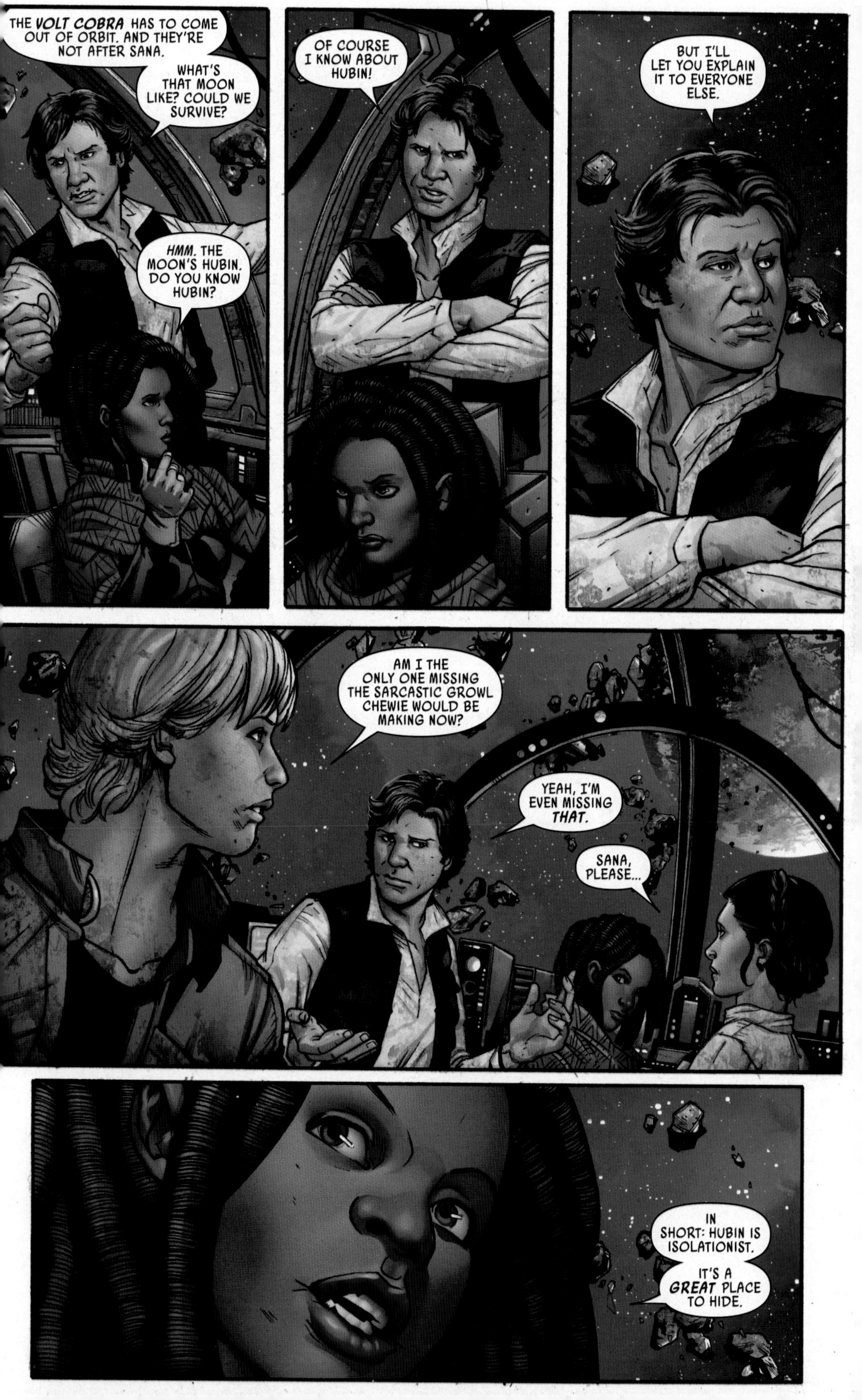
THE VOLT COBRA HAS TO COME OUT OF ORBIT. AND THEY'RE NOT AFTER SANA.
WHAT'S THAT MOON LIKE? COULD WE SURVIVE?
HMM. THE MOON'S HUBIN. DO YOU KNOW HUBIN?
OF COURSE I KNOW ABOUT HUBIN!
BUT I'LL LET YOU EXPLAIN IT TO EVERYONE ELSE.
AM I THE ONLY ONE MISSING THE SARCASTIC GROWL CHEWIE WOULD BE MAKING NOW?
YEAH, I'M EVEN MISSING THAT.
SANA, PLEASE...
IN SHORT: HUBIN IS ISOLATIONIST.
IT'S A GREAT PLACE TO HIDE.

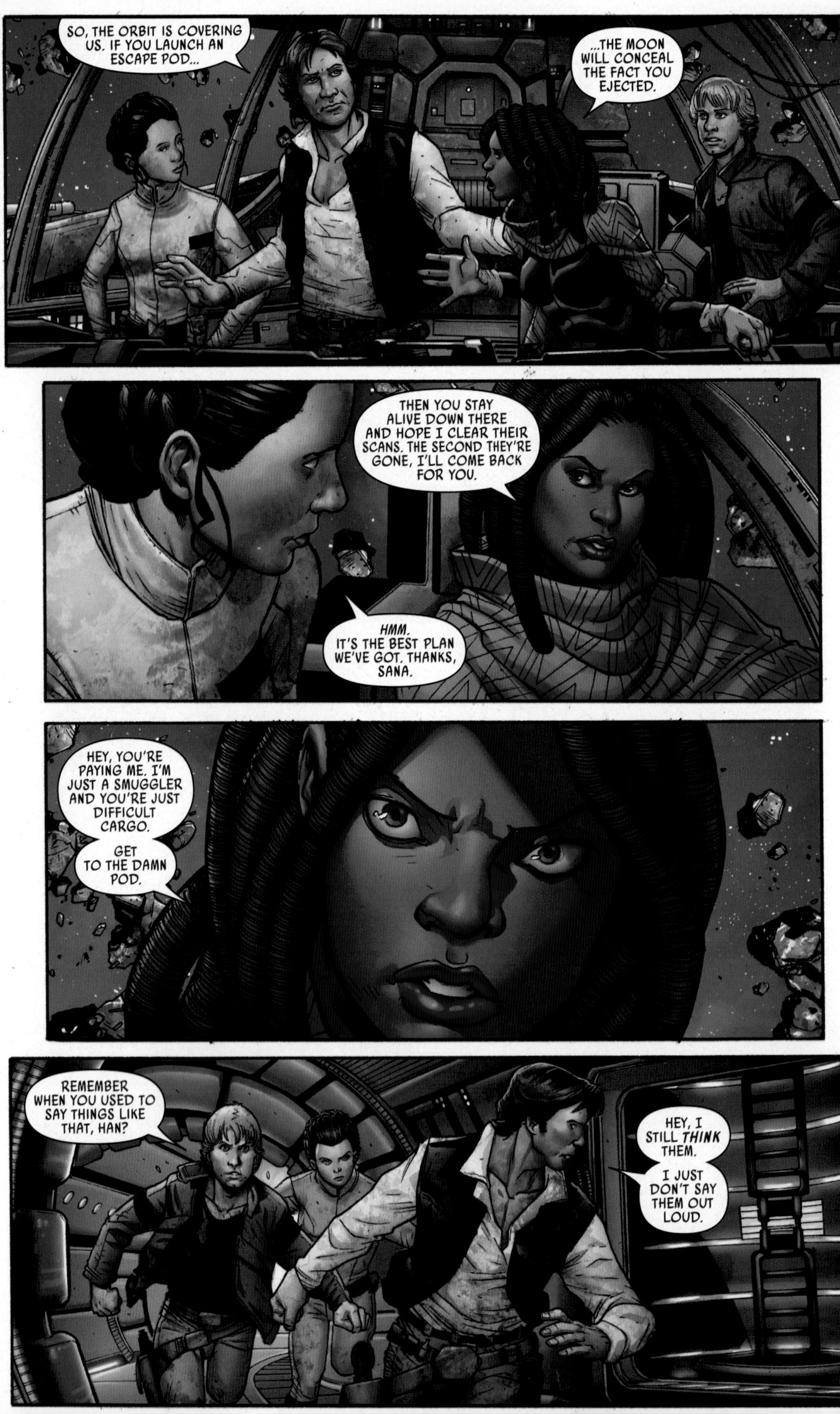
SO, THE ORBIT IS COVERING US. IF YOU LAUNCH AN ESCAPE POD...
...THE MOON WILL CONCEAL THE FACT YOU EJECTED.
THEN YOU STAY ALIVE DOWN THERE AND HOPE I CLEAR THEIR SCANS. THE SECOND THEY'RE GONE, I'LL COME BACK FOR YOU.
HMM. IT'S THE BEST PLAN WE'VE GOT. THANKS, SANA.
HEY, YOU'RE PAYING ME. I'M JUST A SMUGGLER AND YOU'RE JUST DIFFICULT CARGO.
GET TO THE DAMN POD.
REMEMBER WHEN YOU USED TO SAY THINGS LIKE THAT, HAN?
HEY, I STILL THINK THEM.
I JUST DON'T SAY THEM OUT LOUD.

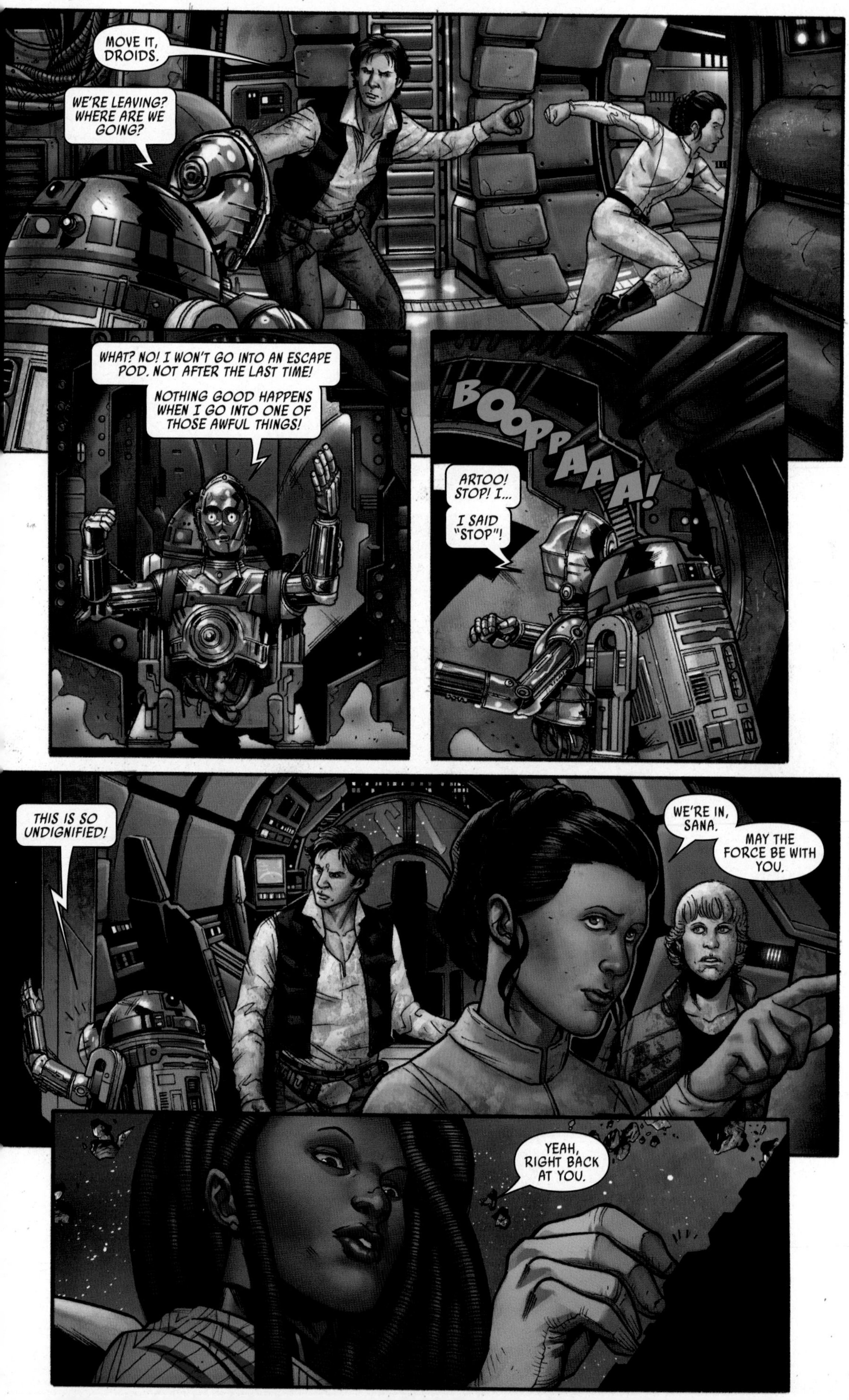
MOVE IT, DROIDS.
WE'RE LEAVING? WHERE ARE WE GOING?
WHAT? NO! I WON'T GO INTO AN ESCAPE POD. NOT AFTER THE LAST TIME!
NOTHING GOOD HAPPENS WHEN I GO INTO ONE OF THOSE AWFUL THINGS!
BOOPPAAAA!
ARTOO! STOP! I...
I SAID "STOP"!
THIS IS SO UNDIGNIFIED!
WE'RE IN, SANA.
MAY THE FORCE BE WITH YOU.
YEAH, RIGHT BACK AT YOU.

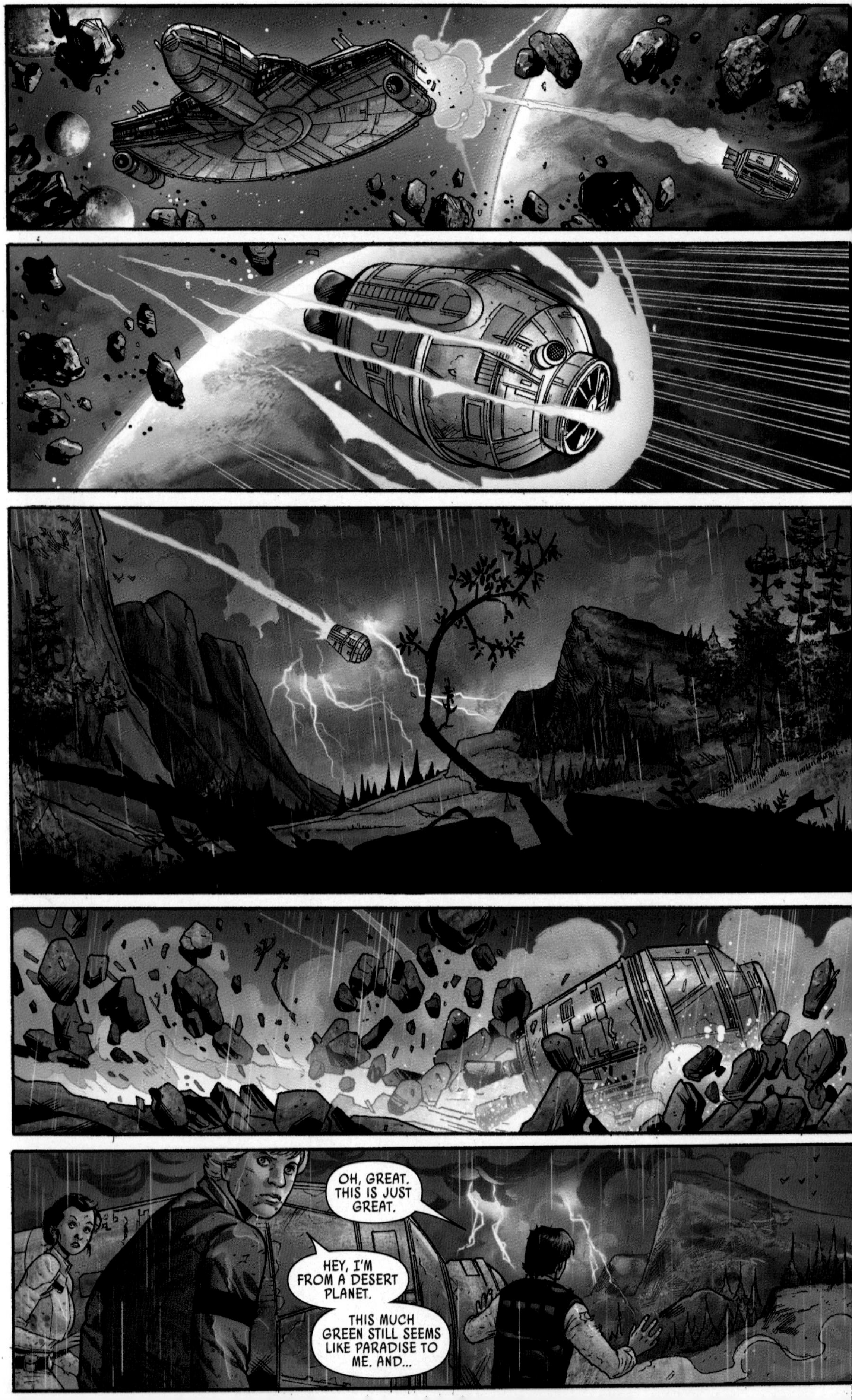
OH, GREAT. THIS IS JUST GREAT.
HEY, I'M FROM A DESERT PLANET.
THIS MUCH GREEN STILL SEEMS LIKE PARADISE TO ME. AND...

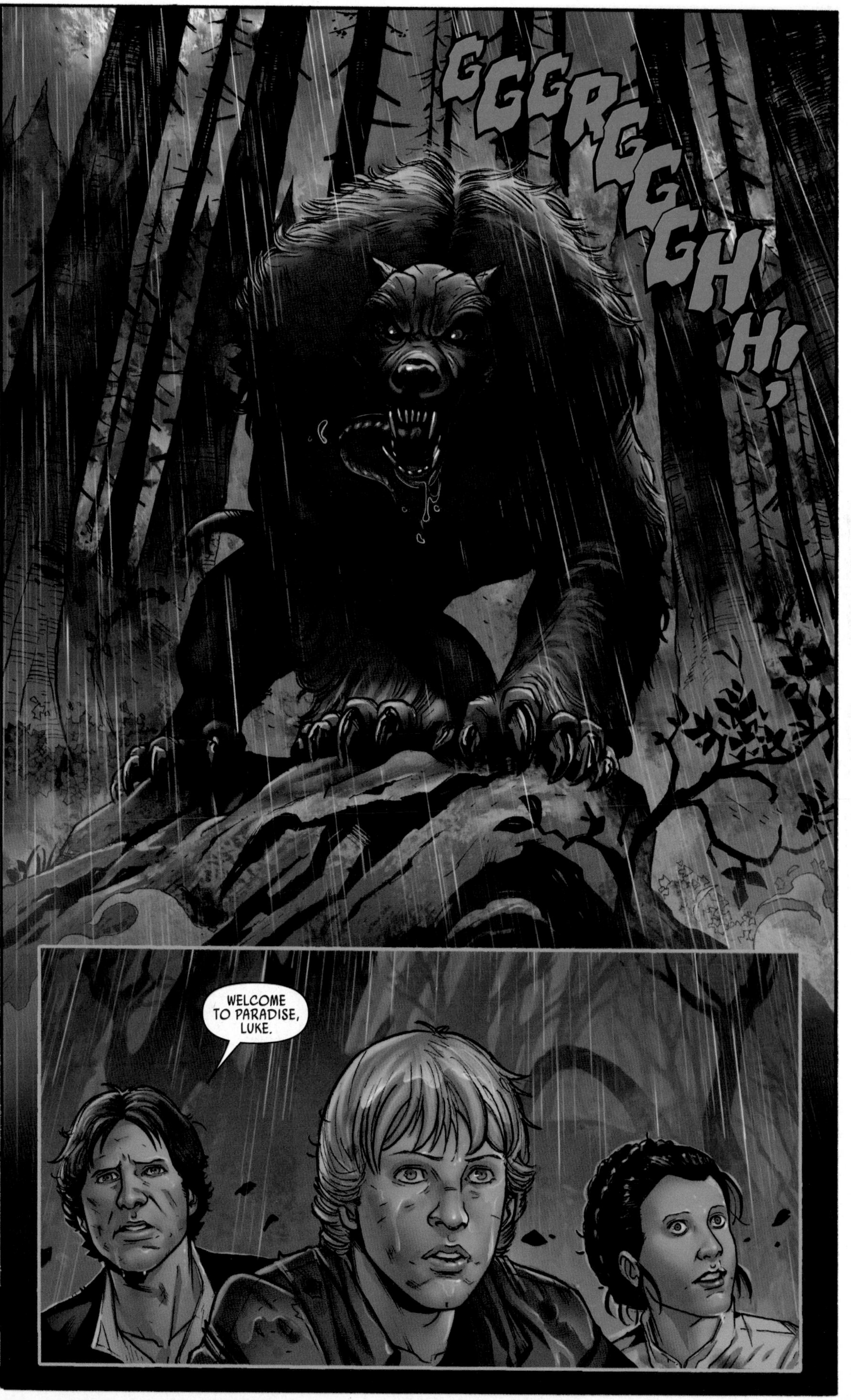
GGGRGGGGHH!
WELCOME TO PARADISE, LUKE.

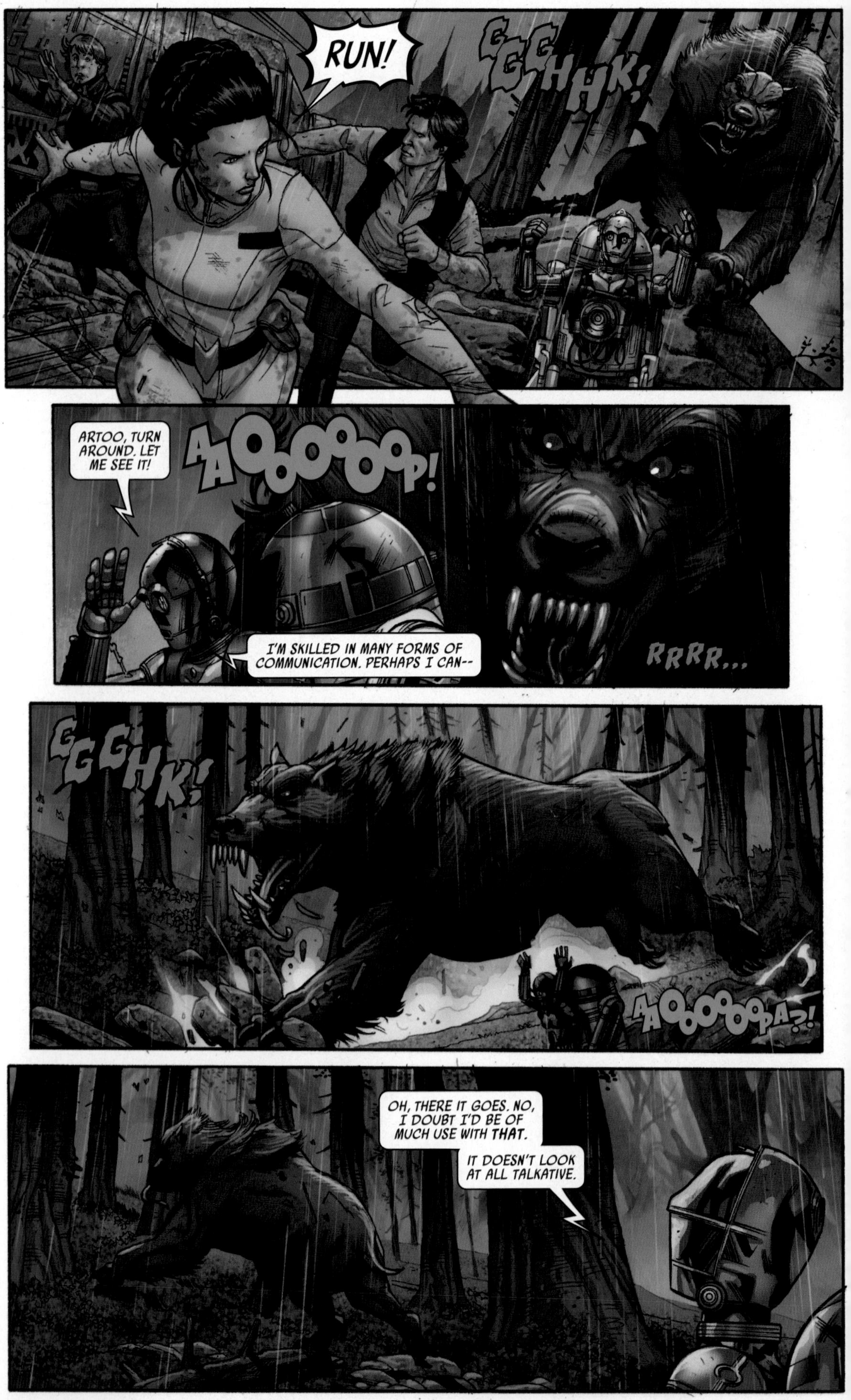
RUN!
GGGHHHK!
ARTOO, TURN AROUND. LET ME SEE IT!
AAOOOOOOOP!
I'M SKILLED IN MANY FORMS OF COMMUNICATION. PERHAPS I CAN--
RRRR...
GGGHK!
AAOOOOOOPA?!
OH, THERE IT GOES. NO, I DOUBT I'D BE OF MUCH USE WITH THAT.
IT DOESN'T LOOK AT ALL TALKATIVE.

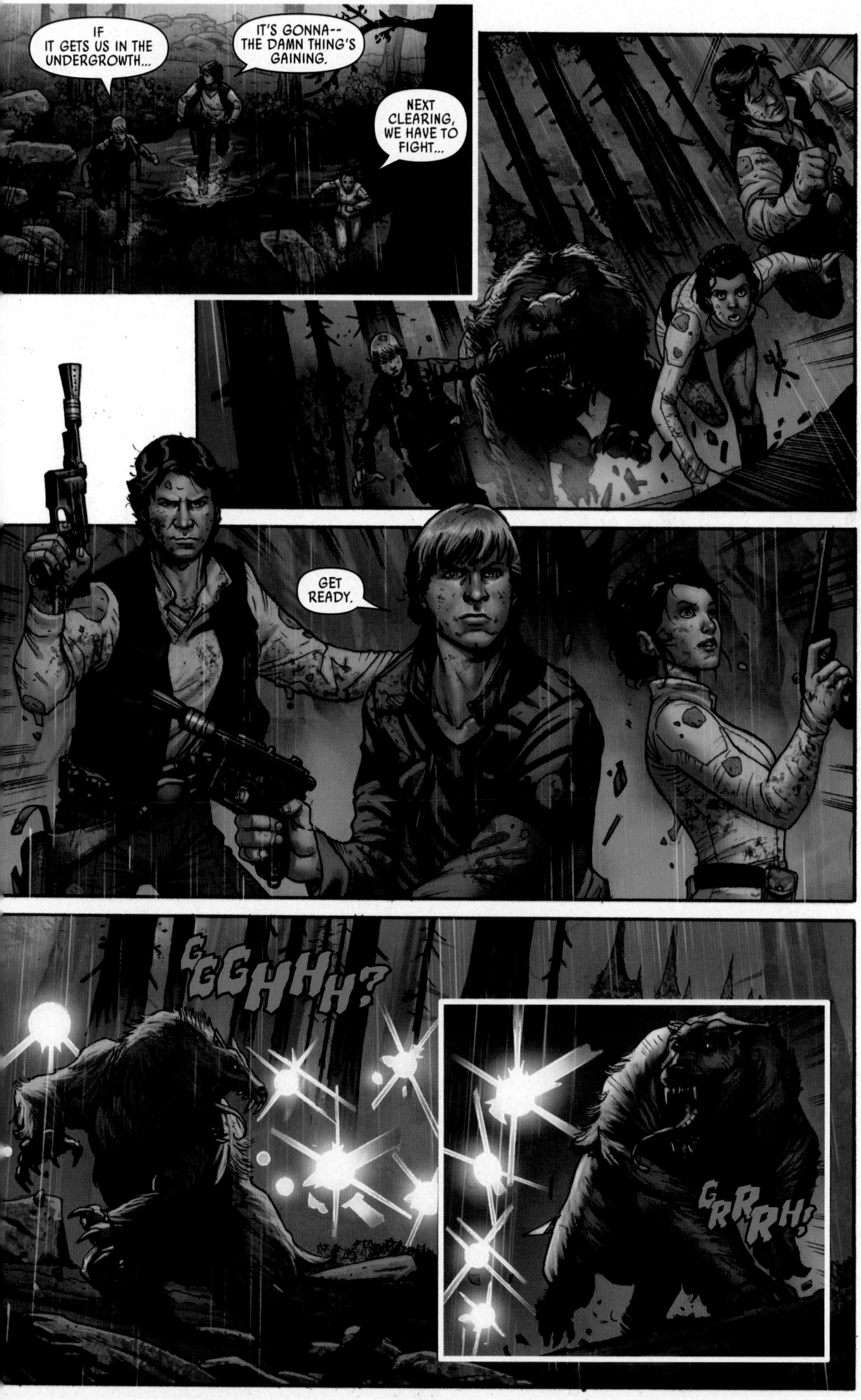
IF IT GETS US IN THE UNDERGROWTH...
IT'S GONNA-- THE DAMN THING'S GAINING.
NEXT CLEARING, WE HAVE TO FIGHT...
GET READY.
GGHHHH?
GRRRH!

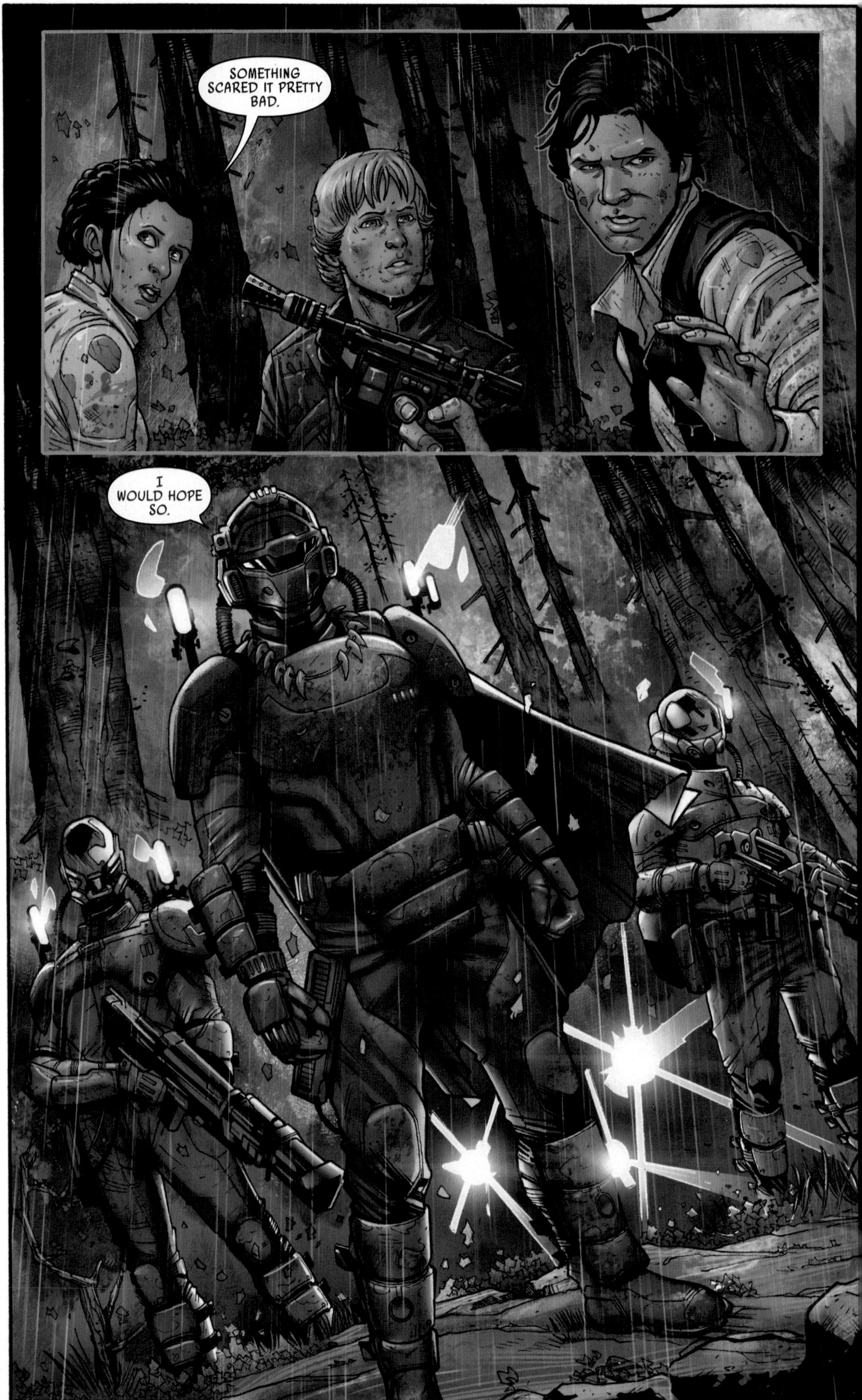
SOMETHING SCARED IT PRETTY BAD.
I WOULD HOPE SO.

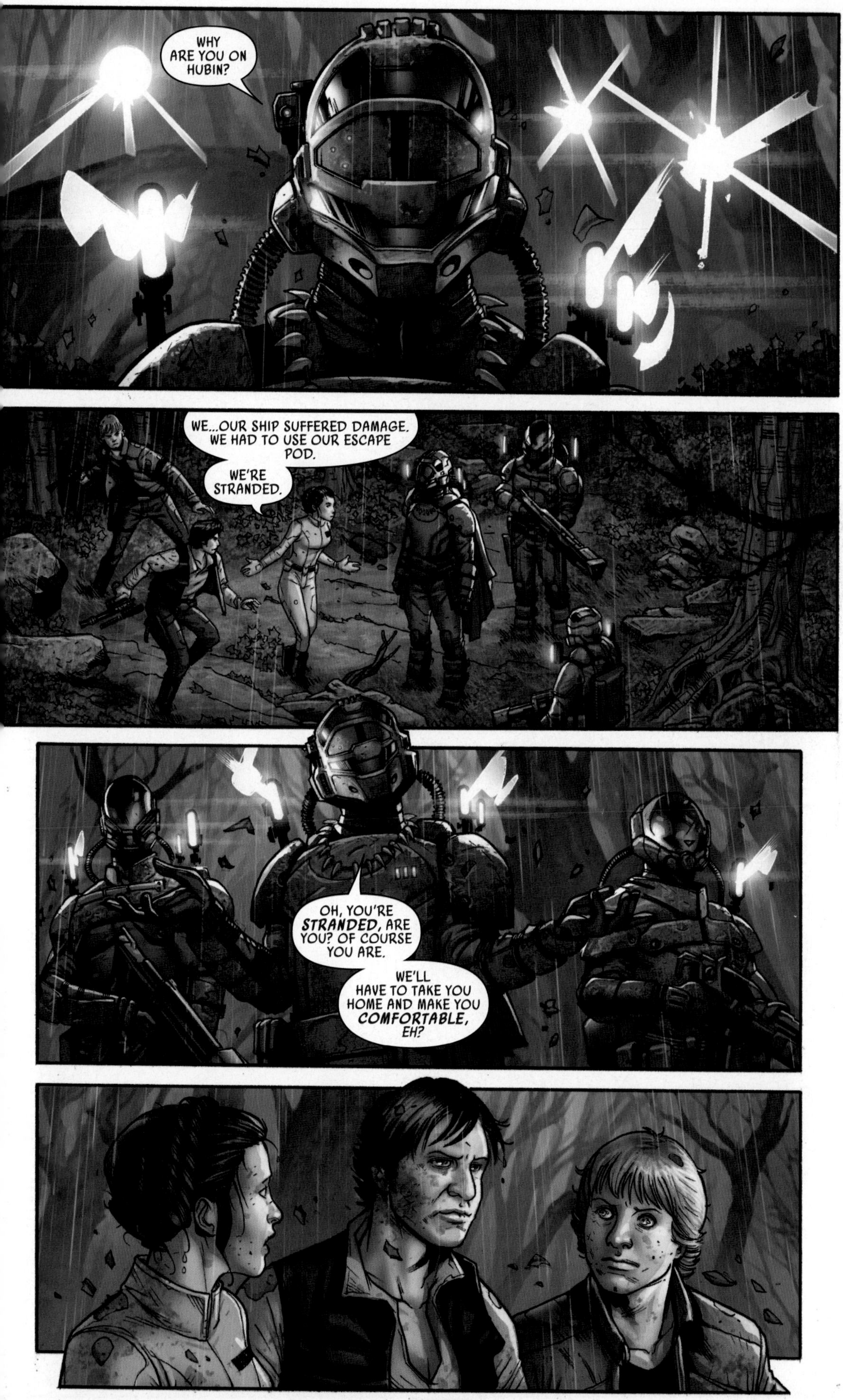
WHY ARE YOU ON HUBIN?
WE...OUR SHIP SUFFERED DAMAGE. WE HAD TO USE OUR ESCAPE POD.
WE'RE STRANDED.
OH, YOU'RE STRANDED, ARE YOU? OF COURSE YOU ARE.
WE'LL HAVE TO TAKE YOU HOME AND MAKE YOU COMFORTABLE, EH?

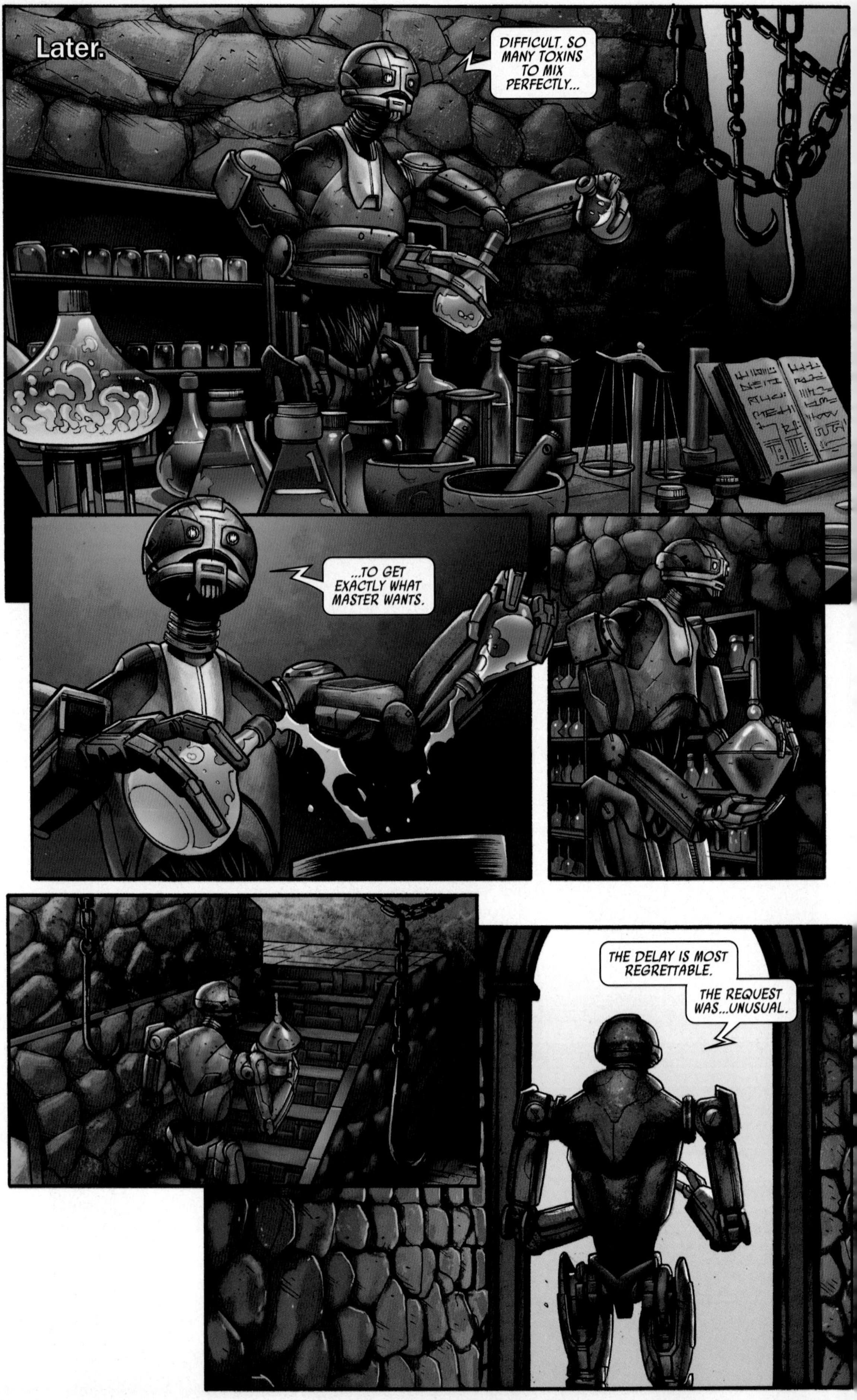
Later.
DIFFICULT. SO MANY TOXINS TO MIX PERFECTLY...
...TO GET EXACTLY WHAT MASTER WANTS.
THE DELAY IS MOST REGRETTABLE.
THE REQUEST WAS...UNUSUAL.

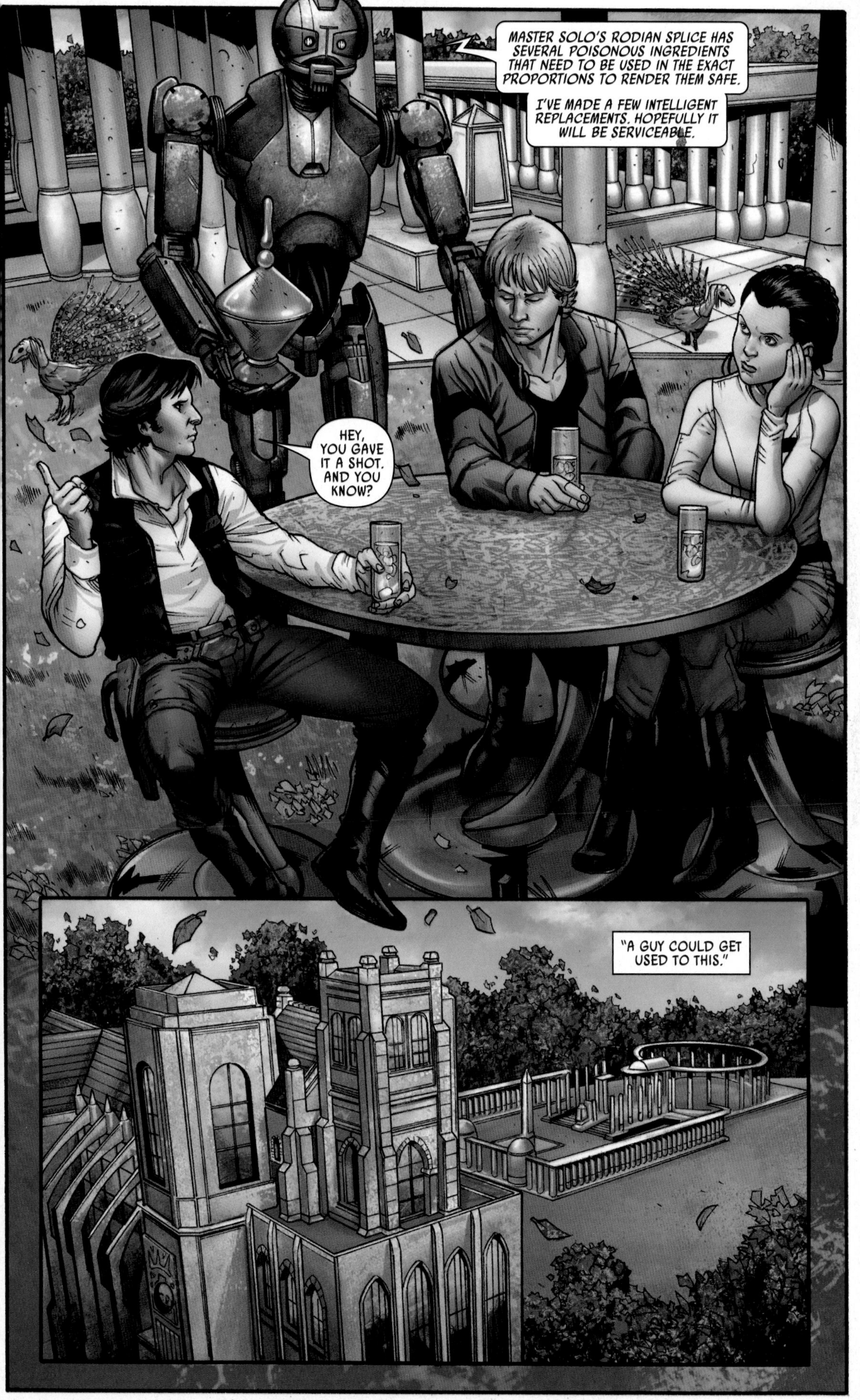
MASTER SOLO'S RODIAN SPLICE HAS SEVERAL POISONOUS INGREDIENTS THAT NEED TO BE USED IN THE EXACT PROPORTIONS TO RENDER THEM SAFE.
I'VE MADE A FEW INTELLIGENT REPLACEMENTS. HOPEFULLY IT WILL BE SERVICEABLE.
HEY, YOU GAVE IT A SHOT. AND YOU KNOW?
"A GUY COULD GET USED TO THIS."

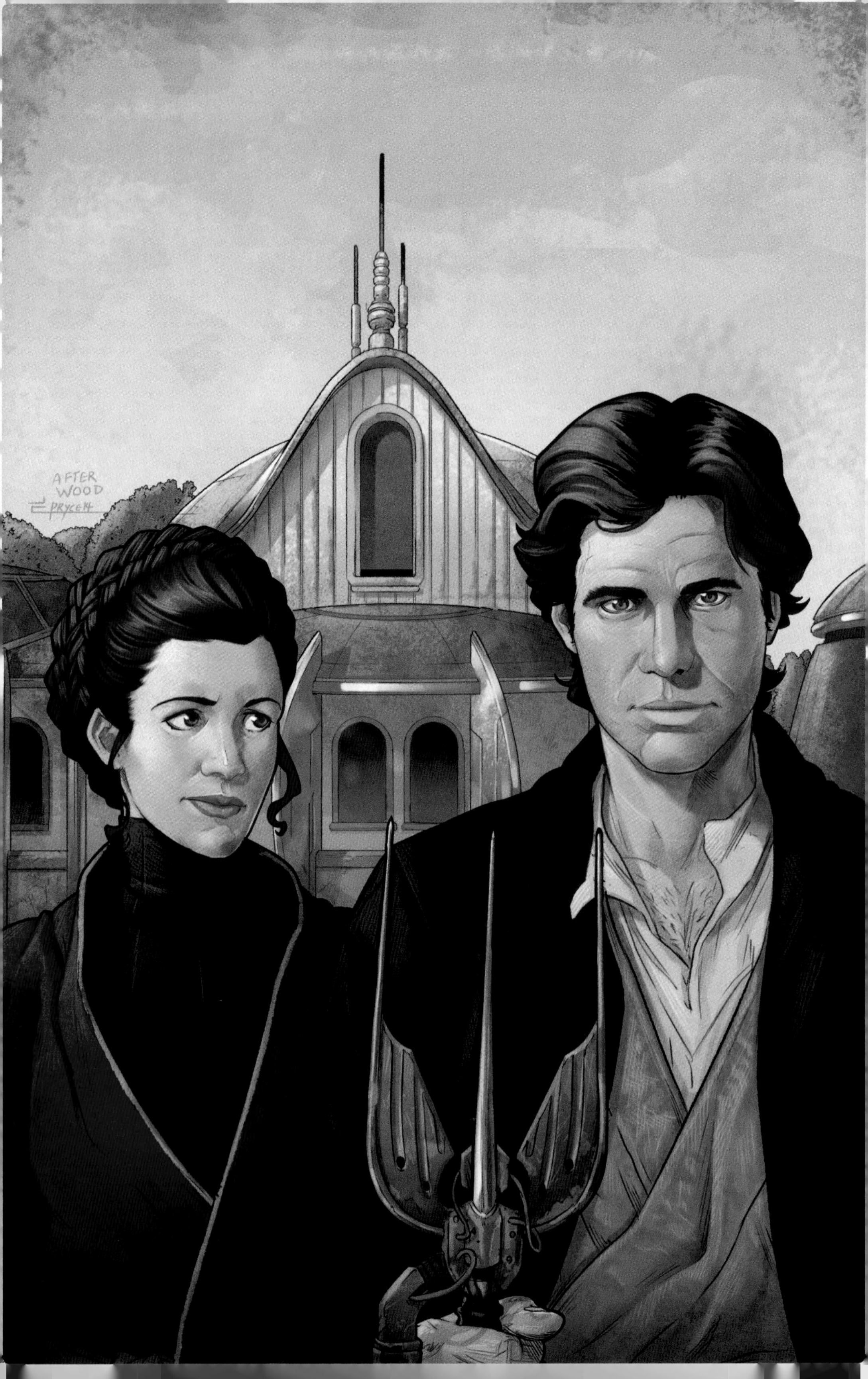
AFTER
WOOD

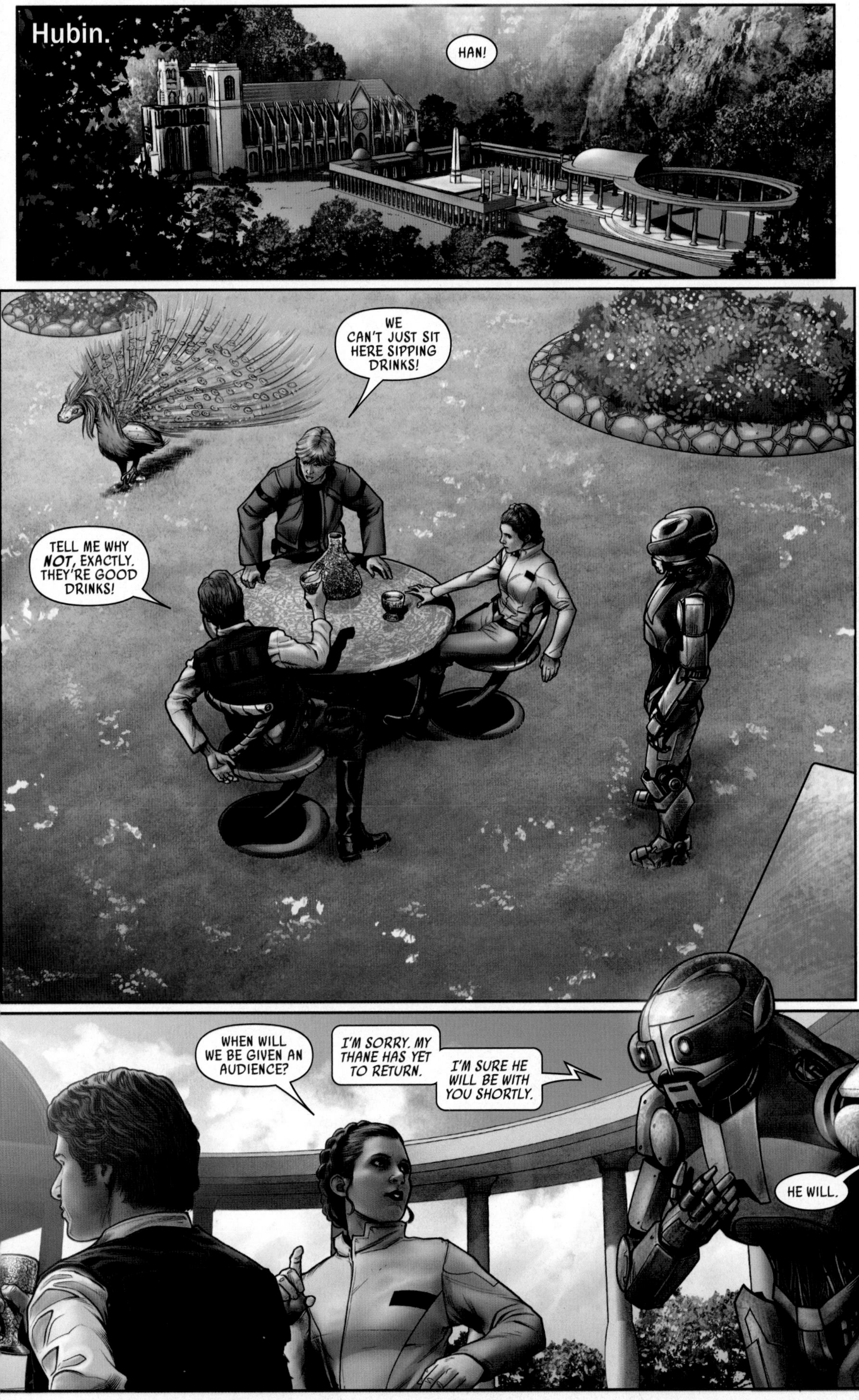
Hubin.
HAN!
WE CAN'T JUST SIT HERE SIPPING DRINKS!
TELL ME WHY *NOT*, EXACTLY. THEY'RE GOOD DRINKS!
WHEN WILL WE BE GIVEN AN AUDIENCE?
I'M SORRY. MY THANE HAS YET TO RETURN.
I'M SURE HE WILL BE WITH YOU SHORTLY.
HE WILL.

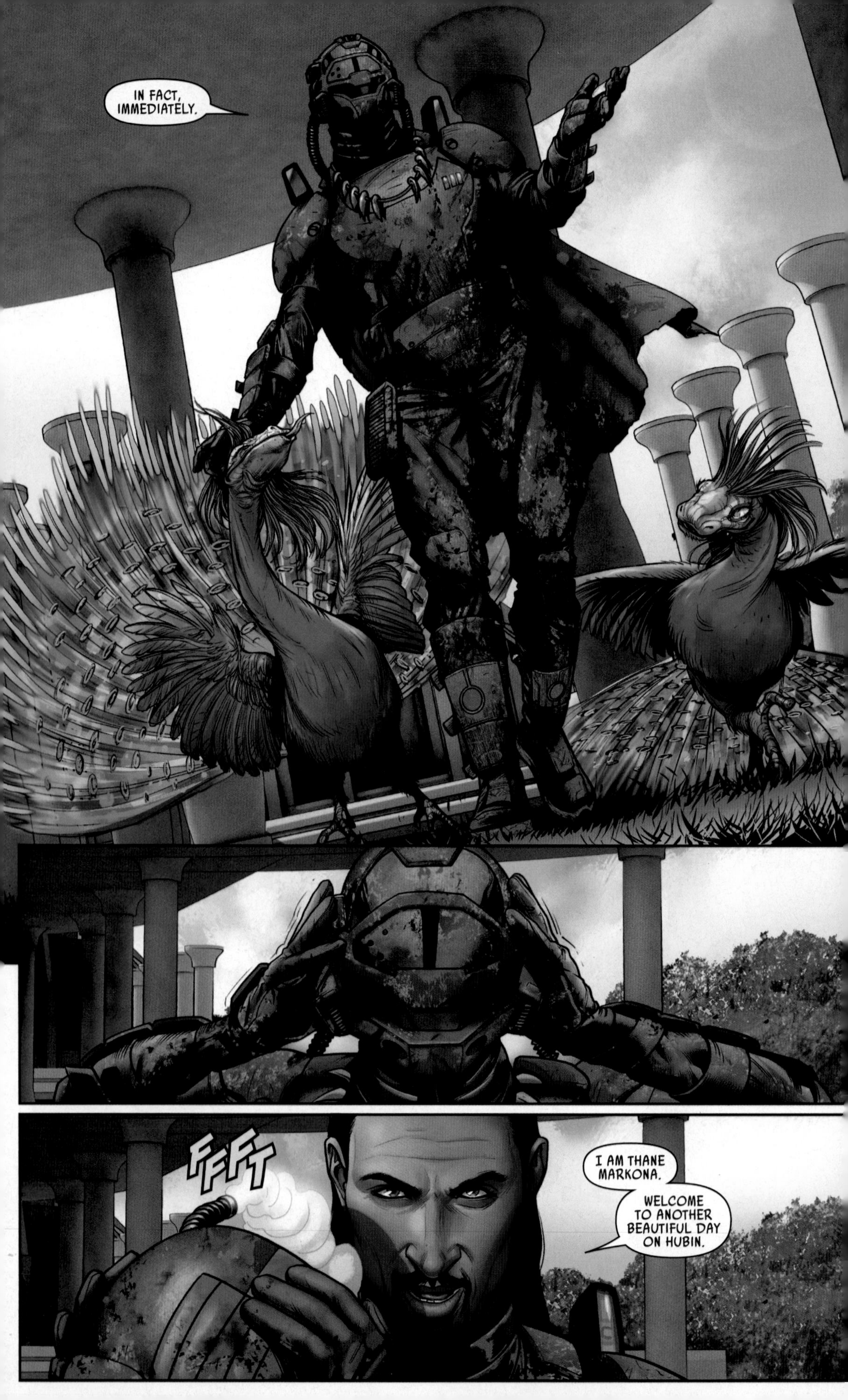
IN FACT, IMMEDIATELY.
FFFT
I AM THANE MARKONA.
WELCOME TO ANOTHER BEAUTIFUL DAY ON HUBIN.

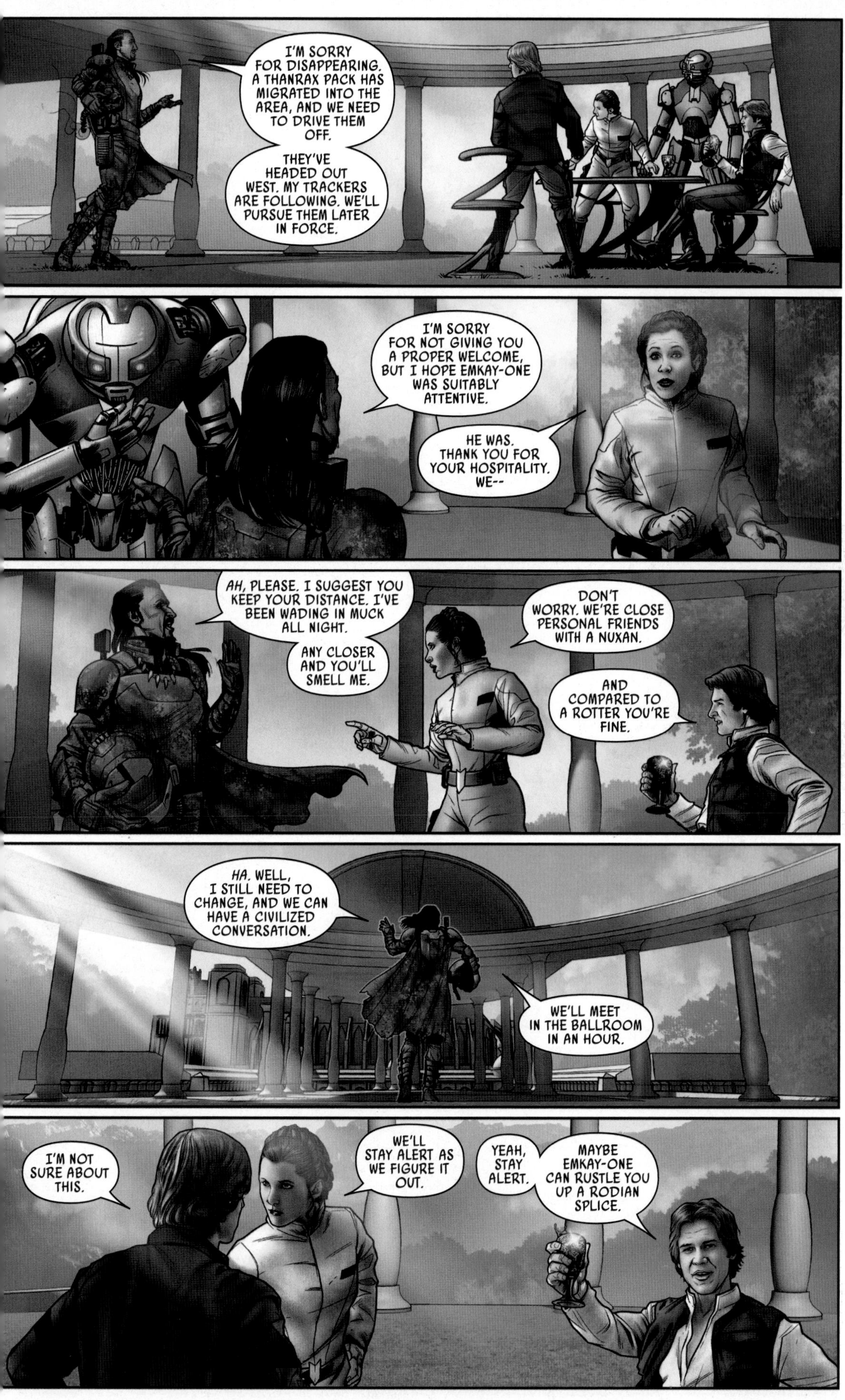

I'M SORRY FOR DISAPPEARING. A THANRAX PACK HAS MIGRATED INTO THE AREA, AND WE NEED TO DRIVE THEM OFF.
THEY'VE HEADED OUT WEST. MY TRACKERS ARE FOLLOWING. WE'LL PURSUE THEM LATER IN FORCE.
I'M SORRY FOR NOT GIVING YOU A PROPER WELCOME, BUT I HOPE EMKAY-ONE WAS SUITABLY ATTENTIVE.
HE WAS. THANK YOU FOR YOUR HOSPITALITY. WE--
AH, PLEASE. I SUGGEST YOU KEEP YOUR DISTANCE. I'VE BEEN WADING IN MUCK ALL NIGHT.
ANY CLOSER AND YOU'LL SMELL ME.
DON'T WORRY. WE'RE CLOSE PERSONAL FRIENDS WITH A NUXAN.
AND COMPARED TO A ROTTER YOU'RE FINE.
HA. WELL, I STILL NEED TO CHANGE, AND WE CAN HAVE A CIVILIZED CONVERSATION.
WE'LL MEET IN THE BALLROOM IN AN HOUR.
I'M NOT SURE ABOUT THIS.
WE'LL STAY ALERT AS WE FIGURE IT OUT.
YEAH, STAY ALERT.
MAYBE EMKAY-ONE CAN RUSTLE YOU UP A RODIAN SPLICE.

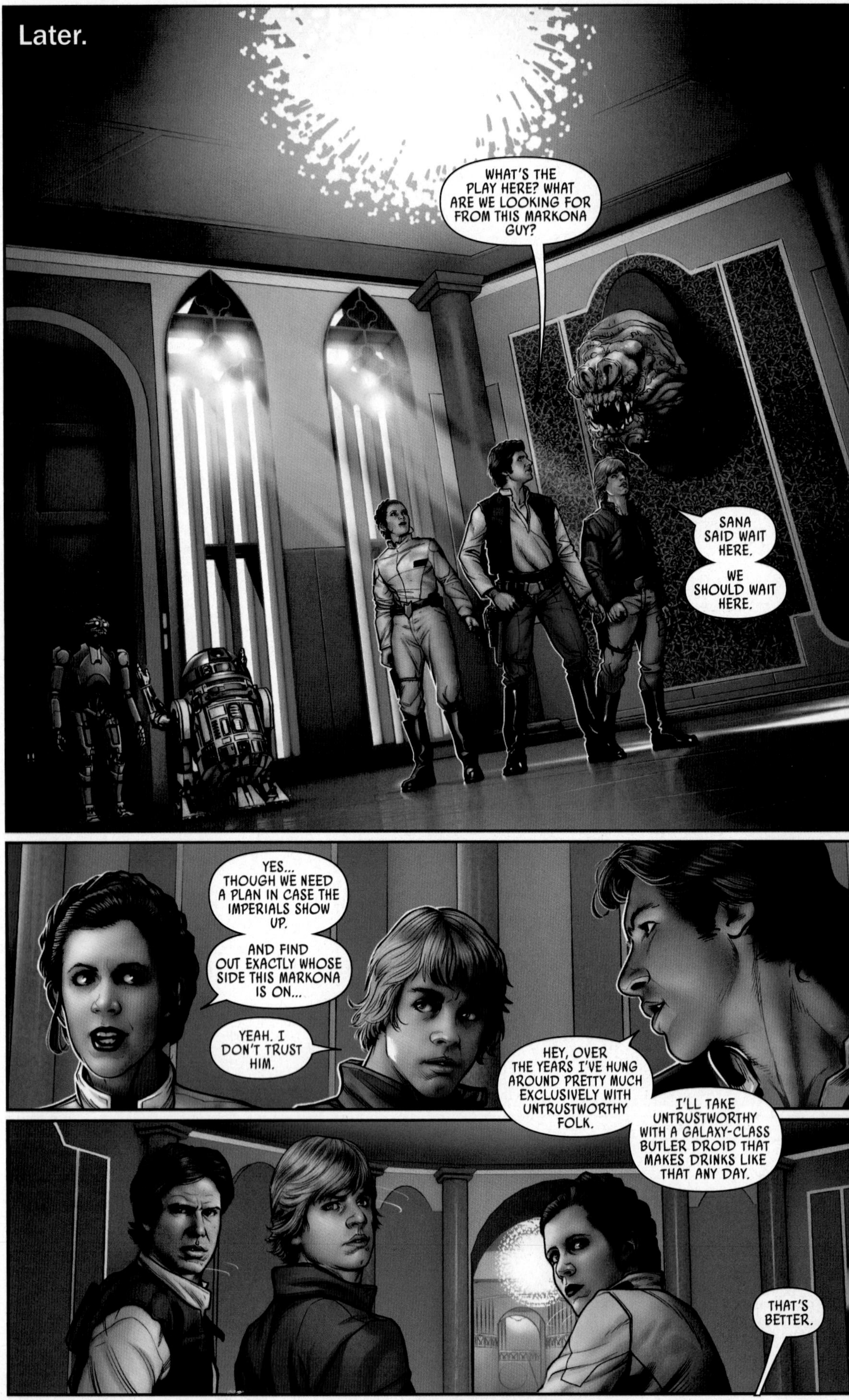
Later.
WHAT'S THE PLAY HERE? WHAT ARE WE LOOKING FOR FROM THIS MARKONA GUY?
SANA SAID WAIT HERE.
WE SHOULD WAIT HERE.
YES... THOUGH WE NEED A PLAN IN CASE THE IMPERIALS SHOW UP.
AND FIND OUT EXACTLY WHOSE SIDE THIS MARKONA IS ON...
YEAH. I DON'T TRUST HIM.
HEY, OVER THE YEARS I'VE HUNG AROUND PRETTY MUCH EXCLUSIVELY WITH UNTRUSTWORTHY FOLK.
I'LL TAKE UNTRUSTWORTHY WITH A GALAXY-CLASS BUTLER DROID THAT MAKES DRINKS LIKE THAT ANY DAY.
THAT'S BETTER.

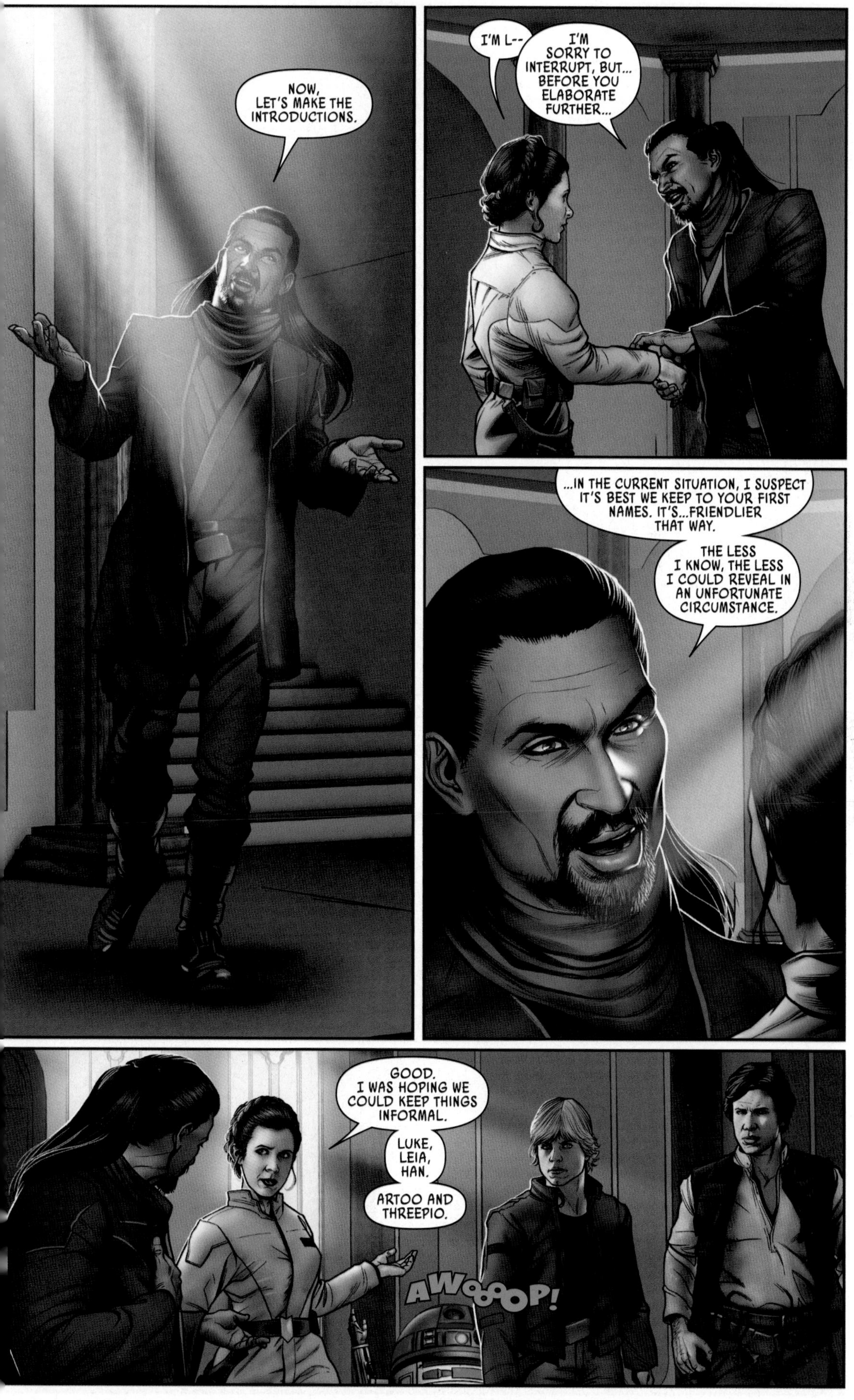
NOW, LET'S MAKE THE INTRODUCTIONS.
I'M L--
I'M SORRY TO INTERRUPT, BUT... BEFORE YOU ELABORATE FURTHER...
...IN THE CURRENT SITUATION, I SUSPECT IT'S BEST WE KEEP TO YOUR FIRST NAMES. IT'S...FRIENDLIER THAT WAY.
THE LESS I KNOW, THE LESS I COULD REVEAL IN AN UNFORTUNATE CIRCUMSTANCE.
GOOD. I WAS HOPING WE COULD KEEP THINGS INFORMAL.
LUKE, LEIA, HAN.
ARTOO AND THREEPIO.
AWOOOOP!

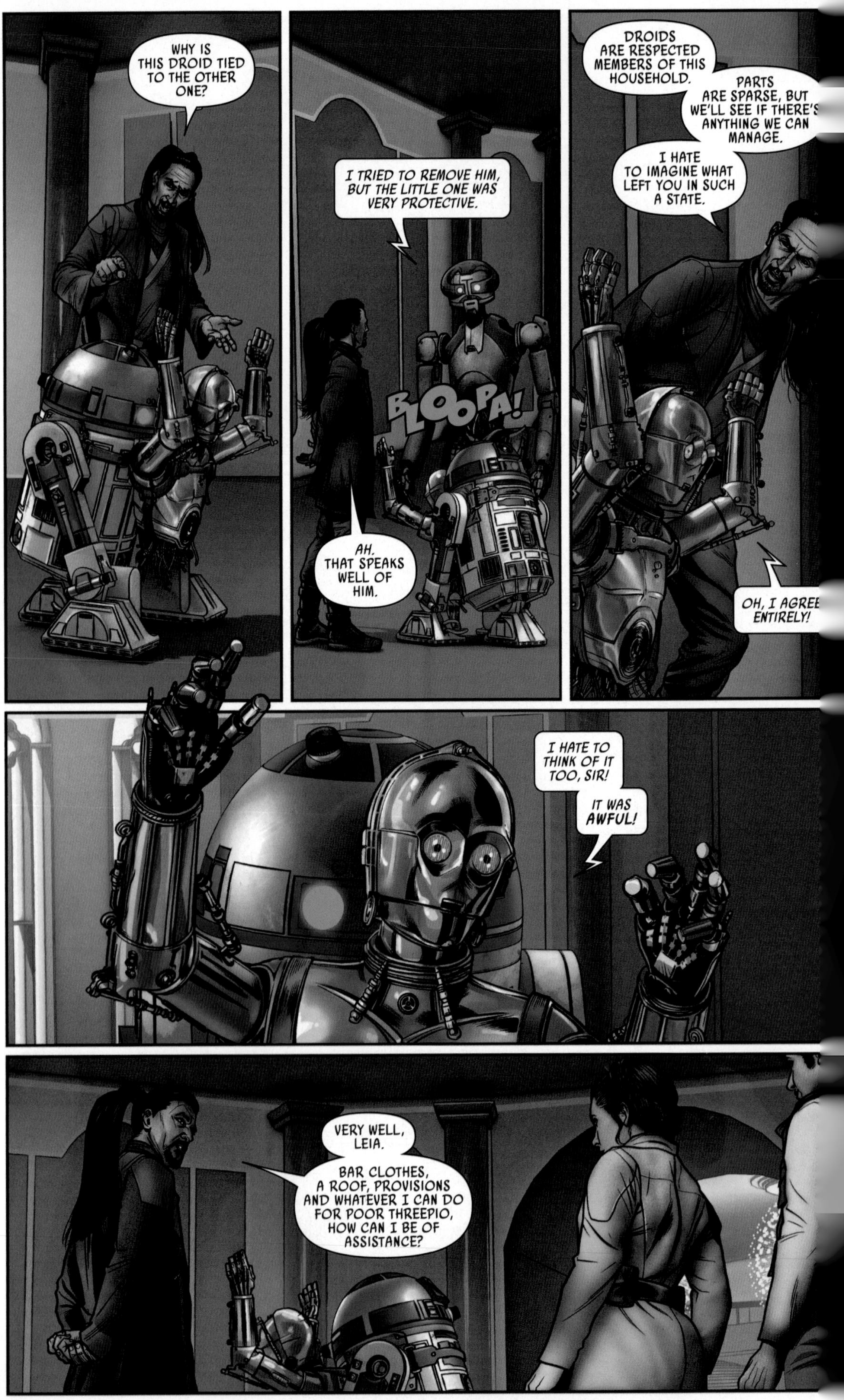
WHY IS THIS DROID TIED TO THE OTHER ONE?
I TRIED TO REMOVE HIM, BUT THE LITTLE ONE WAS VERY PROTECTIVE.
BLOOPA!
AH. THAT SPEAKS WELL OF HIM.
DROIDS ARE RESPECTED MEMBERS OF THIS HOUSEHOLD.
PARTS ARE SPARSE, BUT WE'LL SEE IF THERE'S ANYTHING WE CAN MANAGE.
I HATE TO IMAGINE WHAT LEFT YOU IN SUCH A STATE.
OH, I AGREE ENTIRELY!
I HATE TO THINK OF IT TOO, SIR!
IT WAS AWFUL!
VERY WELL, LEIA.
BAR CLOTHES, A ROOF, PROVISIONS AND WHATEVER I CAN DO FOR POOR THREEPIO, HOW CAN I BE OF ASSISTANCE?

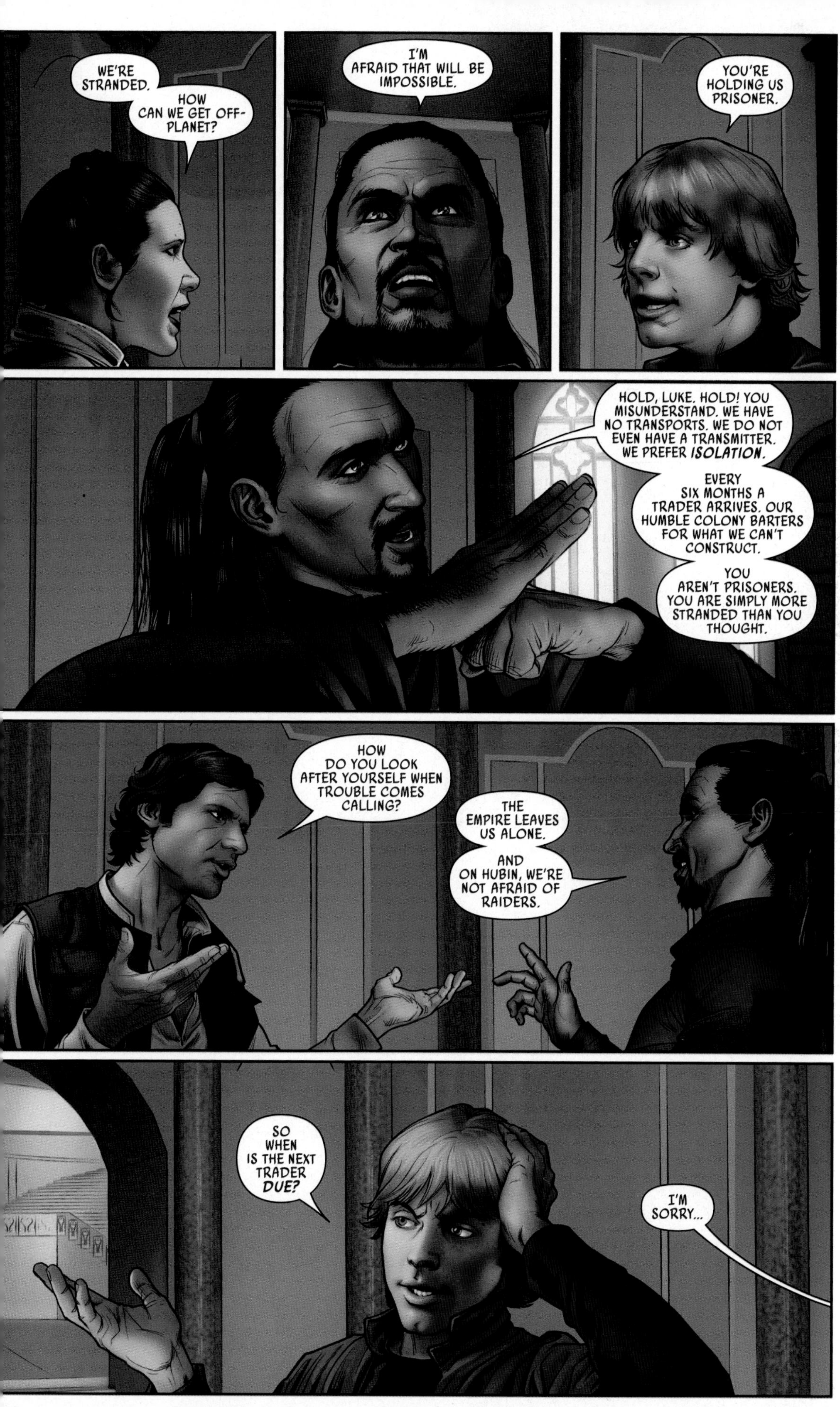
WE'RE STRANDED.
HOW CAN WE GET OFF-PLANET?
I'M AFRAID THAT WILL BE IMPOSSIBLE.
YOU'RE HOLDING US PRISONER.
HOLD, LUKE. HOLD! YOU MISUNDERSTAND. WE HAVE NO TRANSPORTS. WE DO NOT EVEN HAVE A TRANSMITTER. WE PREFER *ISOLATION*.
EVERY SIX MONTHS A TRADER ARRIVES. OUR HUMBLE COLONY BARTERS FOR WHAT WE CAN'T CONSTRUCT.
YOU AREN'T PRISONERS. YOU ARE SIMPLY MORE STRANDED THAN YOU THOUGHT.
HOW DO YOU LOOK AFTER YOURSELF WHEN TROUBLE COMES CALLING?
THE EMPIRE LEAVES US ALONE.
AND ON HUBIN, WE'RE NOT AFRAID OF RAIDERS.
SO WHEN IS THE NEXT TRADER *DUE*?
I'M SORRY...

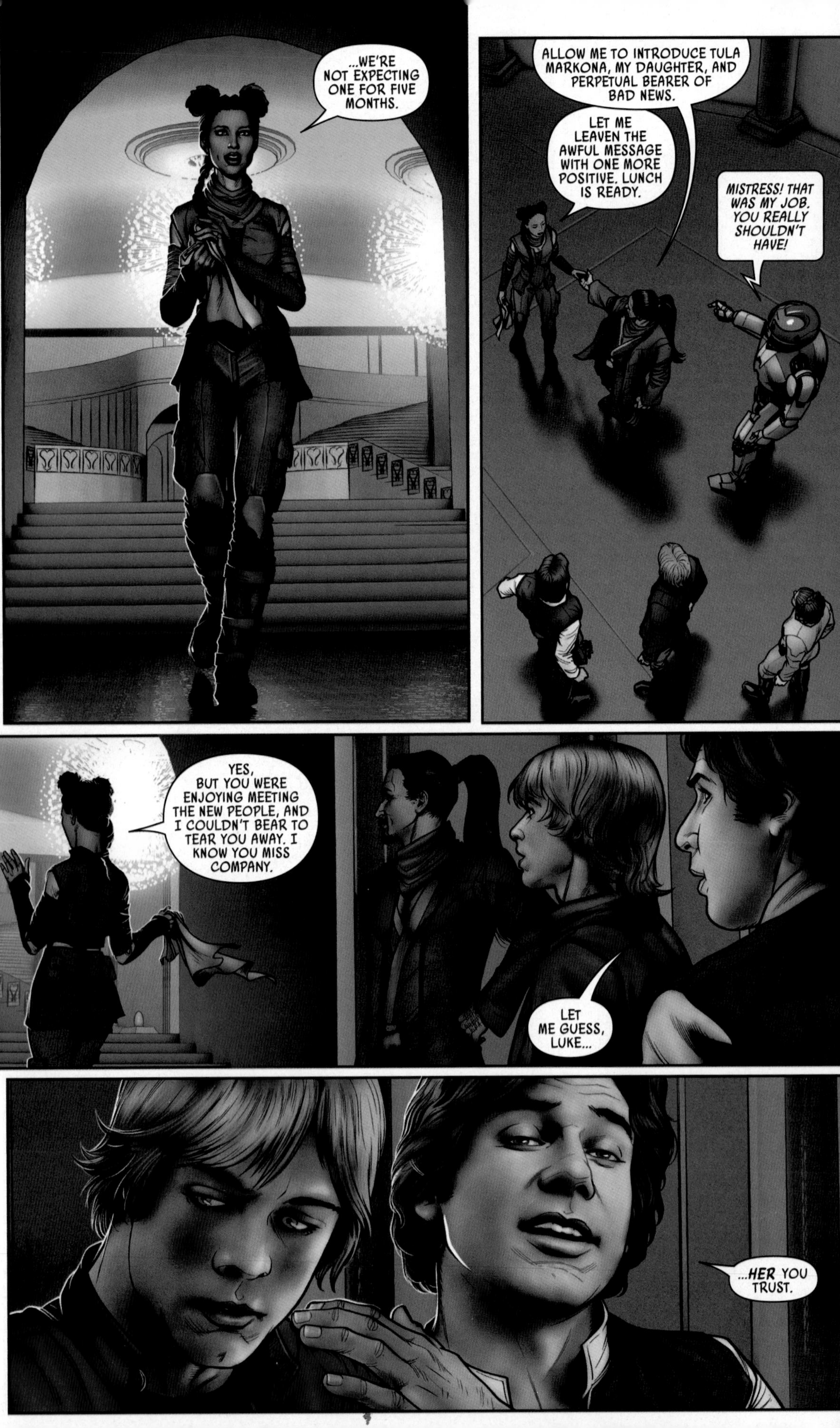

...WE'RE NOT EXPECTING ONE FOR FIVE MONTHS.
ALLOW ME TO INTRODUCE TULA MARKONA, MY DAUGHTER, AND PERPETUAL BEARER OF BAD NEWS.
LET ME LEAVEN THE AWFUL MESSAGE WITH ONE MORE POSITIVE. LUNCH IS READY.
MISTRESS! THAT WAS MY JOB. YOU REALLY SHOULDN'T HAVE!
YES, BUT YOU WERE ENJOYING MEETING THE NEW PEOPLE, AND I COULDN'T BEAR TO TEAR YOU AWAY. I KNOW YOU MISS COMPANY.
LET ME GUESS, LUKE...
...HER YOU TRUST.

WHEN I THINK OF ISOLATIONIST HERMITS, I DON'T TEND TO ENVISAGE MANSIONS...

SELF-SUFFICIENT NEEDN'T MEAN POVERTY.

WE CAME HERE WITH QUITE SOME SURPLUS.

WHY DOES THE EMPIRE LEAVE YOU ALONE?

WE PAY TITHES, BUT THIS WORLD IS SIMPLY NOT MUCH USE TO THEM.

IN MY PREVIOUS CAREER, I EARNED RIGHTS TO THE MOON. THIS IS...MY RETIREMENT.

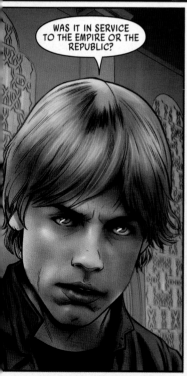

WAS IT IN SERVICE TO THE EMPIRE OR THE REPUBLIC?

CAN YOU IDENTIFY WHEN ONE ENDED AND THE OTHER BEGAN?

AS SOMEONE WHO LIVED THROUGH THOSE TIMES, I'M UNSURE I COULD MARK THAT LINE, LUKE.

YOU HAVE MY HOSPITALITY HERE FOR AS LONG AS YOU STAY.

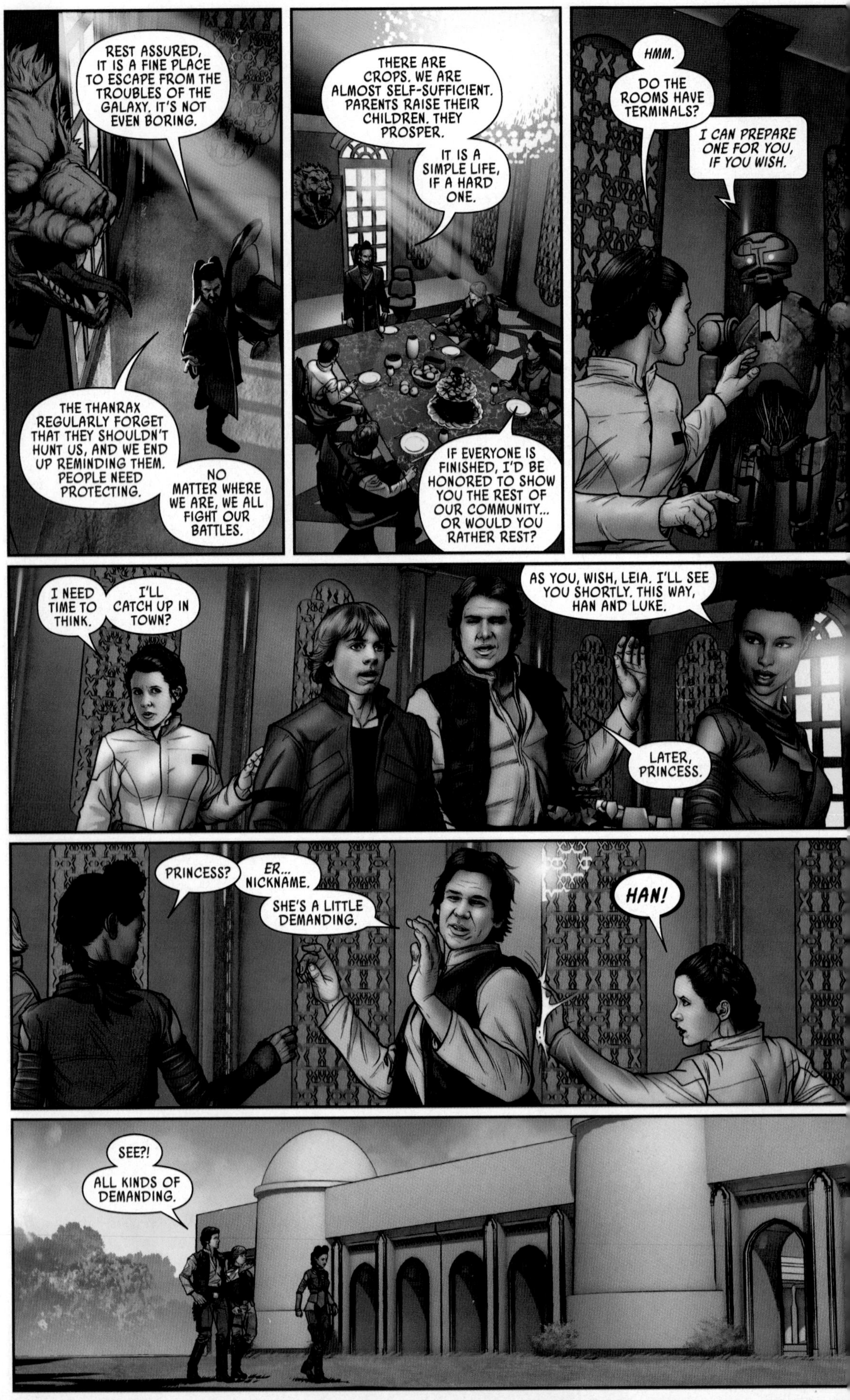
REST ASSURED, IT IS A FINE PLACE TO ESCAPE FROM THE TROUBLES OF THE GALAXY. IT'S NOT EVEN BORING.
THE THANRAX REGULARLY FORGET THAT THEY SHOULDN'T HUNT US, AND WE END UP REMINDING THEM. PEOPLE NEED PROTECTING.
NO MATTER WHERE WE ARE, WE ALL FIGHT OUR BATTLES.
THERE ARE CROPS. WE ARE ALMOST SELF-SUFFICIENT. PARENTS RAISE THEIR CHILDREN. THEY PROSPER.
IT IS A SIMPLE LIFE, IF A HARD ONE.
IF EVERYONE IS FINISHED, I'D BE HONORED TO SHOW YOU THE REST OF OUR COMMUNITY... OR WOULD YOU RATHER REST?
HMM.
DO THE ROOMS HAVE TERMINALS?
I CAN PREPARE ONE FOR YOU, IF YOU WISH.
I NEED TIME TO THINK.
I'LL CATCH UP IN TOWN?
AS YOU, WISH, LEIA. I'LL SEE YOU SHORTLY. THIS WAY, HAN AND LUKE.
LATER, PRINCESS.
PRINCESS?
ER... NICKNAME.
SHE'S A LITTLE DEMANDING.
HAN!
SEE?!
ALL KINDS OF DEMANDING.

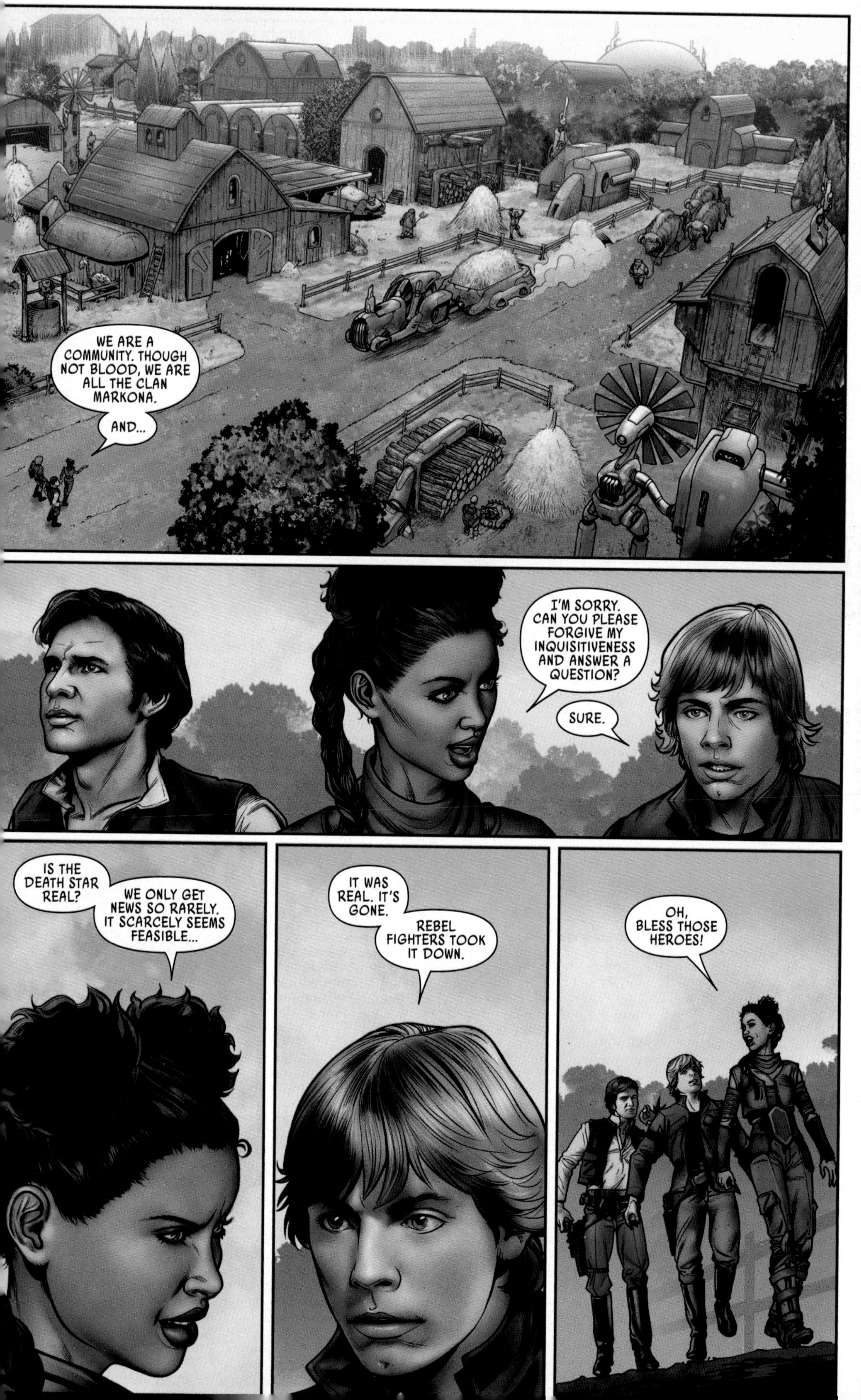
WE ARE A COMMUNITY. THOUGH NOT BLOOD, WE ARE ALL THE CLAN MARKONA.
AND...
I'M SORRY. CAN YOU PLEASE FORGIVE MY INQUISITIVENESS AND ANSWER A QUESTION?
SURE.
IS THE DEATH STAR REAL?
WE ONLY GET NEWS SO RARELY. IT SCARCELY SEEMS FEASIBLE...
IT WAS REAL. IT'S GONE.
REBEL FIGHTERS TOOK IT DOWN.
OH, BLESS THOSE HEROES!

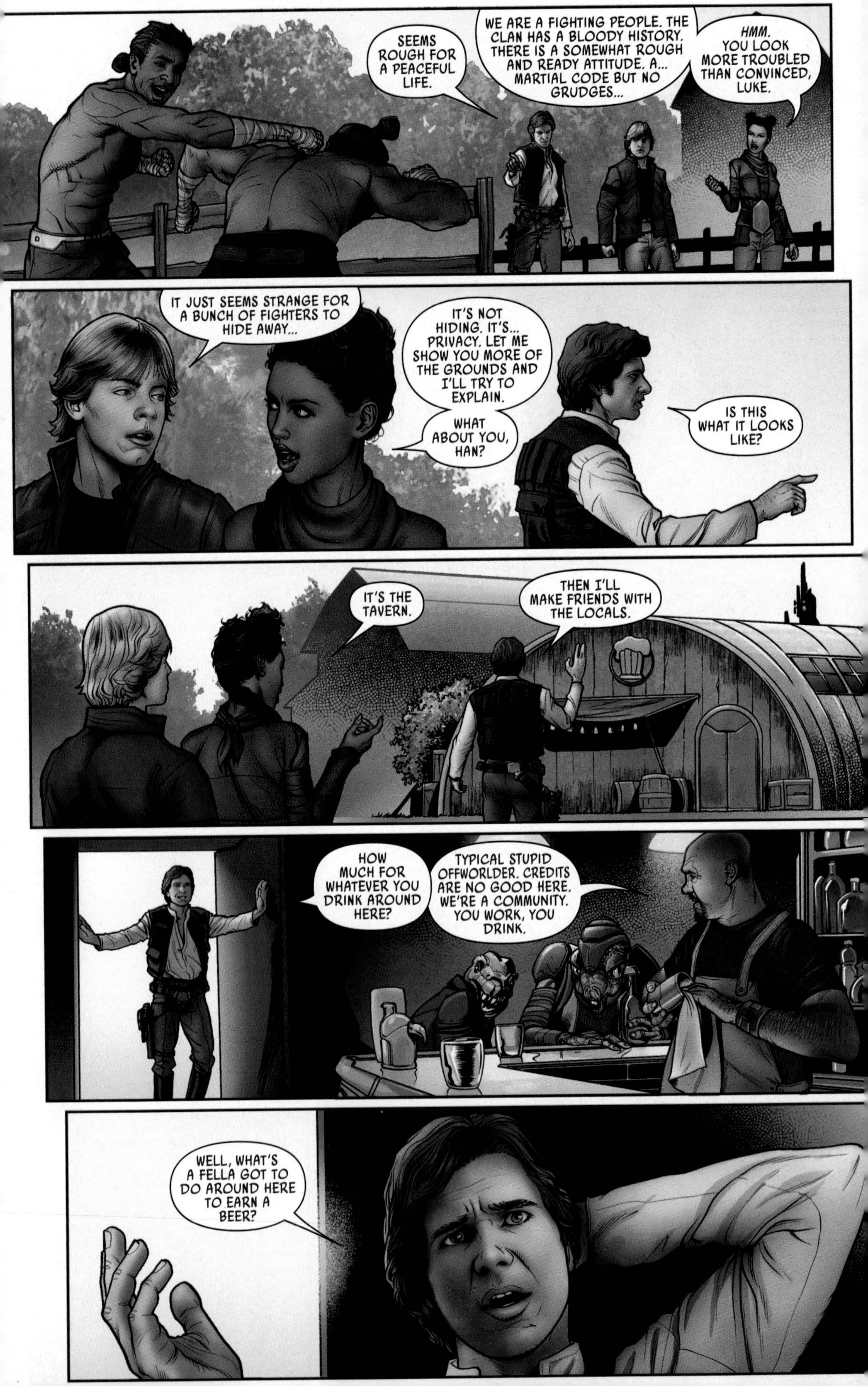
SEEMS ROUGH FOR A PEACEFUL LIFE.
WE ARE A FIGHTING PEOPLE. THE CLAN HAS A BLOODY HISTORY. THERE IS A SOMEWHAT ROUGH AND READY ATTITUDE. A... MARTIAL CODE BUT NO GRUDGES...
HMM. YOU LOOK MORE TROUBLED THAN CONVINCED, LUKE.
IT JUST SEEMS STRANGE FOR A BUNCH OF FIGHTERS TO HIDE AWAY...
IT'S NOT HIDING. IT'S... PRIVACY. LET ME SHOW YOU MORE OF THE GROUNDS AND I'LL TRY TO EXPLAIN.
WHAT ABOUT YOU, HAN?
IS THIS WHAT IT LOOKS LIKE?
IT'S THE TAVERN.
THEN I'LL MAKE FRIENDS WITH THE LOCALS.
HOW MUCH FOR WHATEVER YOU DRINK AROUND HERE?
TYPICAL STUPID OFFWORLDER. CREDITS ARE NO GOOD HERE. WE'RE A COMMUNITY. YOU WORK, YOU DRINK.
WELL, WHAT'S A FELLA GOT TO DO AROUND HERE TO EARN A BEER?

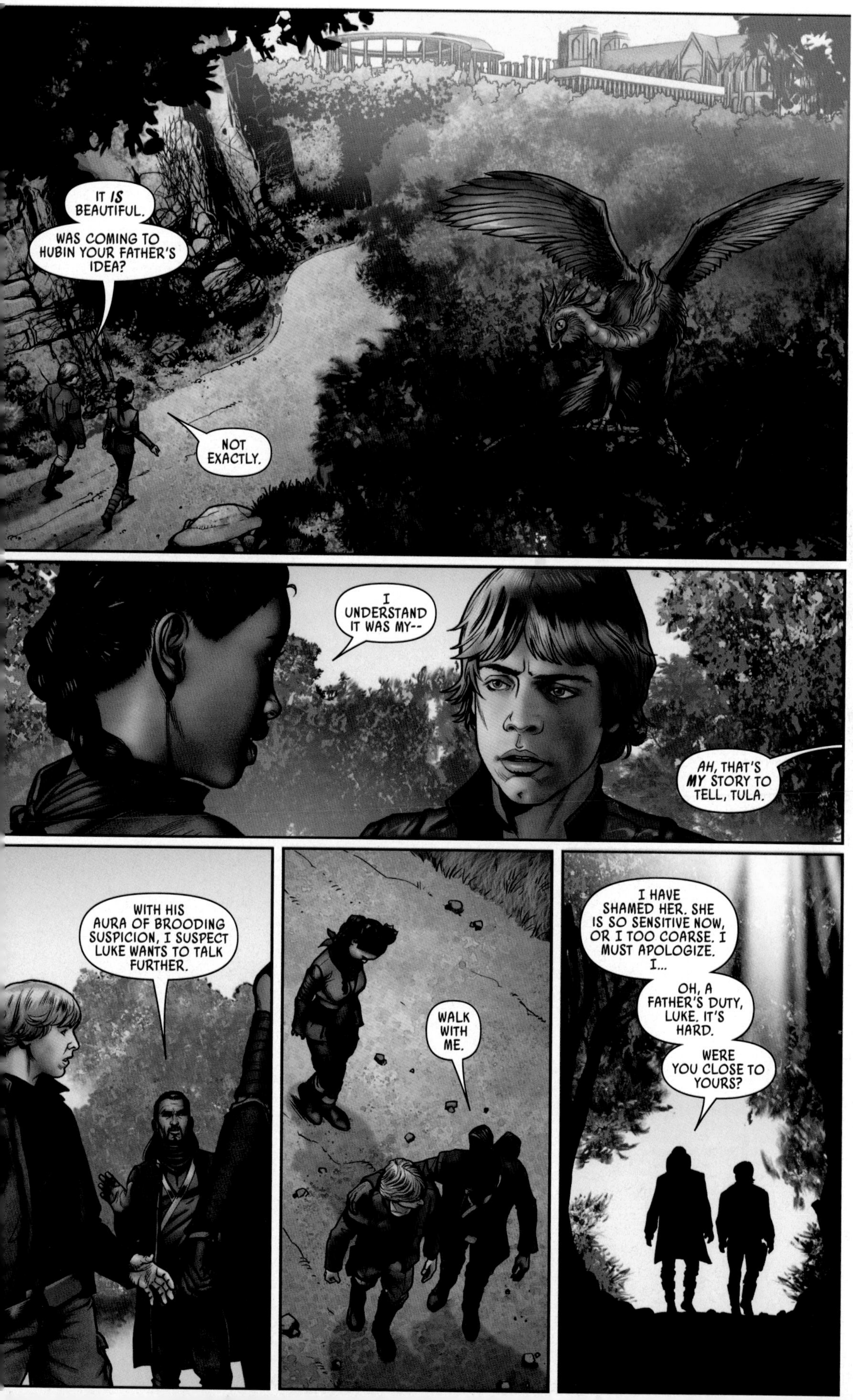
IT IS BEAUTIFUL.
WAS COMING TO HUBIN YOUR FATHER'S IDEA?
NOT EXACTLY.
I UNDERSTAND IT WAS MY--
AH, THAT'S MY STORY TO TELL, TULA.
WITH HIS AURA OF BROODING SUSPICION, I SUSPECT LUKE WANTS TO TALK FURTHER.
WALK WITH ME.
I HAVE SHAMED HER. SHE IS SO SENSITIVE NOW, OR I TOO COARSE. I MUST APOLOGIZE. I...
OH, A FATHER'S DUTY, LUKE. IT'S HARD.
WERE YOU CLOSE TO YOURS?

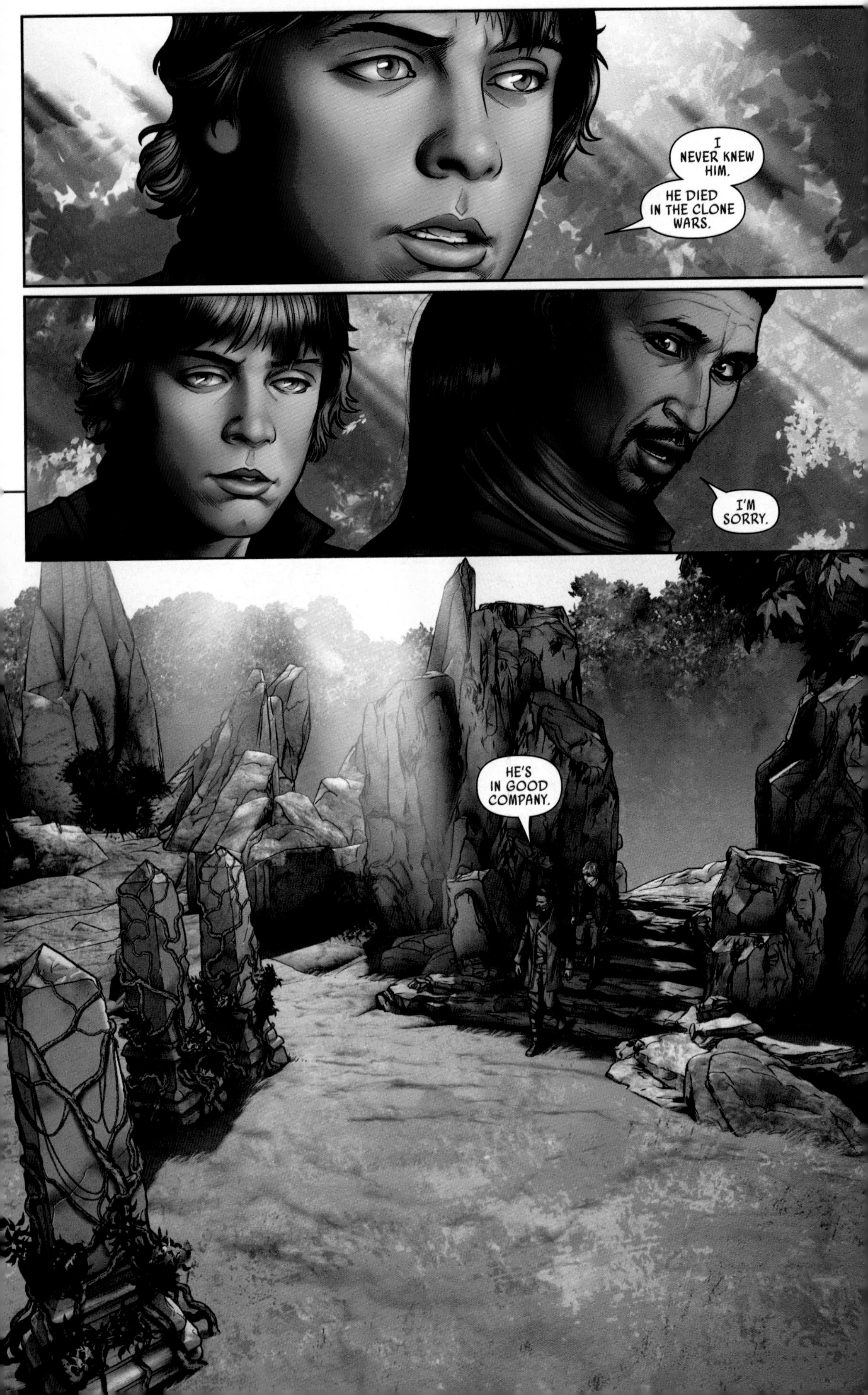

I NEVER KNEW HIM.
HE DIED IN THE CLONE WARS.
I'M SORRY.
HE'S IN GOOD COMPANY.

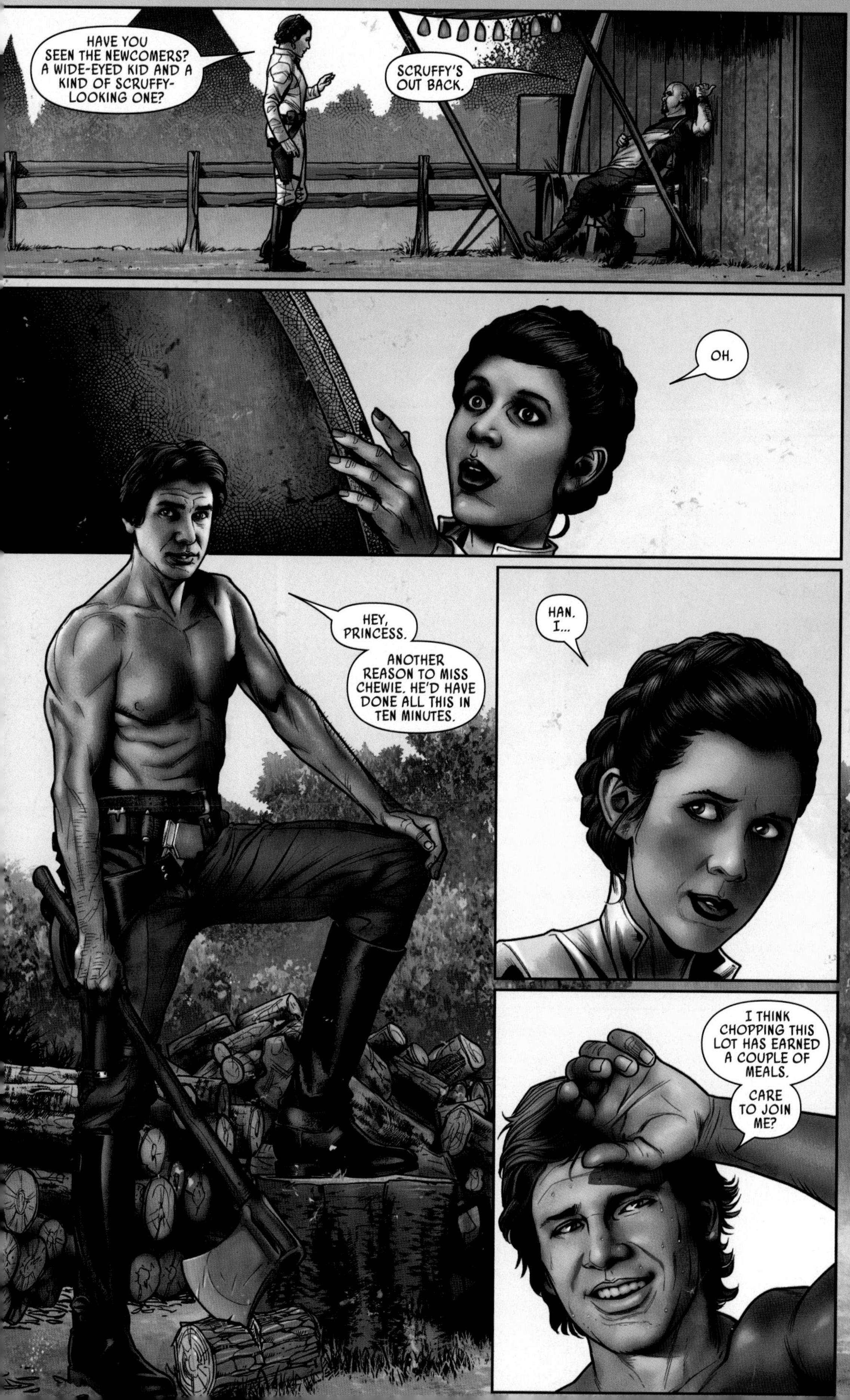

HAVE YOU SEEN THE NEWCOMERS? A WIDE-EYED KID AND A KIND OF SCRUFFY-LOOKING ONE?
SCRUFFY'S OUT BACK.
OH.
HEY, PRINCESS.
ANOTHER REASON TO MISS CHEWIE. HE'D HAVE DONE ALL THIS IN TEN MINUTES.
HAN. I...
I THINK CHOPPING THIS LOT HAS EARNED A COUPLE OF MEALS.
CARE TO JOIN ME?

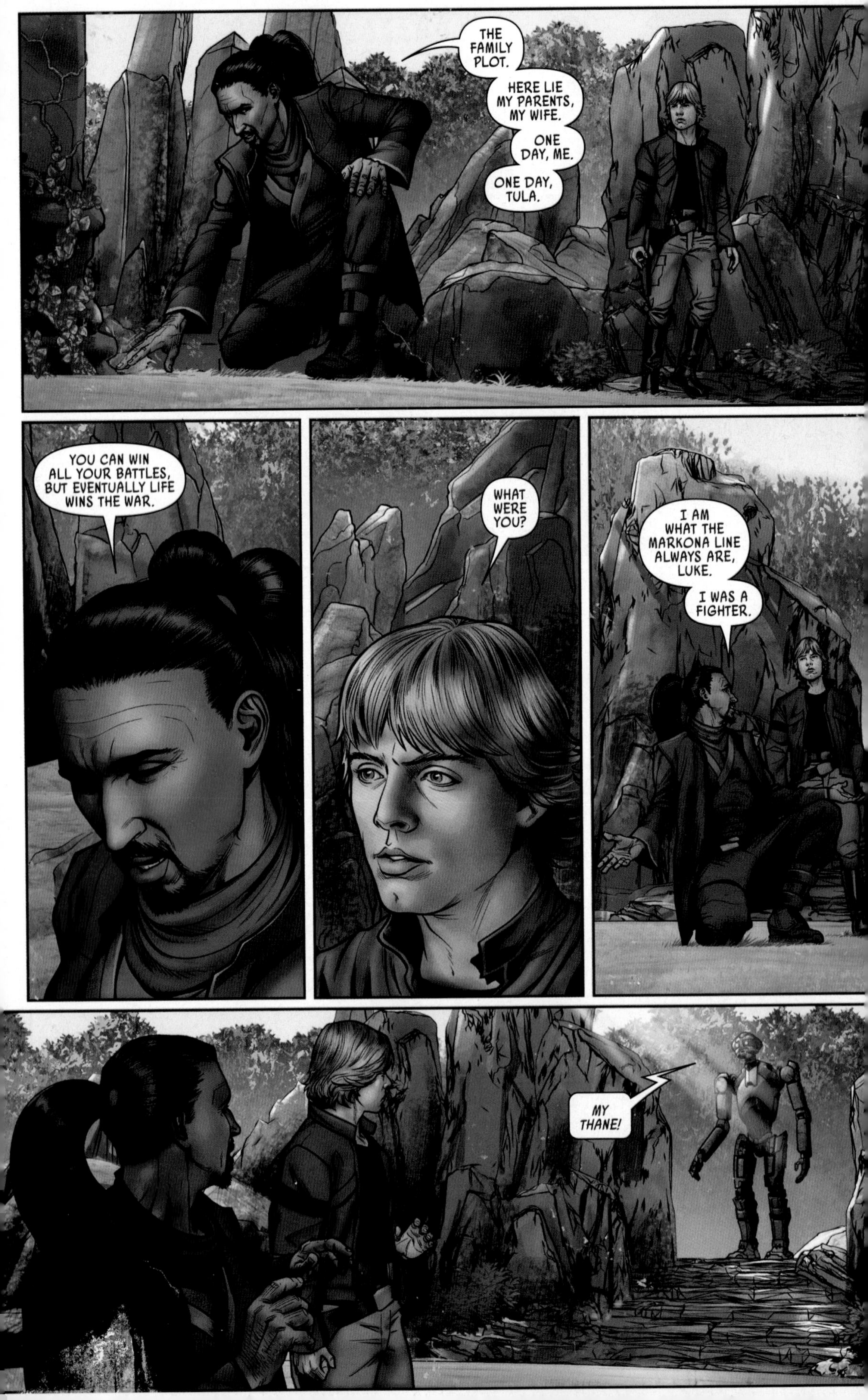
THE FAMILY PLOT.
HERE LIE MY PARENTS, MY WIFE.
ONE DAY, ME.
ONE DAY, TULA.
YOU CAN WIN ALL YOUR BATTLES, BUT EVENTUALLY LIFE WINS THE WAR.
WHAT WERE YOU?
I AM WHAT THE MARKONA LINE ALWAYS ARE, LUKE.
I WAS A FIGHTER.
MY THANE!

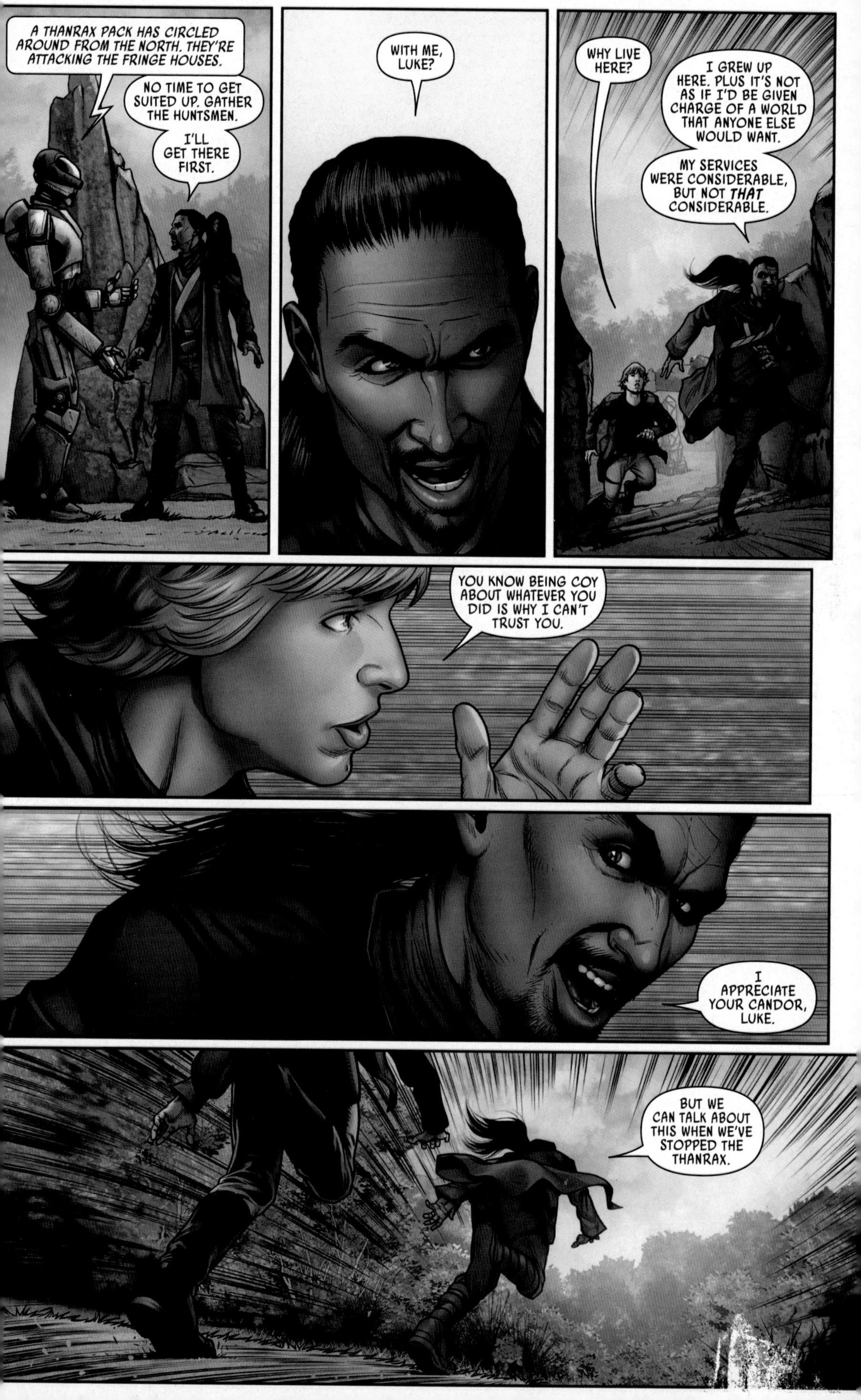
A THANRAX PACK HAS CIRCLED AROUND FROM THE NORTH. THEY'RE ATTACKING THE FRINGE HOUSES.
NO TIME TO GET SUITED UP. GATHER THE HUNTSMEN.
I'LL GET THERE FIRST.
WITH ME, LUKE?
WHY LIVE HERE?
I GREW UP HERE. PLUS IT'S NOT AS IF I'D BE GIVEN CHARGE OF A WORLD THAT ANYONE ELSE WOULD WANT.
MY SERVICES WERE CONSIDERABLE, BUT NOT *THAT* CONSIDERABLE.
YOU KNOW BEING COY ABOUT WHATEVER YOU DID IS WHY I CAN'T TRUST YOU.
I APPRECIATE YOUR CANDOR, LUKE.
BUT WE CAN TALK ABOUT THIS WHEN WE'VE STOPPED THE THANRAX.

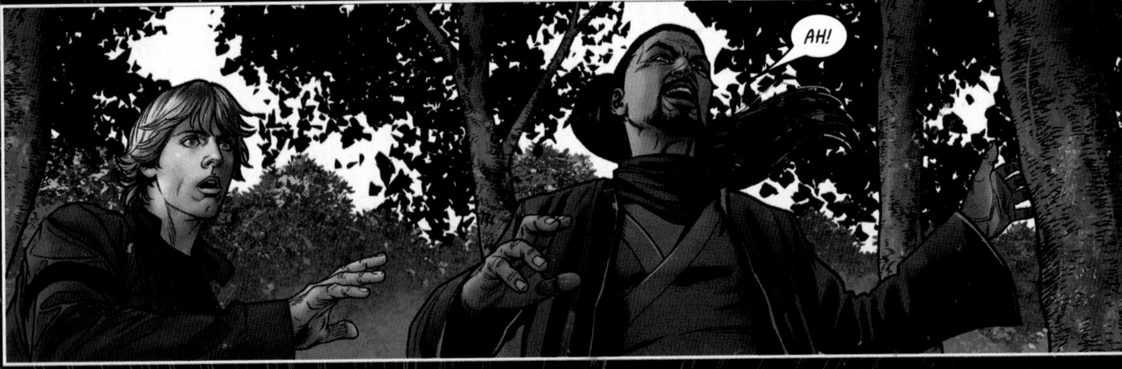
AH!

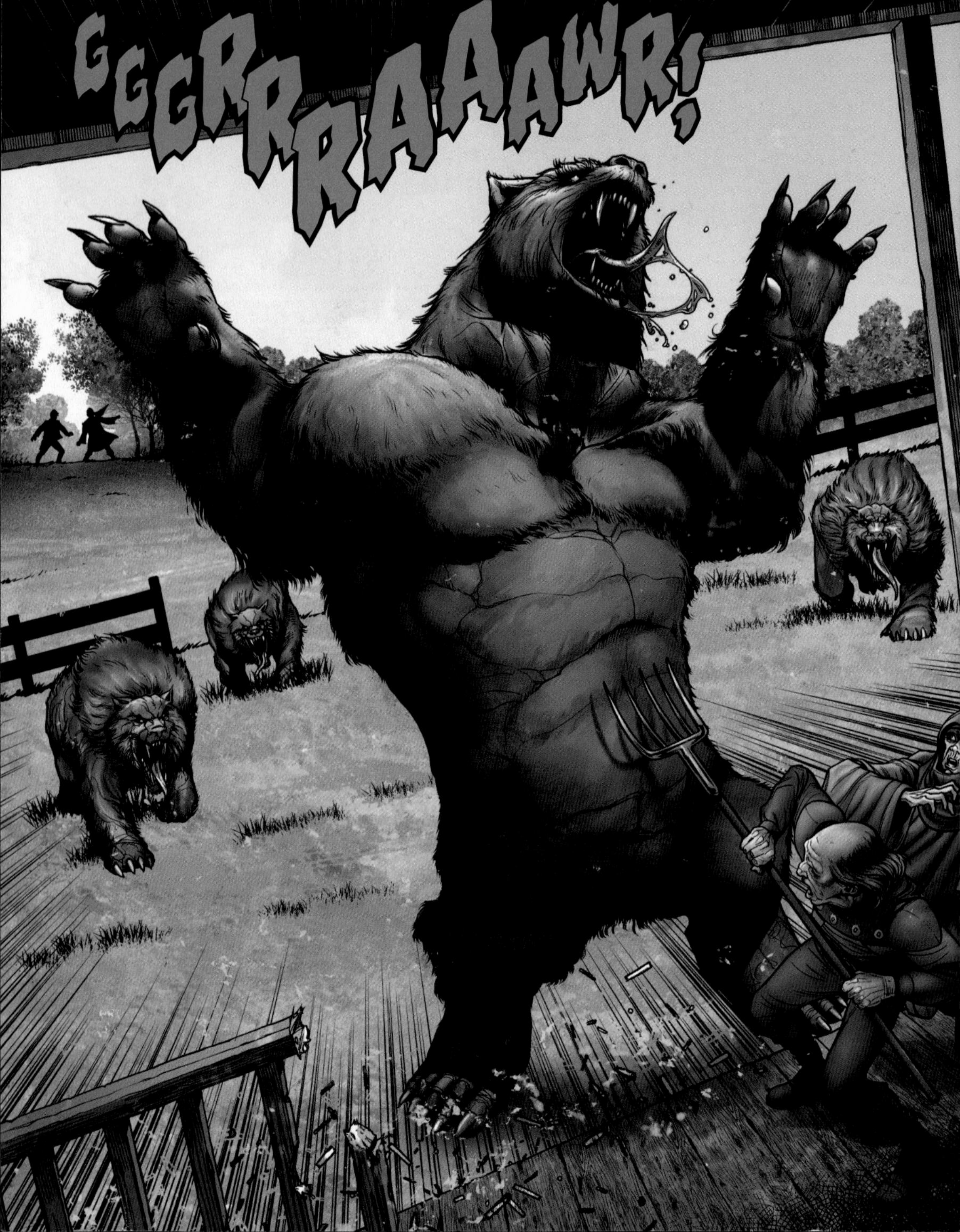
GGGRRRAAAAWR!

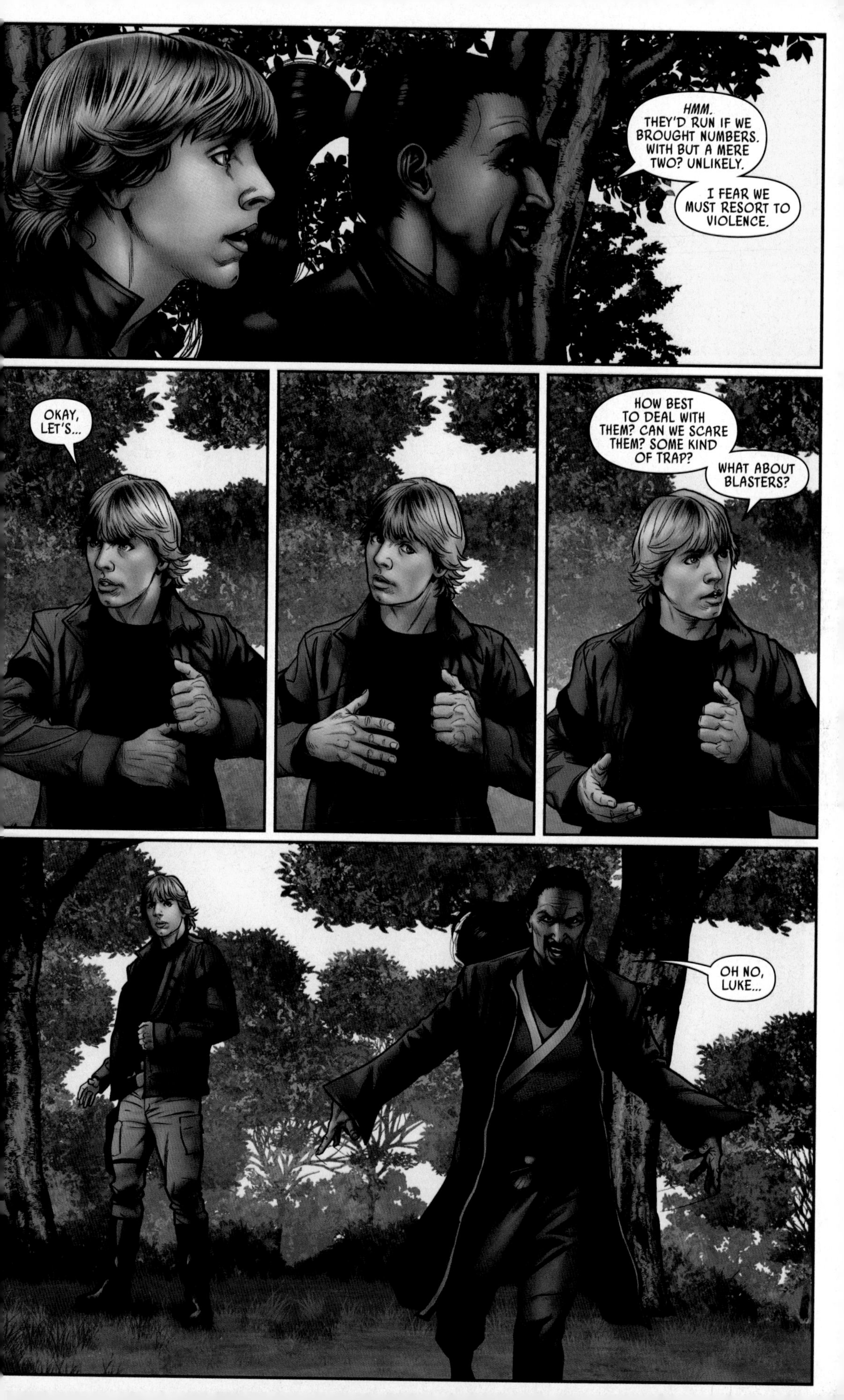
HMM. THEY'D RUN IF WE BROUGHT NUMBERS. WITH BUT A MERE TWO? UNLIKELY.
I FEAR WE MUST RESORT TO VIOLENCE.
OKAY, LET'S...
HOW BEST TO DEAL WITH THEM? CAN WE SCARE THEM? SOME KIND OF TRAP?
WHAT ABOUT BLASTERS?
OH NO, LUKE...

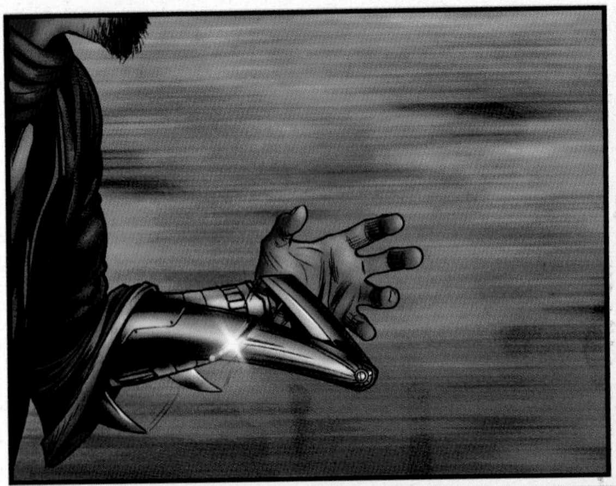

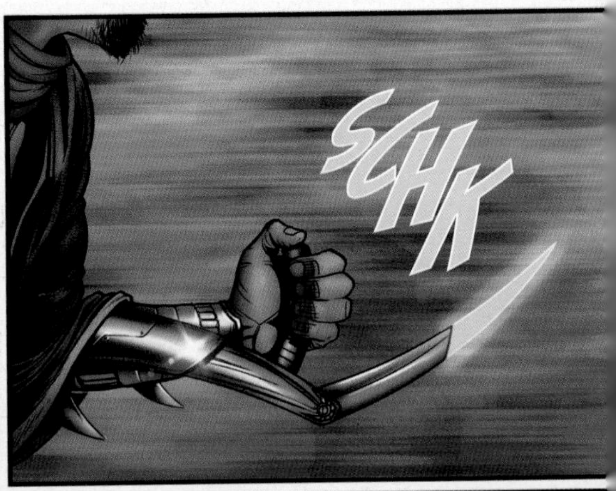
SCHK

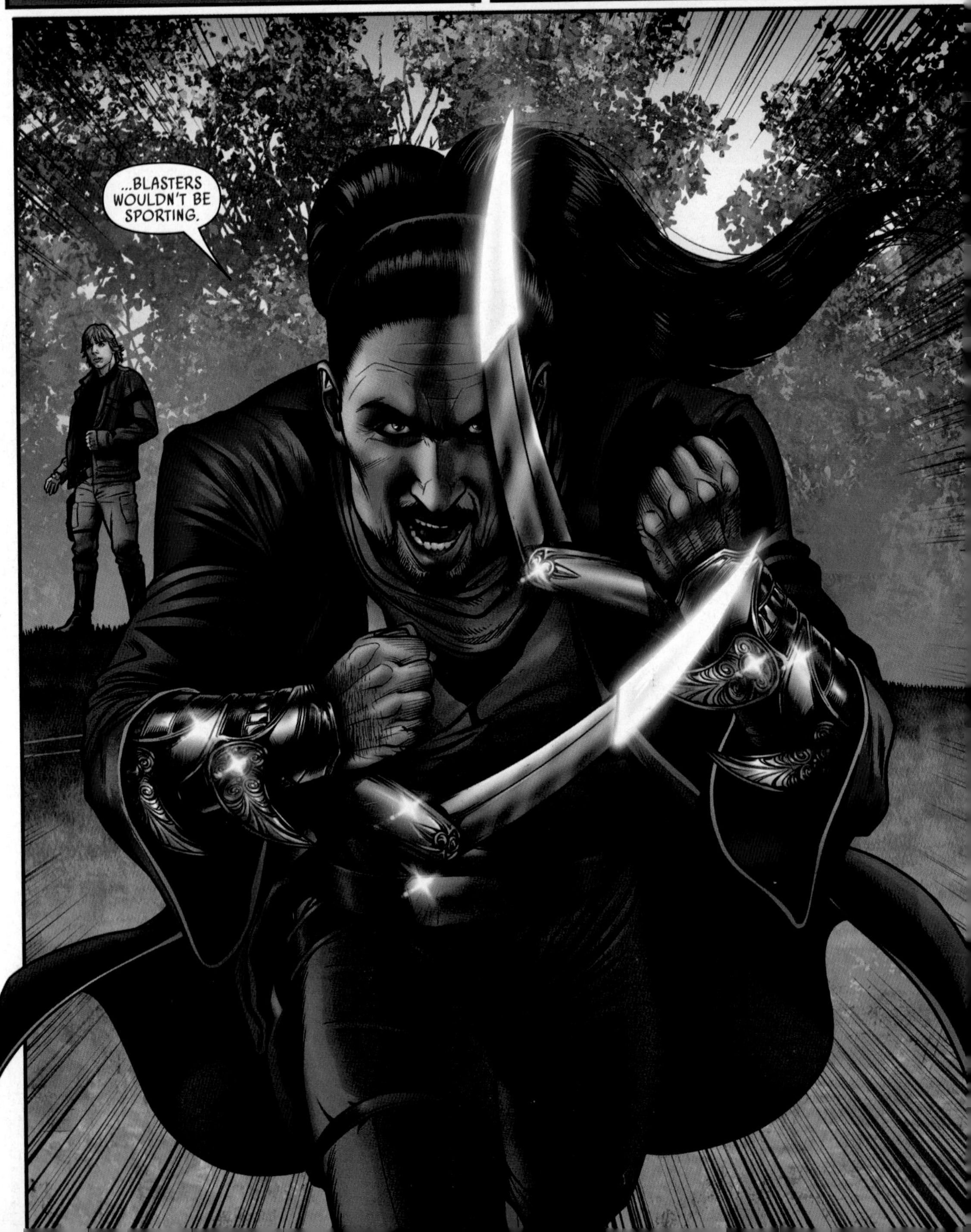
...BLASTERS WOULDN'T BE SPORTING.

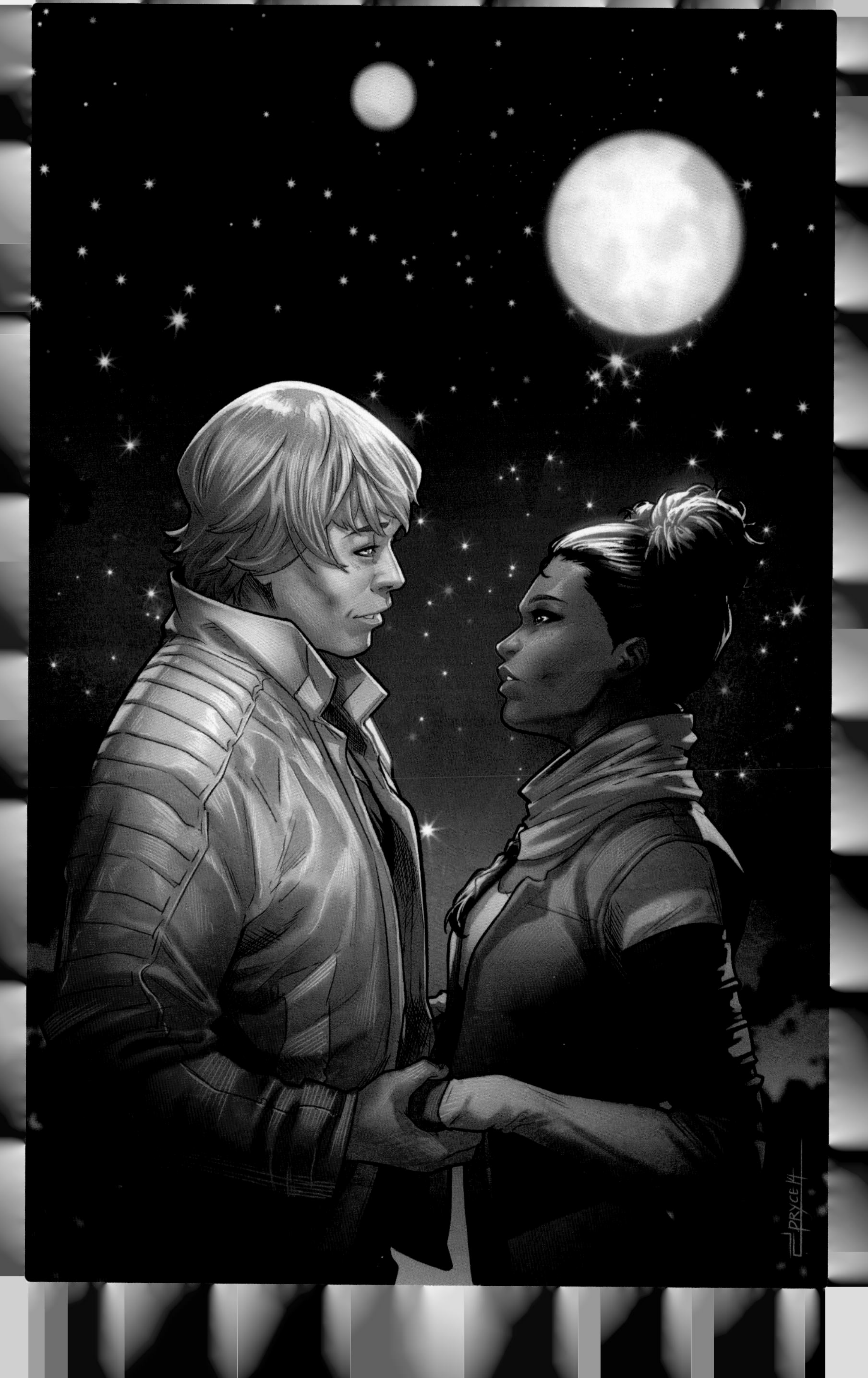

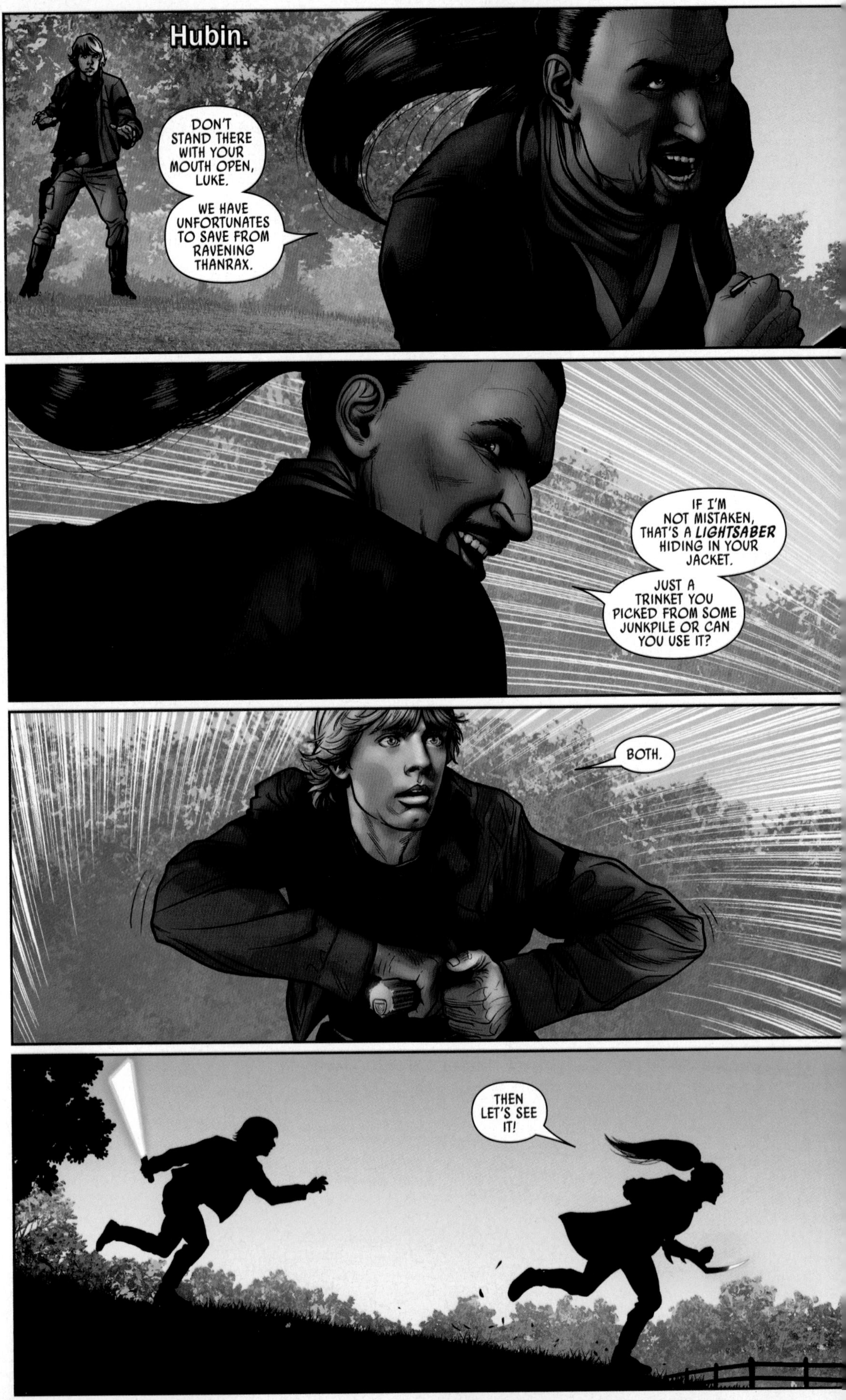

Hubin.
DON'T STAND THERE WITH YOUR MOUTH OPEN, LUKE.
WE HAVE UNFORTUNATES TO SAVE FROM RAVENING THANRAX.
IF I'M NOT MISTAKEN, THAT'S A LIGHTSABER HIDING IN YOUR JACKET.
JUST A TRINKET YOU PICKED FROM SOME JUNKPILE OR CAN YOU USE IT?
BOTH.
THEN LET'S SEE IT!

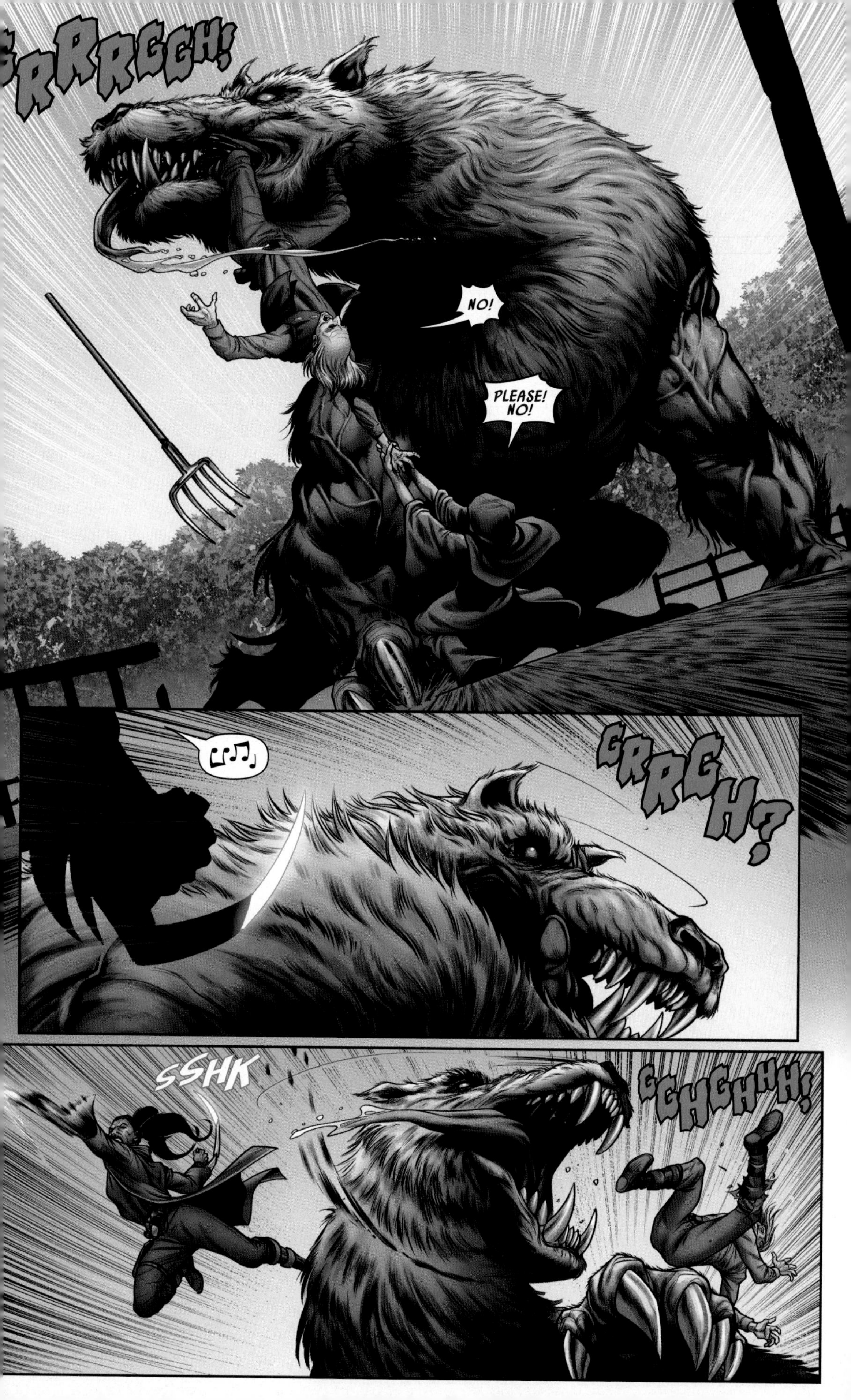

RRRGGH!
NO!
PLEASE! NO!
GRRGH?
SSHK
GGHGHHH!

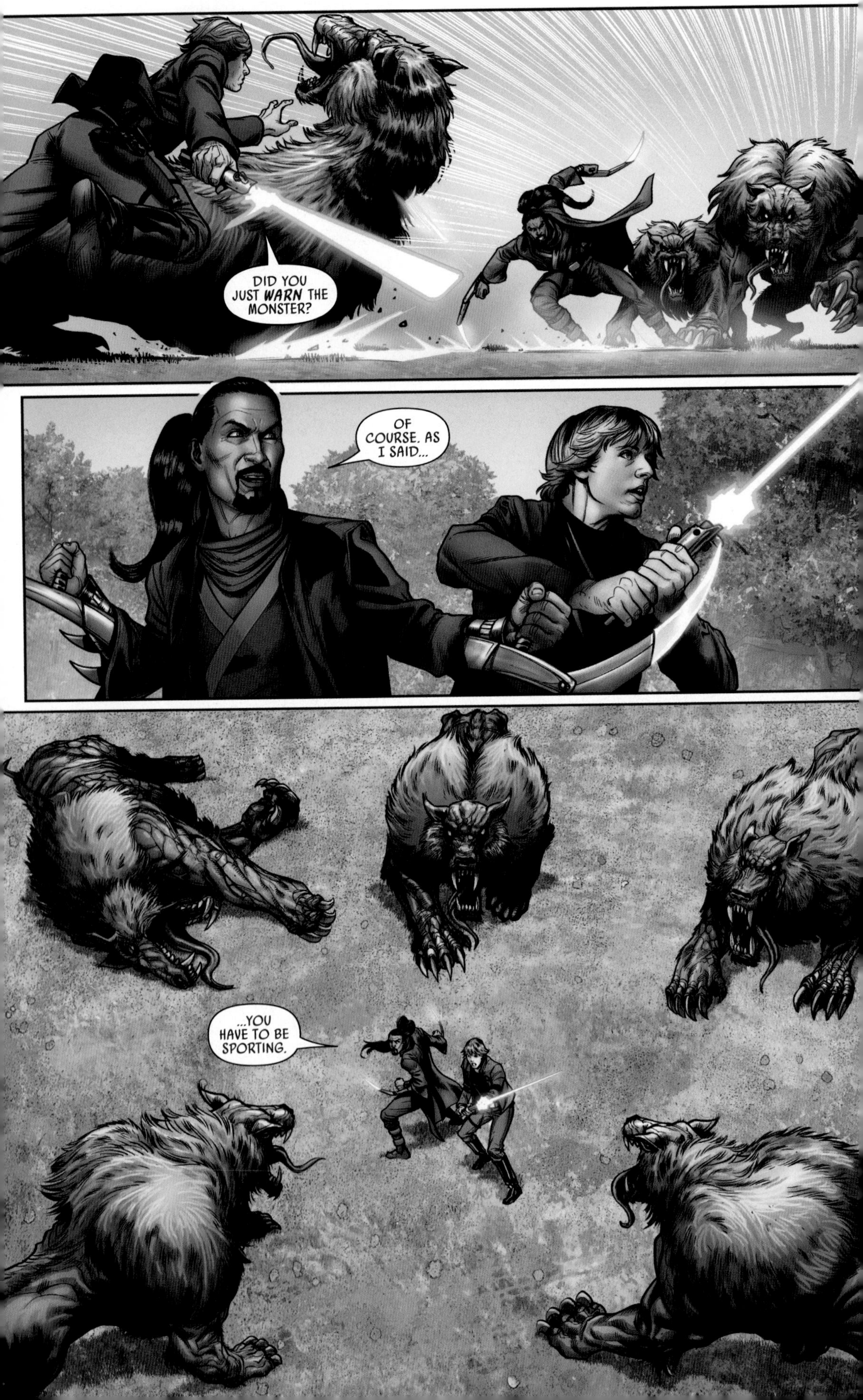
DID YOU JUST *WARN* THE MONSTER?
OF COURSE. AS I SAID...
...YOU HAVE TO BE SPORTING.

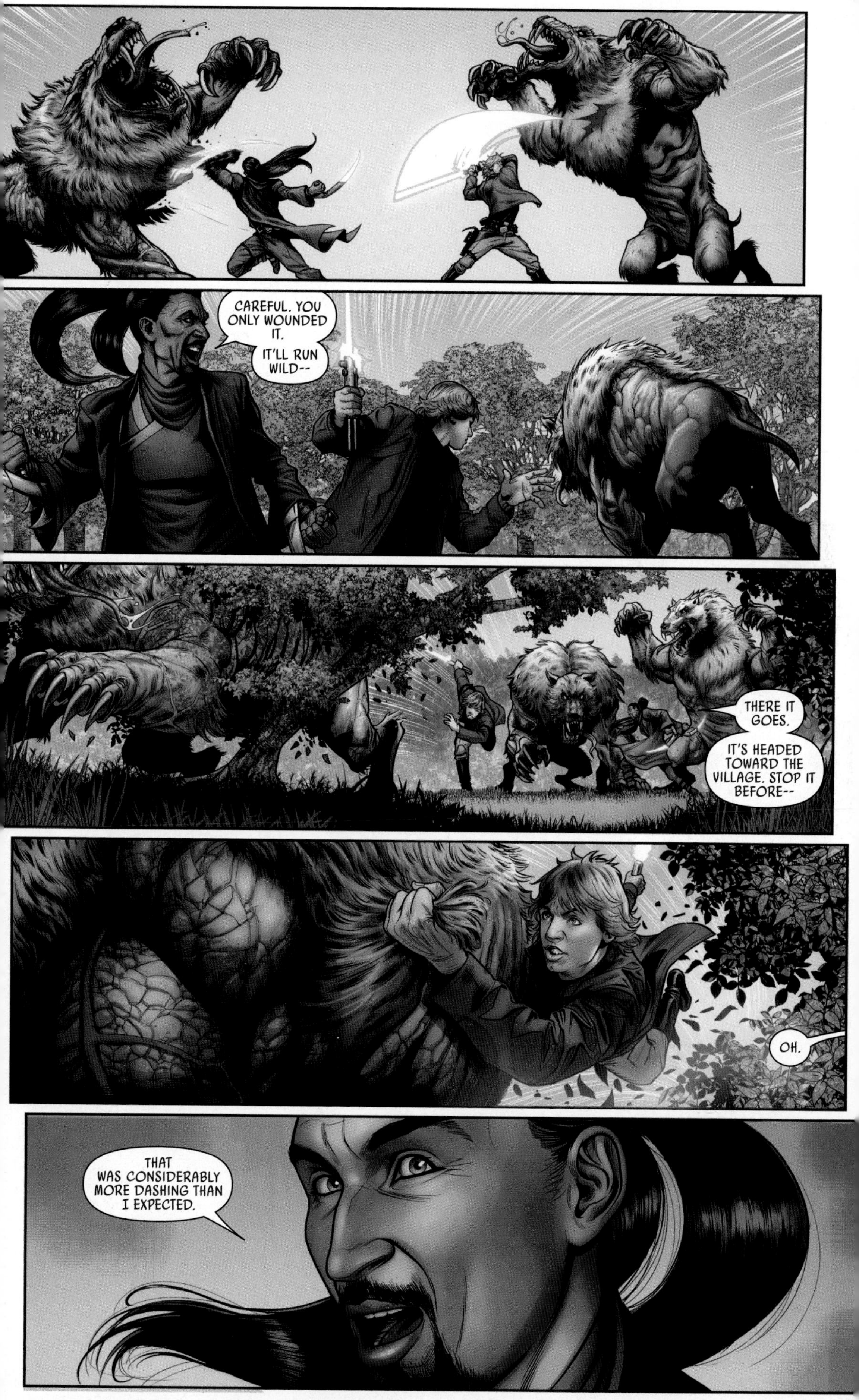
CAREFUL. YOU ONLY WOUNDED IT.
IT'LL RUN WILD--
THERE IT GOES.
IT'S HEADED TOWARD THE VILLAGE. STOP IT BEFORE--
OH.
THAT WAS CONSIDERABLY MORE DASHING THAN I EXPECTED.

Nearby.

SO, WHY ASK MARKONA IF YOU COULD HAVE A PRIVATE TERMINAL?

JUST... THINKING. PLANNING.

YOU KNOW ME. AFTER THE DISASTER OF MAKO-TA, QUEEN TRIOS OF BLASTED SHU-TORUN LEFT ME A WHOLE LOT TO CHEW OVER...

THANK YOU.

YOU KNOW, THIS IS SURPRISINGLY PLEASANT.

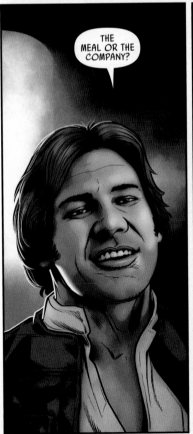

THE MEAL OR THE COMPANY?

LET'S SAY BOTH.

YOU KNOW, I HATE TO RUIN THE MOMENT BY SUGGESTING THERE'S ANYTHING IN COMMON BETWEEN A SMUGGLER AND ROYALTY, BUT I WAS THINKING THE SAME THING.

WHEN WAS THE LAST TIME WE HAD A QUIET MEA--

THANRAX! THANRAX!

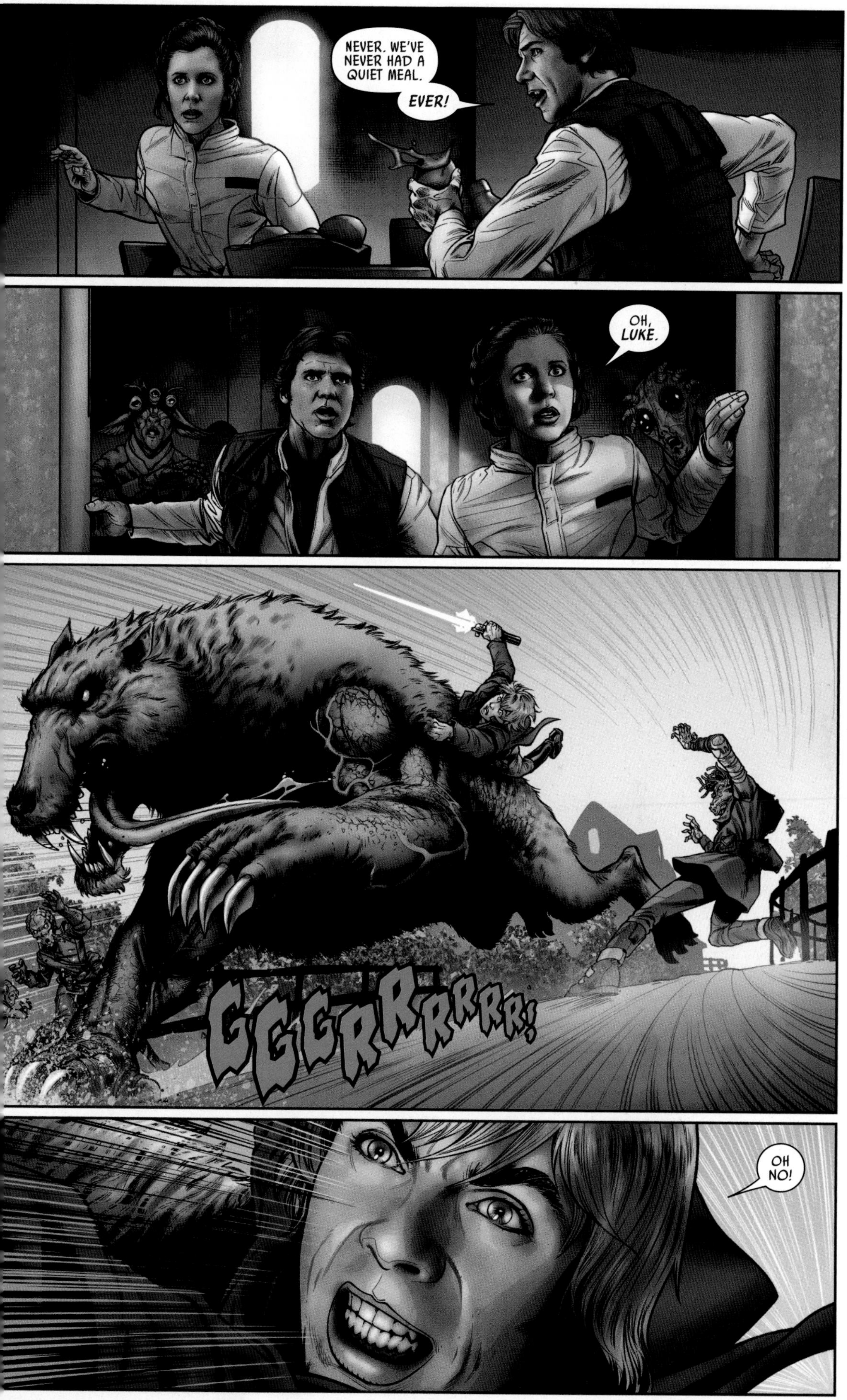
NEVER. WE'VE NEVER HAD A QUIET MEAL.
EVER!
OH, LUKE.
GGGRRRRRR!
OH NO!

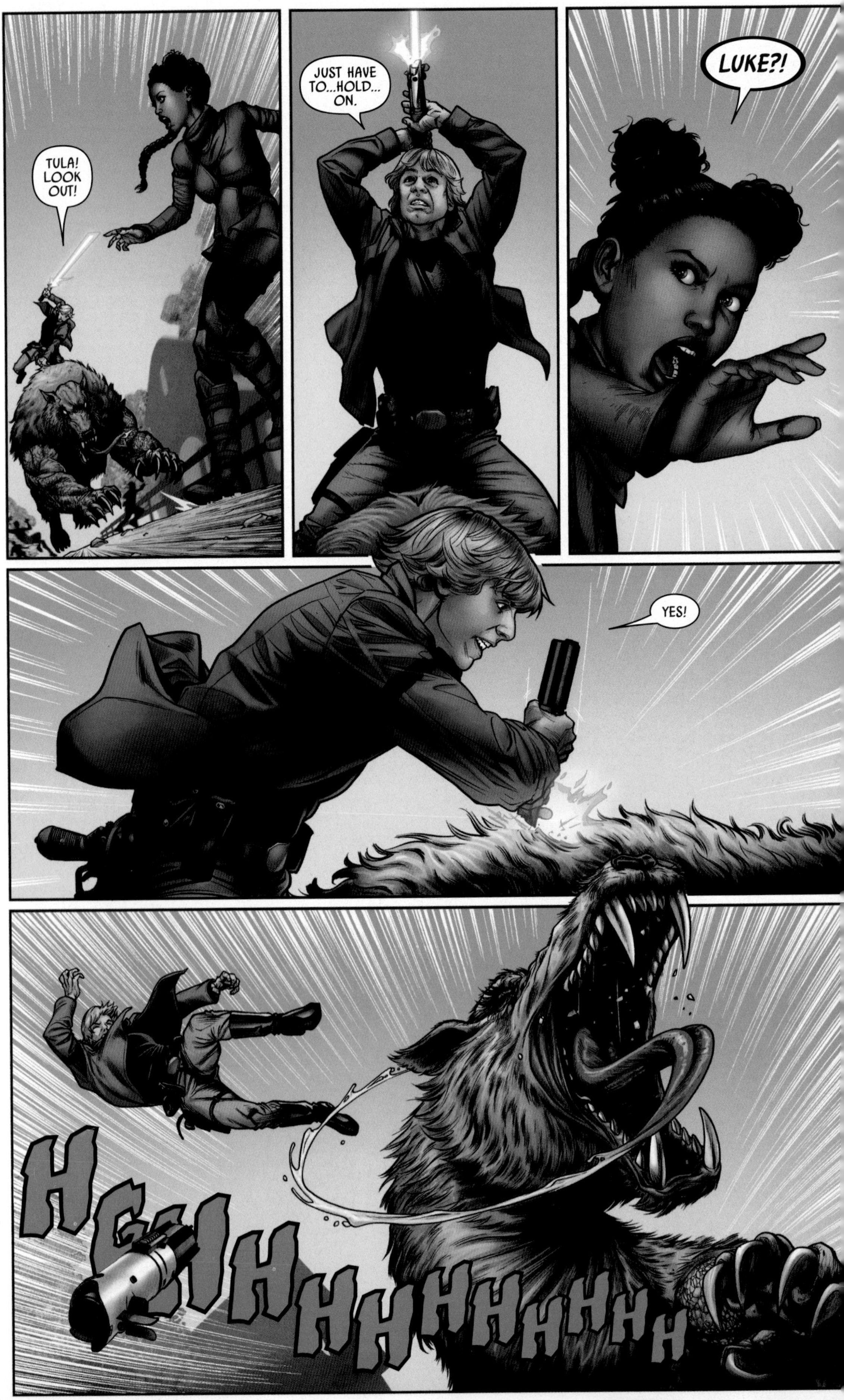
TULA! LOOK OUT!
JUST HAVE TO...HOLD... ON.
LUKE?!
YES!
HGIIHHHHHHHHHH

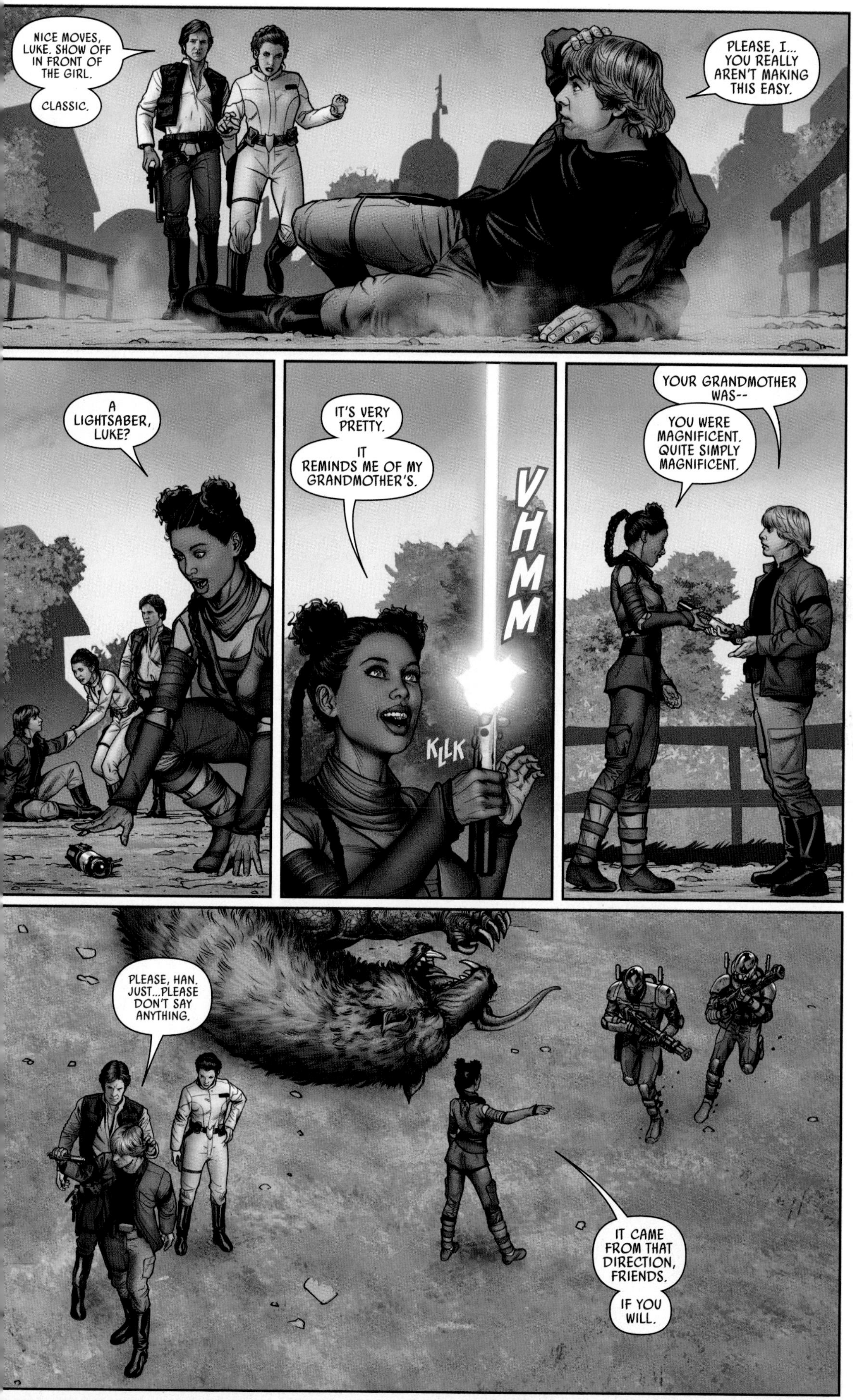
NICE MOVES, LUKE. SHOW OFF IN FRONT OF THE GIRL.
CLASSIC.
PLEASE, I... YOU REALLY AREN'T MAKING THIS EASY.
A LIGHTSABER, LUKE?
IT'S VERY PRETTY.
IT REMINDS ME OF MY GRANDMOTHER'S.
VHMM
KLLK
YOUR GRANDMOTHER WAS--
YOU WERE MAGNIFICENT. QUITE SIMPLY MAGNIFICENT.
PLEASE, HAN. JUST...PLEASE DON'T SAY ANYTHING.
IT CAME FROM THAT DIRECTION, FRIENDS.
IF YOU WILL.

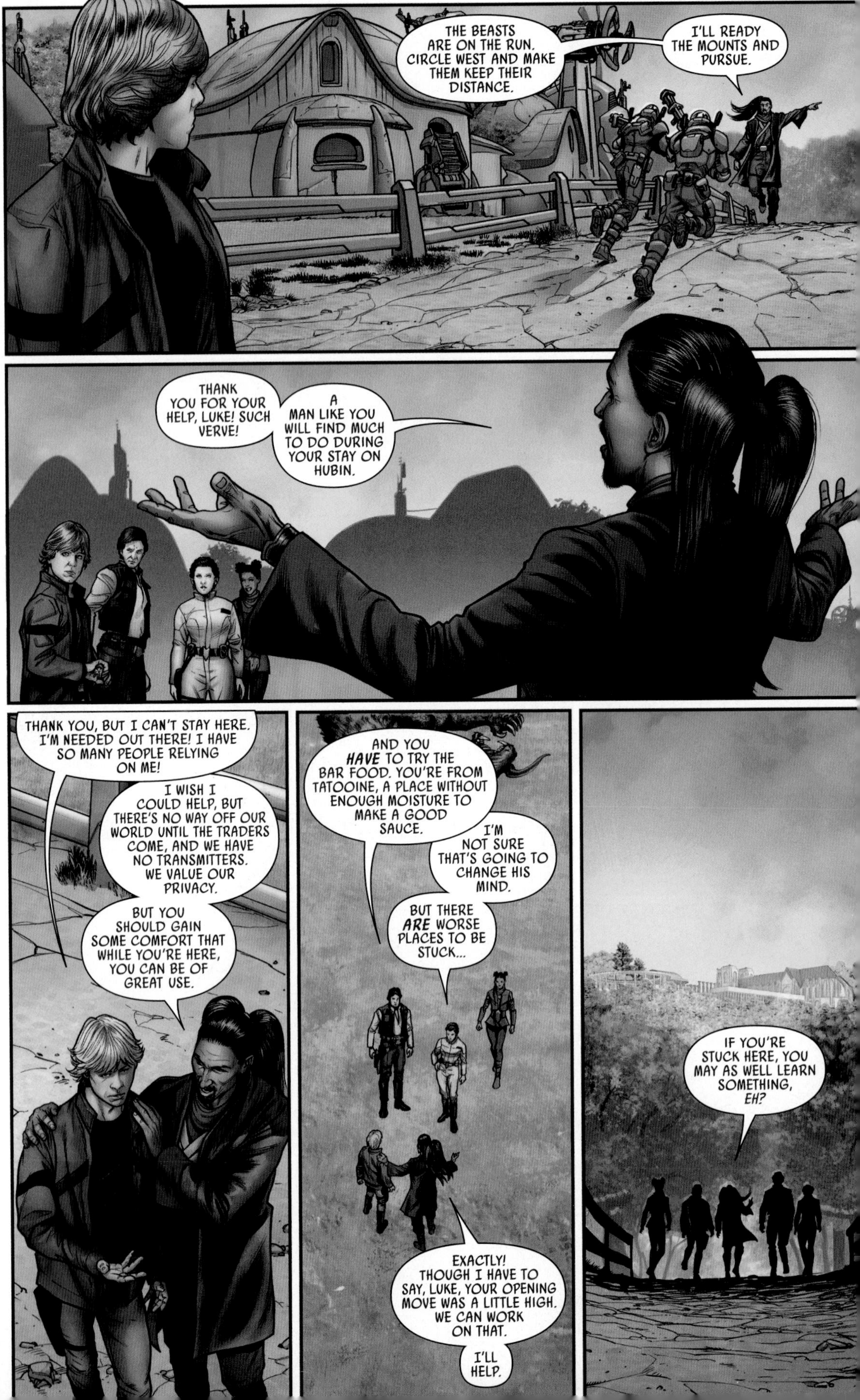
THE BEASTS ARE ON THE RUN. CIRCLE WEST AND MAKE THEM KEEP THEIR DISTANCE.
I'LL READY THE MOUNTS AND PURSUE.
THANK YOU FOR YOUR HELP, LUKE! SUCH VERVE!
A MAN LIKE YOU WILL FIND MUCH TO DO DURING YOUR STAY ON HUBIN.
THANK YOU, BUT I CAN'T STAY HERE. I'M NEEDED OUT THERE! I HAVE SO MANY PEOPLE RELYING ON ME!
I WISH I COULD HELP, BUT THERE'S NO WAY OFF OUR WORLD UNTIL THE TRADERS COME, AND WE HAVE NO TRANSMITTERS. WE VALUE OUR PRIVACY.
BUT YOU SHOULD GAIN SOME COMFORT THAT WHILE YOU'RE HERE, YOU CAN BE OF GREAT USE.
AND YOU *HAVE* TO TRY THE BAR FOOD. YOU'RE FROM TATOOINE, A PLACE WITHOUT ENOUGH MOISTURE TO MAKE A GOOD SAUCE.
I'M NOT SURE THAT'S GOING TO CHANGE HIS MIND.
BUT THERE *ARE* WORSE PLACES TO BE STUCK...
EXACTLY! THOUGH I HAVE TO SAY, LUKE, YOUR OPENING MOVE WAS A LITTLE HIGH. WE CAN WORK ON THAT.
I'LL HELP.
IF YOU'RE STUCK HERE, YOU MAY AS WELL LEARN SOMETHING, *EH?*

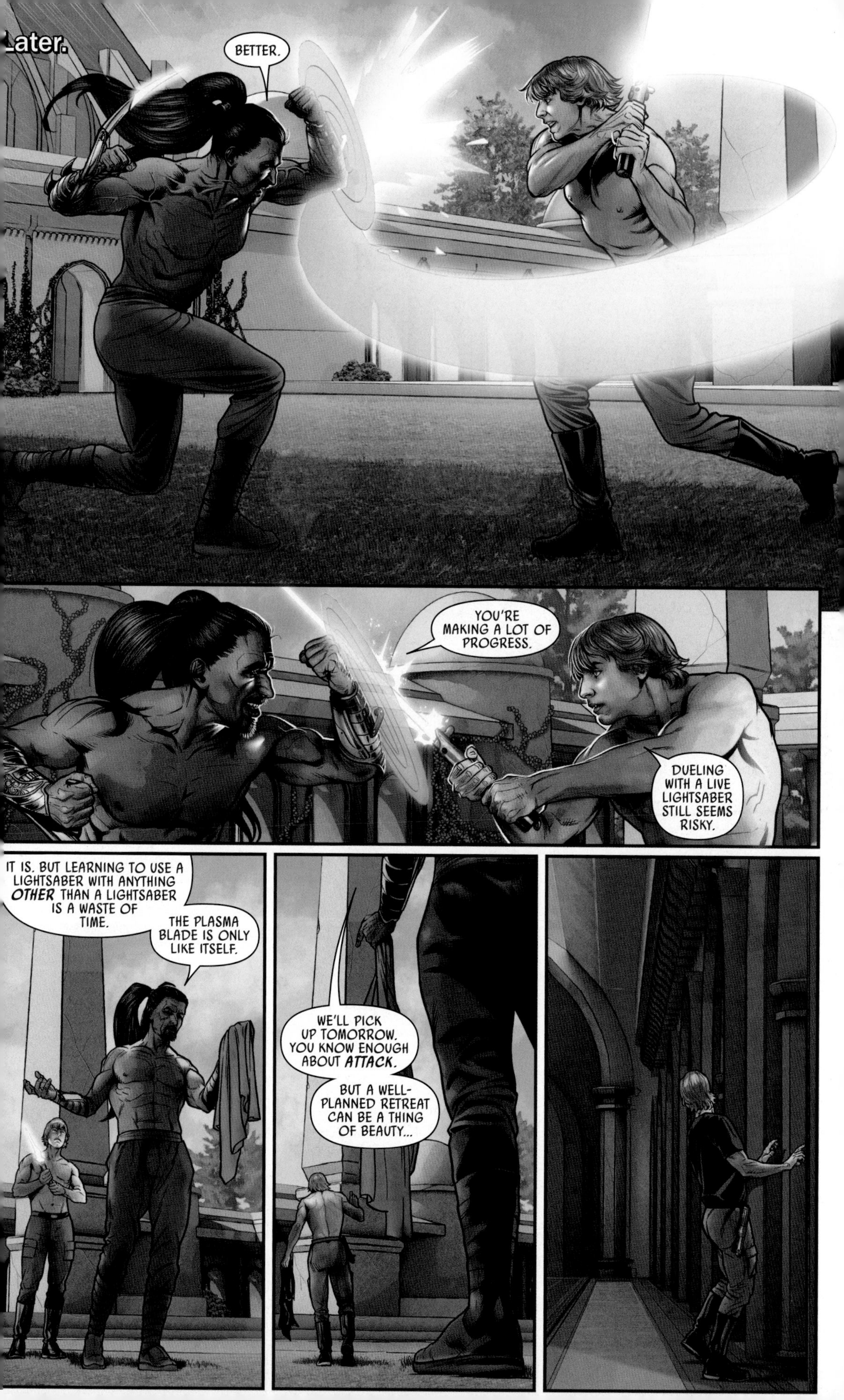
Later.
BETTER.
YOU'RE MAKING A LOT OF PROGRESS.
DUELING WITH A LIVE LIGHTSABER STILL SEEMS RISKY.
IT IS. BUT LEARNING TO USE A LIGHTSABER WITH ANYTHING OTHER THAN A LIGHTSABER IS A WASTE OF TIME.
THE PLASMA BLADE IS ONLY LIKE ITSELF.
WE'LL PICK UP TOMORROW. YOU KNOW ENOUGH ABOUT ATTACK.
BUT A WELL-PLANNED RETREAT CAN BE A THING OF BEAUTY...

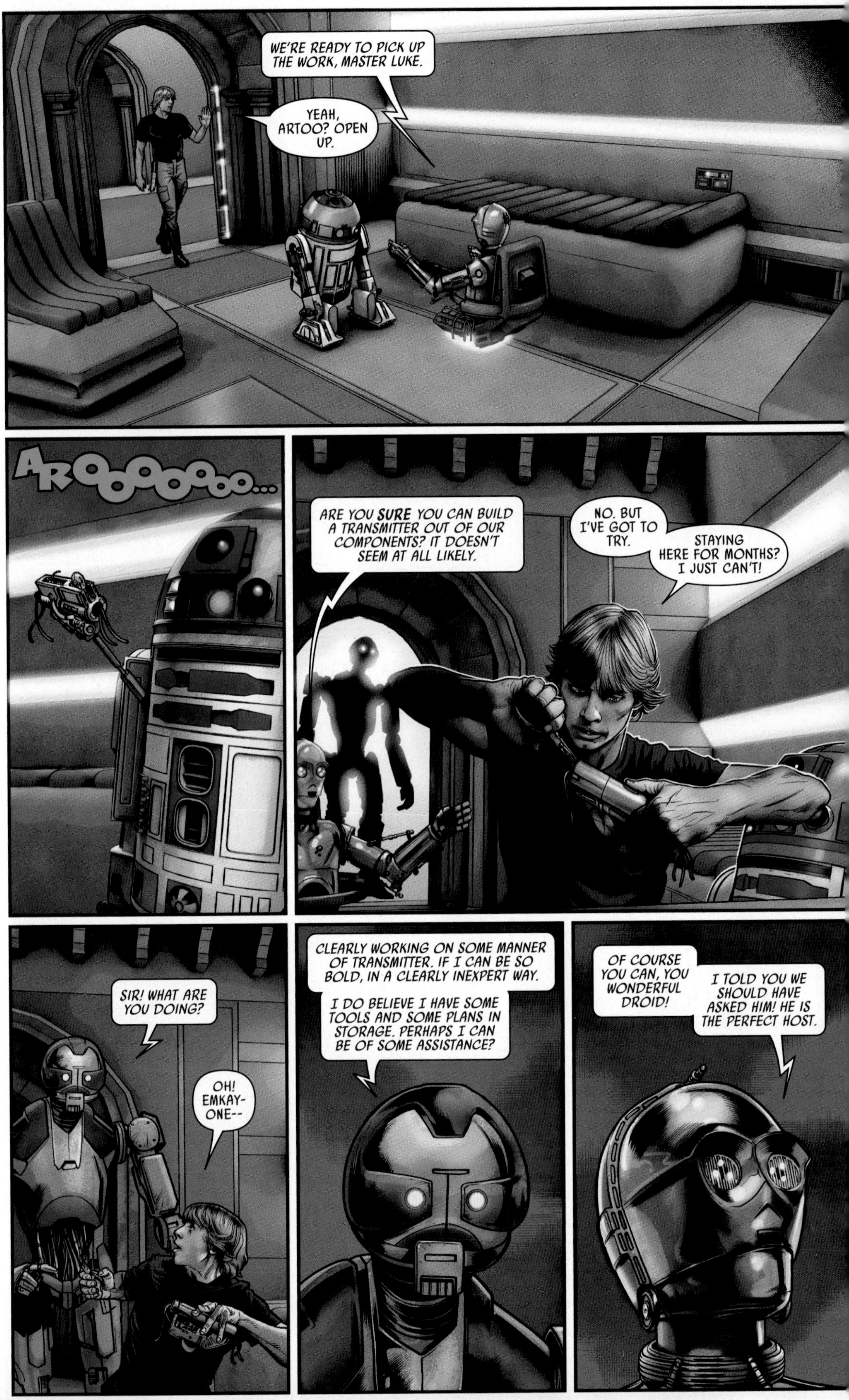
WE'RE READY TO PICK UP THE WORK, MASTER LUKE.
YEAH, ARTOO? OPEN UP.
AROOOOOOOO...
ARE YOU SURE YOU CAN BUILD A TRANSMITTER OUT OF OUR COMPONENTS? IT DOESN'T SEEM AT ALL LIKELY.
NO. BUT I'VE GOT TO TRY.
STAYING HERE FOR MONTHS? I JUST CAN'T!
SIR! WHAT ARE YOU DOING?
OH! EMKAY-ONE--
CLEARLY WORKING ON SOME MANNER OF TRANSMITTER. IF I CAN BE SO BOLD, IN A CLEARLY INEXPERT WAY.
I DO BELIEVE I HAVE SOME TOOLS AND SOME PLANS IN STORAGE. PERHAPS I CAN BE OF SOME ASSISTANCE?
OF COURSE YOU CAN, YOU WONDERFUL DROID!
I TOLD YOU WE SHOULD HAVE ASKED HIM! HE IS THE PERFECT HOST.

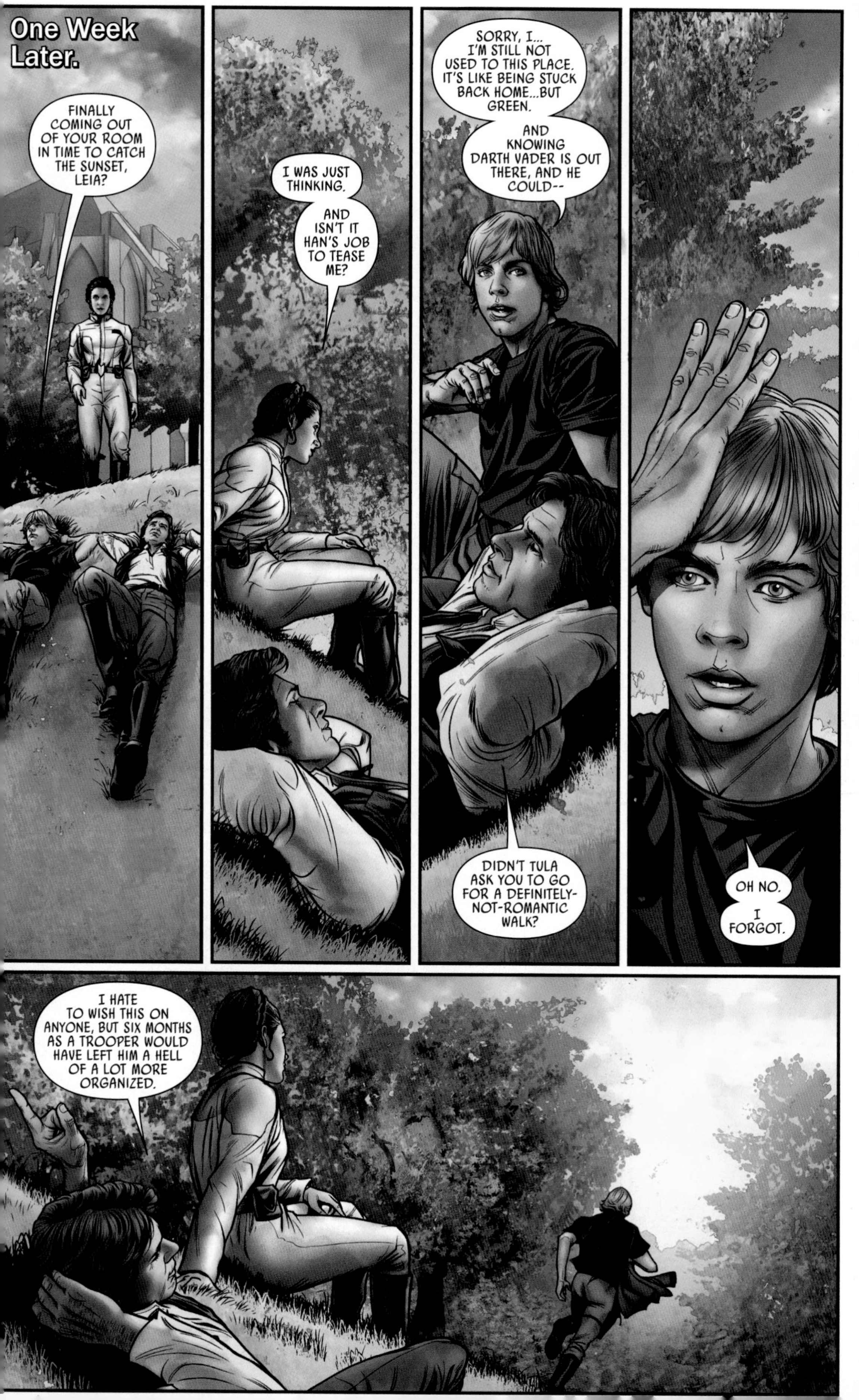
One Week Later.
FINALLY COMING OUT OF YOUR ROOM IN TIME TO CATCH THE SUNSET, LEIA?
I WAS JUST THINKING.
AND ISN'T IT HAN'S JOB TO TEASE ME?
SORRY, I... I'M STILL NOT USED TO THIS PLACE. IT'S LIKE BEING STUCK BACK HOME...BUT GREEN.
AND KNOWING DARTH VADER IS OUT THERE, AND HE COULD--
DIDN'T TULA ASK YOU TO GO FOR A DEFINITELY-NOT-ROMANTIC WALK?
OH NO.
I FORGOT.
I HATE TO WISH THIS ON ANYONE, BUT SIX MONTHS AS A TROOPER WOULD HAVE LEFT HIM A HELL OF A LOT MORE ORGANIZED.

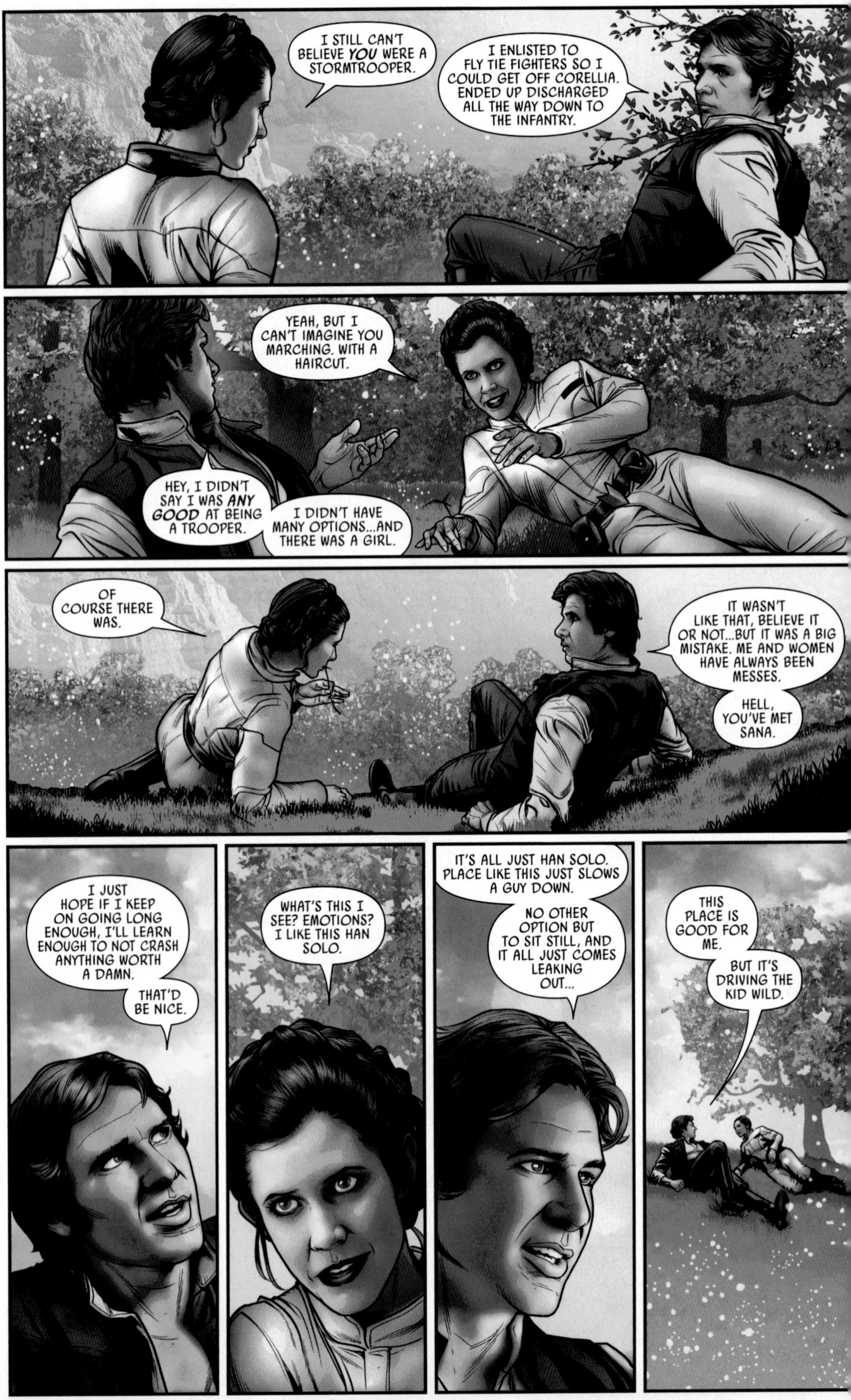

I STILL CAN'T BELIEVE *YOU* WERE A STORMTROOPER.
I ENLISTED TO FLY TIE FIGHTERS SO I COULD GET OFF CORELLIA. ENDED UP DISCHARGED ALL THE WAY DOWN TO THE INFANTRY.
YEAH, BUT I CAN'T IMAGINE YOU MARCHING. WITH A HAIRCUT.
HEY, I DIDN'T SAY I WAS *ANY GOOD* AT BEING A TROOPER.
I DIDN'T HAVE MANY OPTIONS...AND THERE WAS A GIRL.
OF COURSE THERE WAS.
IT WASN'T LIKE THAT, BELIEVE IT OR NOT...BUT IT WAS A BIG MISTAKE. ME AND WOMEN HAVE ALWAYS BEEN MESSES.
HELL, YOU'VE MET SANA.
I JUST HOPE IF I KEEP ON GOING LONG ENOUGH, I'LL LEARN ENOUGH TO NOT CRASH ANYTHING WORTH A DAMN.
THAT'D BE NICE.
WHAT'S THIS I SEE? EMOTIONS? I LIKE THIS HAN SOLO.
IT'S ALL JUST HAN SOLO. PLACE LIKE THIS JUST SLOWS A GUY DOWN.
NO OTHER OPTION BUT TO SIT STILL, AND IT ALL JUST COMES LEAKING OUT...
THIS PLACE IS GOOD FOR ME.
BUT IT'S DRIVING THE KID WILD.

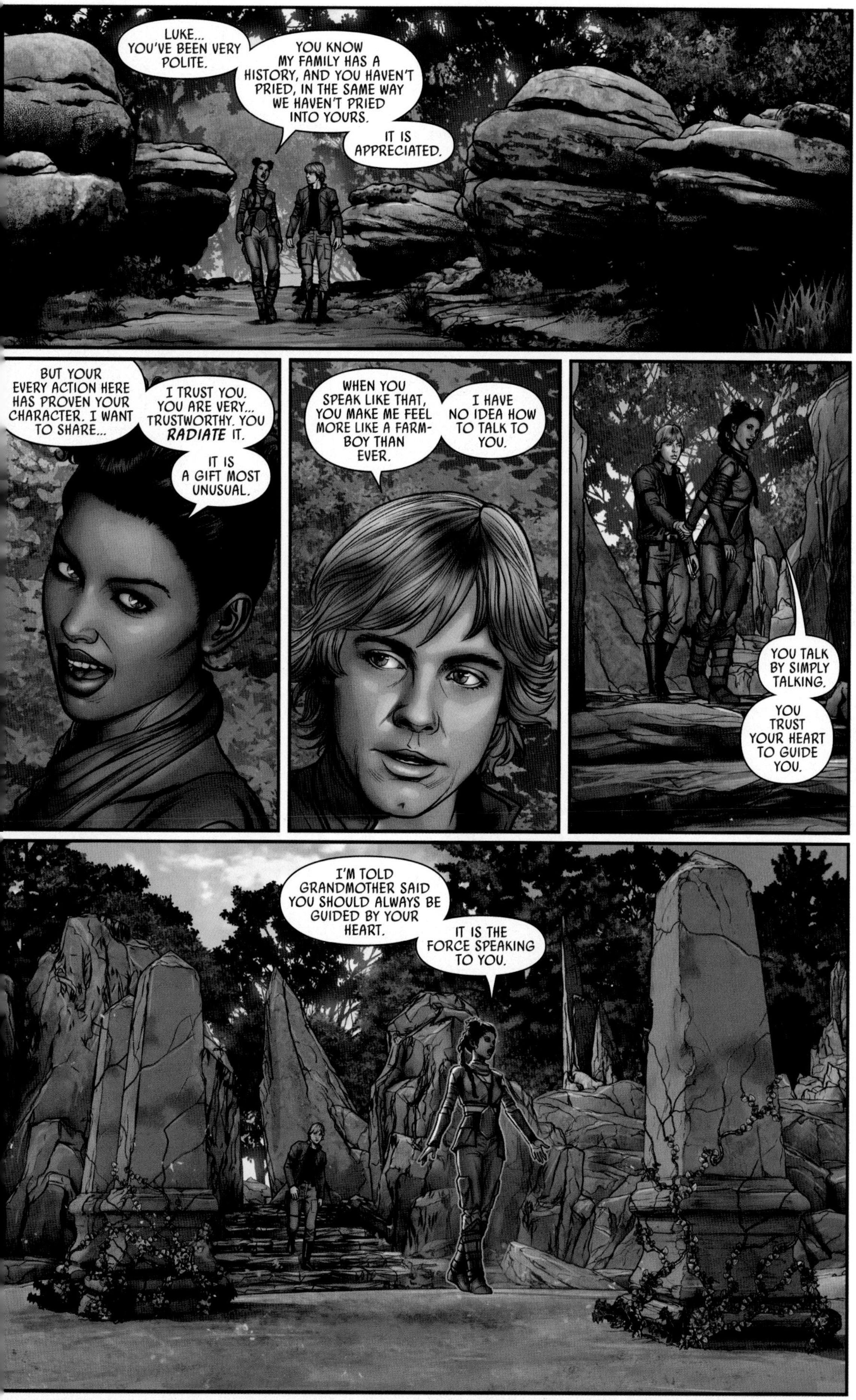
LUKE... YOU'VE BEEN VERY POLITE.
YOU KNOW MY FAMILY HAS A HISTORY, AND YOU HAVEN'T PRIED, IN THE SAME WAY WE HAVEN'T PRIED INTO YOURS.
IT IS APPRECIATED.
BUT YOUR EVERY ACTION HERE HAS PROVEN YOUR CHARACTER. I WANT TO SHARE...
I TRUST YOU. YOU ARE VERY... TRUSTWORTHY. YOU *RADIATE* IT.
IT IS A GIFT MOST UNUSUAL.
WHEN YOU SPEAK LIKE THAT, YOU MAKE ME FEEL MORE LIKE A FARM-BOY THAN EVER.
I HAVE NO IDEA HOW TO TALK TO YOU.
YOU TALK BY SIMPLY TALKING.
YOU TRUST YOUR HEART TO GUIDE YOU.
I'M TOLD GRANDMOTHER SAID YOU SHOULD ALWAYS BE GUIDED BY YOUR HEART.
IT IS THE FORCE SPEAKING TO YOU.

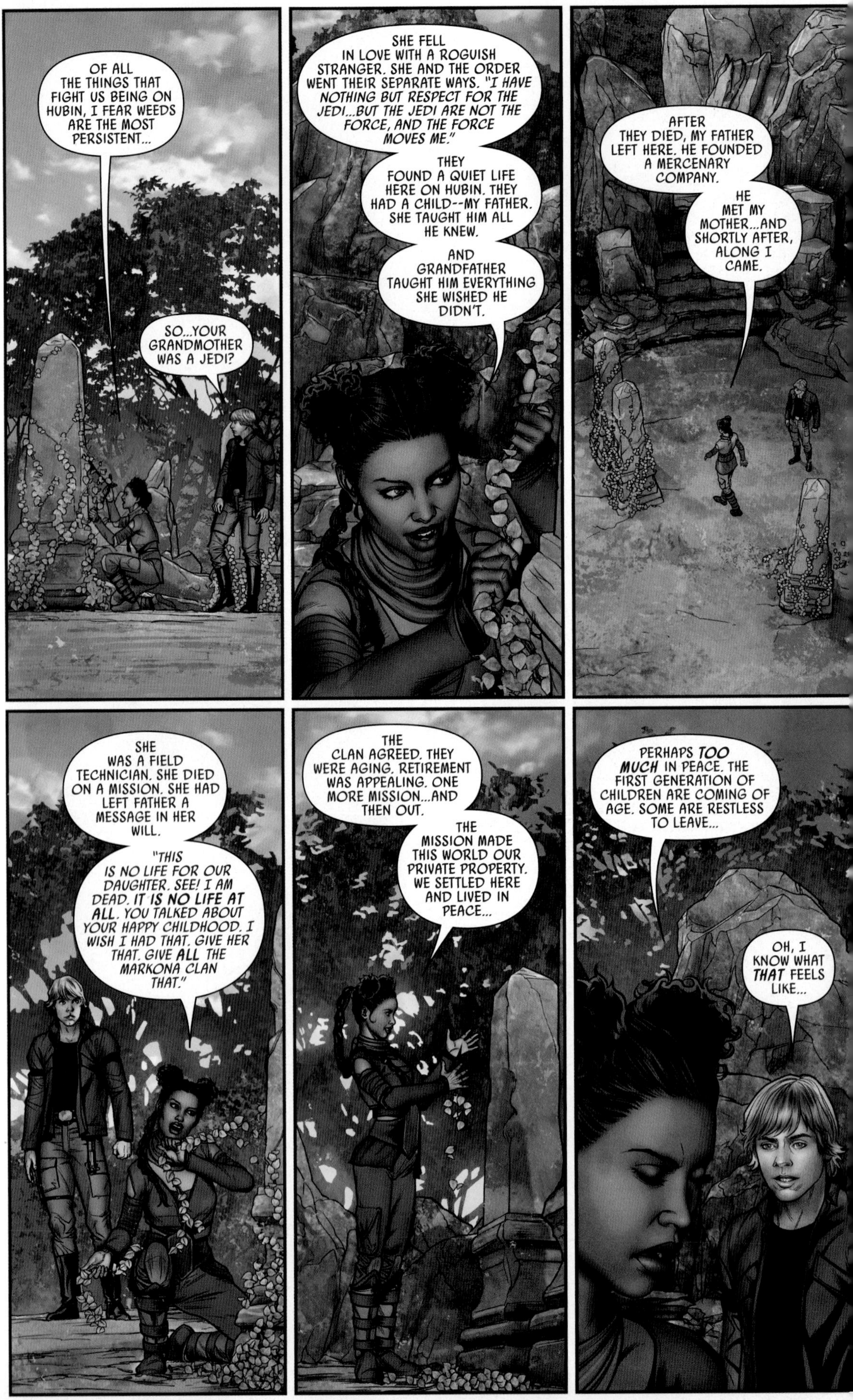
OF ALL THE THINGS THAT FIGHT US BEING ON HUBIN, I FEAR WEEDS ARE THE MOST PERSISTENT...
SO...YOUR GRANDMOTHER WAS A JEDI?
SHE FELL IN LOVE WITH A ROGUISH STRANGER. SHE AND THE ORDER WENT THEIR SEPARATE WAYS. "I HAVE NOTHING BUT RESPECT FOR THE JEDI...BUT THE JEDI ARE NOT THE FORCE, AND THE FORCE MOVES ME."
THEY FOUND A QUIET LIFE HERE ON HUBIN. THEY HAD A CHILD--MY FATHER. SHE TAUGHT HIM ALL HE KNEW.
AND GRANDFATHER TAUGHT HIM EVERYTHING SHE WISHED HE DIDN'T.
AFTER THEY DIED, MY FATHER LEFT HERE. HE FOUNDED A MERCENARY COMPANY.
HE MET MY MOTHER...AND SHORTLY AFTER, ALONG I CAME.
SHE WAS A FIELD TECHNICIAN. SHE DIED ON A MISSION. SHE HAD LEFT FATHER A MESSAGE IN HER WILL.
"THIS IS NO LIFE FOR OUR DAUGHTER. SEE! I AM DEAD. IT IS NO LIFE AT ALL. YOU TALKED ABOUT YOUR HAPPY CHILDHOOD. I WISH I HAD THAT. GIVE HER THAT. GIVE ALL THE MARKONA CLAN THAT."
THE CLAN AGREED. THEY WERE AGING. RETIREMENT WAS APPEALING. ONE MORE MISSION...AND THEN OUT.
THE MISSION MADE THIS WORLD OUR PRIVATE PROPERTY. WE SETTLED HERE AND LIVED IN PEACE...
PERHAPS TOO MUCH IN PEACE. THE FIRST GENERATION OF CHILDREN ARE COMING OF AGE. SOME ARE RESTLESS TO LEAVE...
OH, I KNOW WHAT THAT FEELS LIKE...

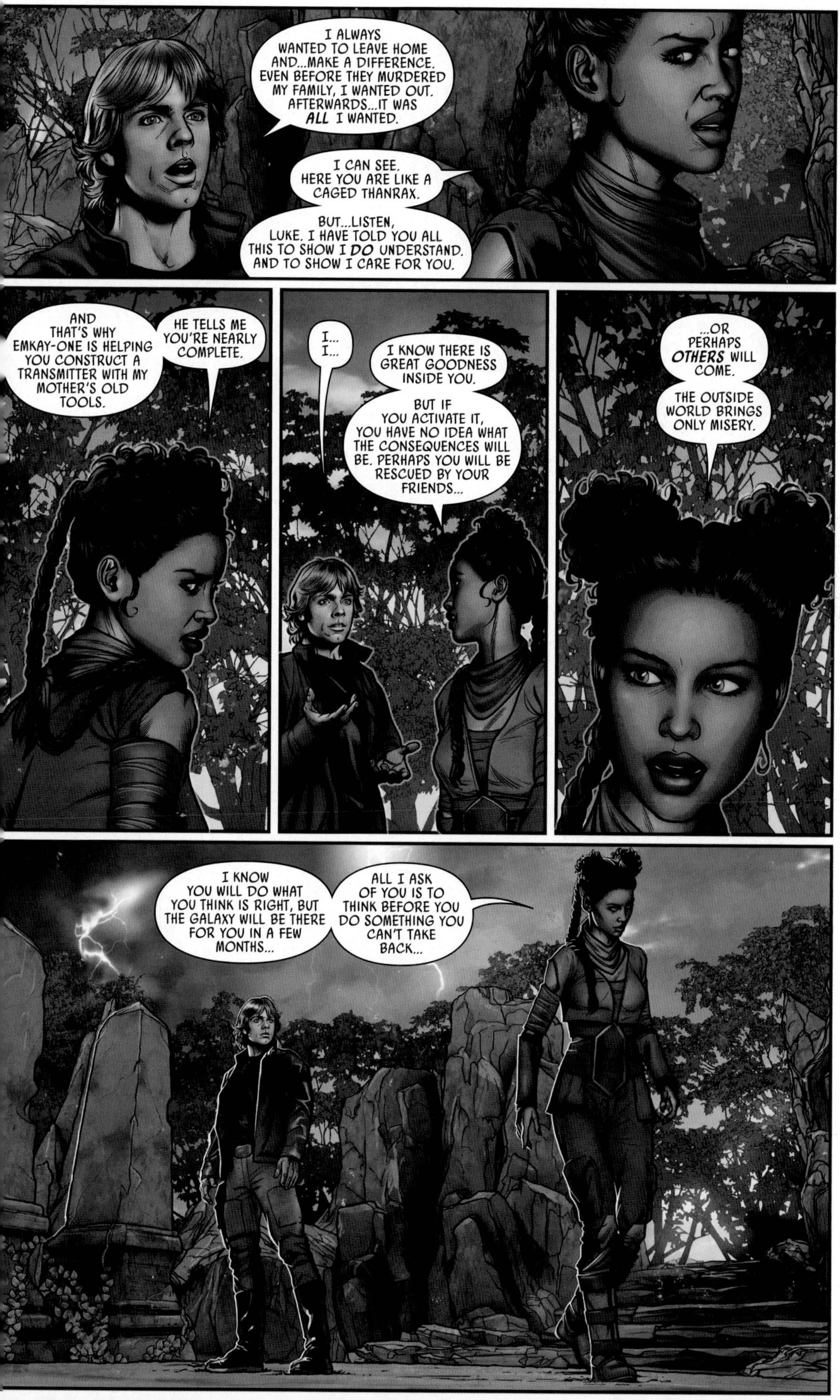

I ALWAYS WANTED TO LEAVE HOME AND...MAKE A DIFFERENCE. EVEN BEFORE THEY MURDERED MY FAMILY, I WANTED OUT. AFTERWARDS...IT WAS ALL I WANTED.
I CAN SEE. HERE YOU ARE LIKE A CAGED THANRAX.
BUT...LISTEN, LUKE. I HAVE TOLD YOU ALL THIS TO SHOW I DO UNDERSTAND. AND TO SHOW I CARE FOR YOU.
AND THAT'S WHY EMKAY-ONE IS HELPING YOU CONSTRUCT A TRANSMITTER WITH MY MOTHER'S OLD TOOLS.
HE TELLS ME YOU'RE NEARLY COMPLETE.
I... I...
I KNOW THERE IS GREAT GOODNESS INSIDE YOU.
BUT IF YOU ACTIVATE IT, YOU HAVE NO IDEA WHAT THE CONSEQUENCES WILL BE. PERHAPS YOU WILL BE RESCUED BY YOUR FRIENDS...
...OR PERHAPS OTHERS WILL COME.
THE OUTSIDE WORLD BRINGS ONLY MISERY.
I KNOW YOU WILL DO WHAT YOU THINK IS RIGHT, BUT THE GALAXY WILL BE THERE FOR YOU IN A FEW MONTHS...
ALL I ASK OF YOU IS TO THINK BEFORE YOU DO SOMETHING YOU CAN'T TAKE BACK...

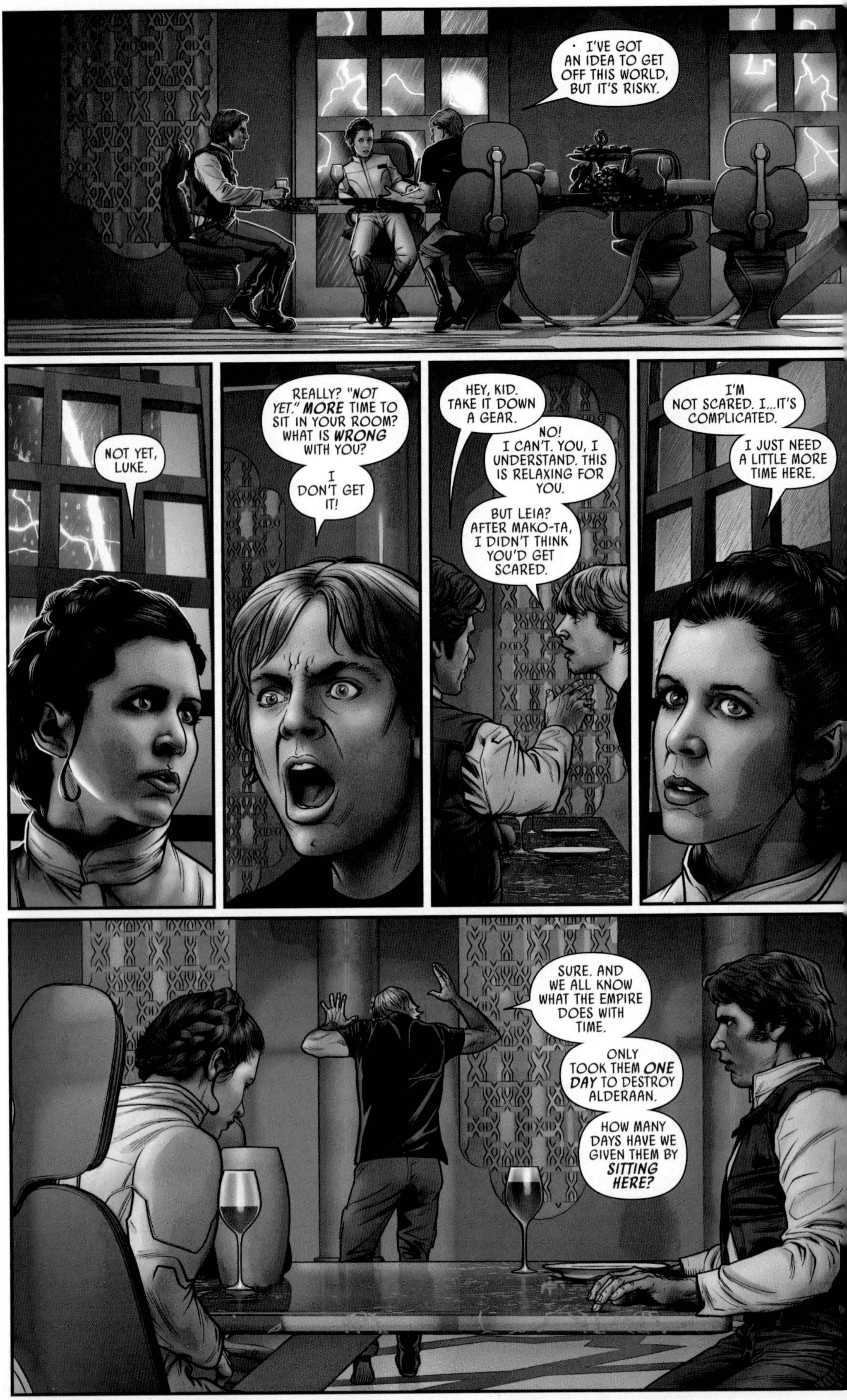
I'VE GOT AN IDEA TO GET OFF THIS WORLD, BUT IT'S RISKY.
NOT YET, LUKE.
REALLY? "NOT YET." MORE TIME TO SIT IN YOUR ROOM? WHAT IS WRONG WITH YOU?
I DON'T GET IT!
HEY, KID. TAKE IT DOWN A GEAR.
NO! I CAN'T. YOU, I UNDERSTAND. THIS IS RELAXING FOR YOU.
BUT LEIA? AFTER MAKO-TA, I DIDN'T THINK YOU'D GET SCARED.
I'M NOT SCARED. I...IT'S COMPLICATED.
I JUST NEED A LITTLE MORE TIME HERE.
SURE. AND WE ALL KNOW WHAT THE EMPIRE DOES WITH TIME.
ONLY TOOK THEM ONE DAY TO DESTROY ALDERAAN.
HOW MANY DAYS HAVE WE GIVEN THEM BY SITTING HERE?

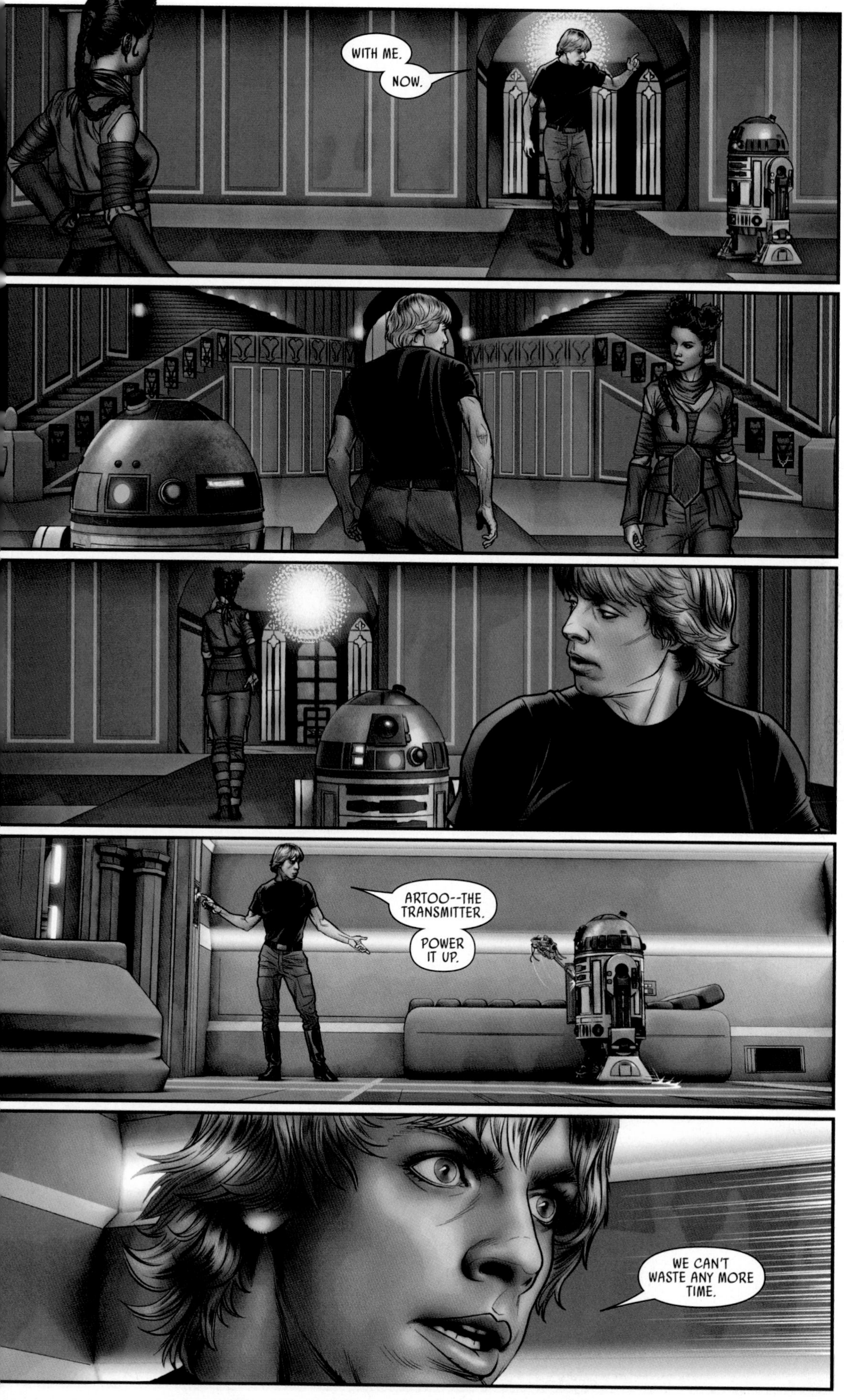
WITH ME.
NOW.
ARTOO--THE TRANSMITTER.
POWER IT UP.
WE CAN'T WASTE ANY MORE TIME.

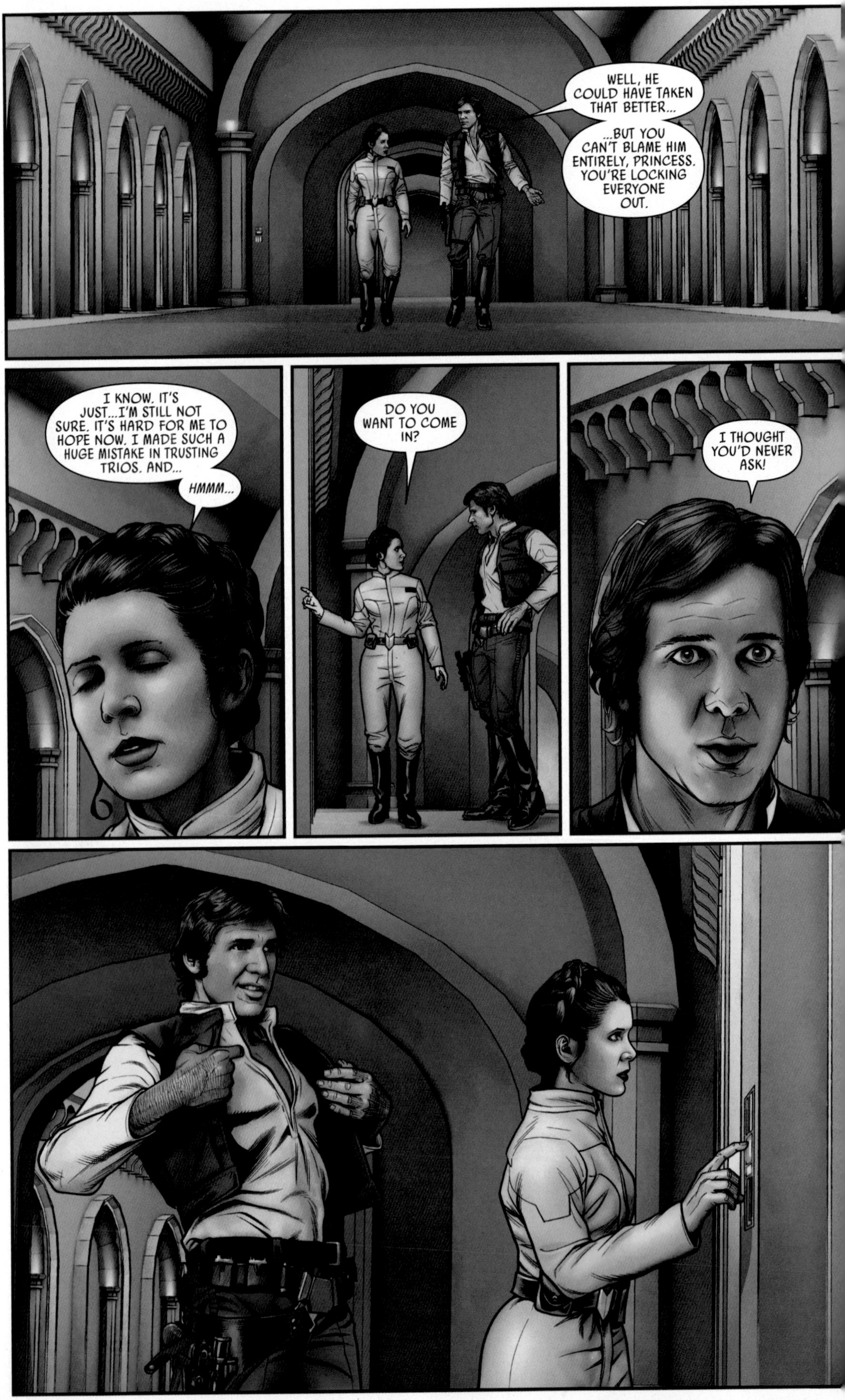
WELL, HE COULD HAVE TAKEN THAT BETTER...
...BUT YOU CAN'T BLAME HIM ENTIRELY, PRINCESS. YOU'RE LOCKING EVERYONE OUT.
I KNOW. IT'S JUST...I'M STILL NOT SURE. IT'S HARD FOR ME TO HOPE NOW. I MADE SUCH A HUGE MISTAKE IN TRUSTING TRIOS. AND...
HMMM...
DO YOU WANT TO COME IN?
I THOUGHT YOU'D NEVER ASK!

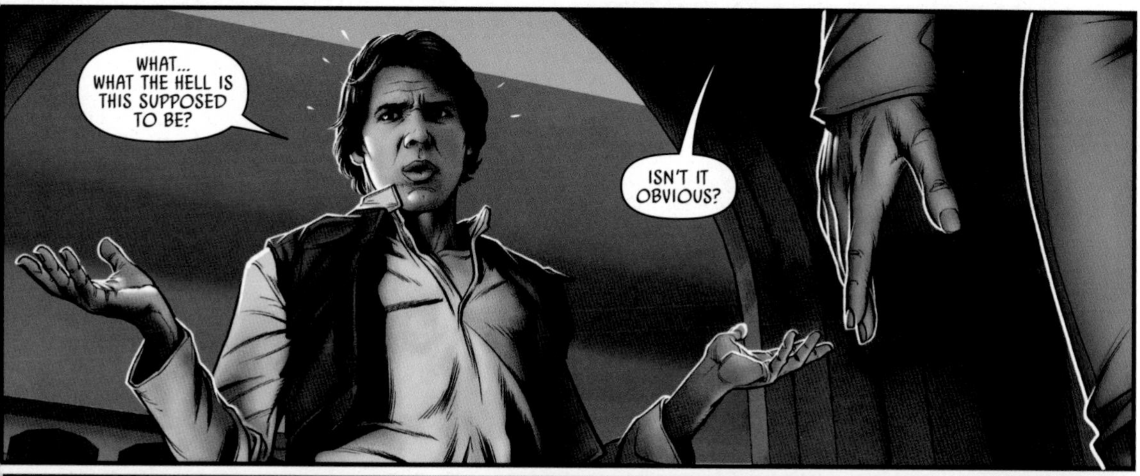
WHAT... WHAT THE HELL IS THIS SUPPOSED TO BE?
ISN'T IT OBVIOUS?

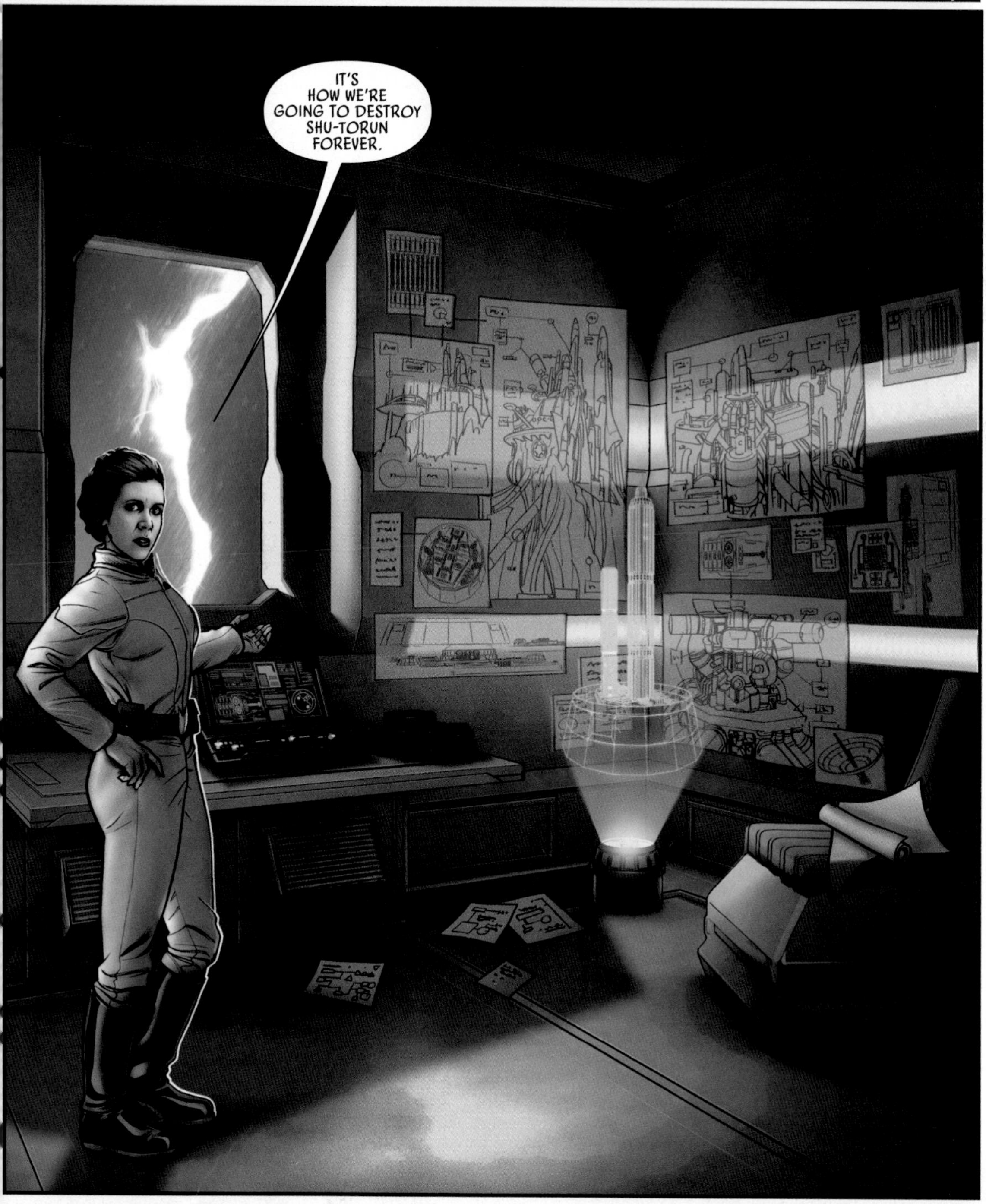
IT'S HOW WE'RE GOING TO DESTROY SHU-TORUN FOREVER.

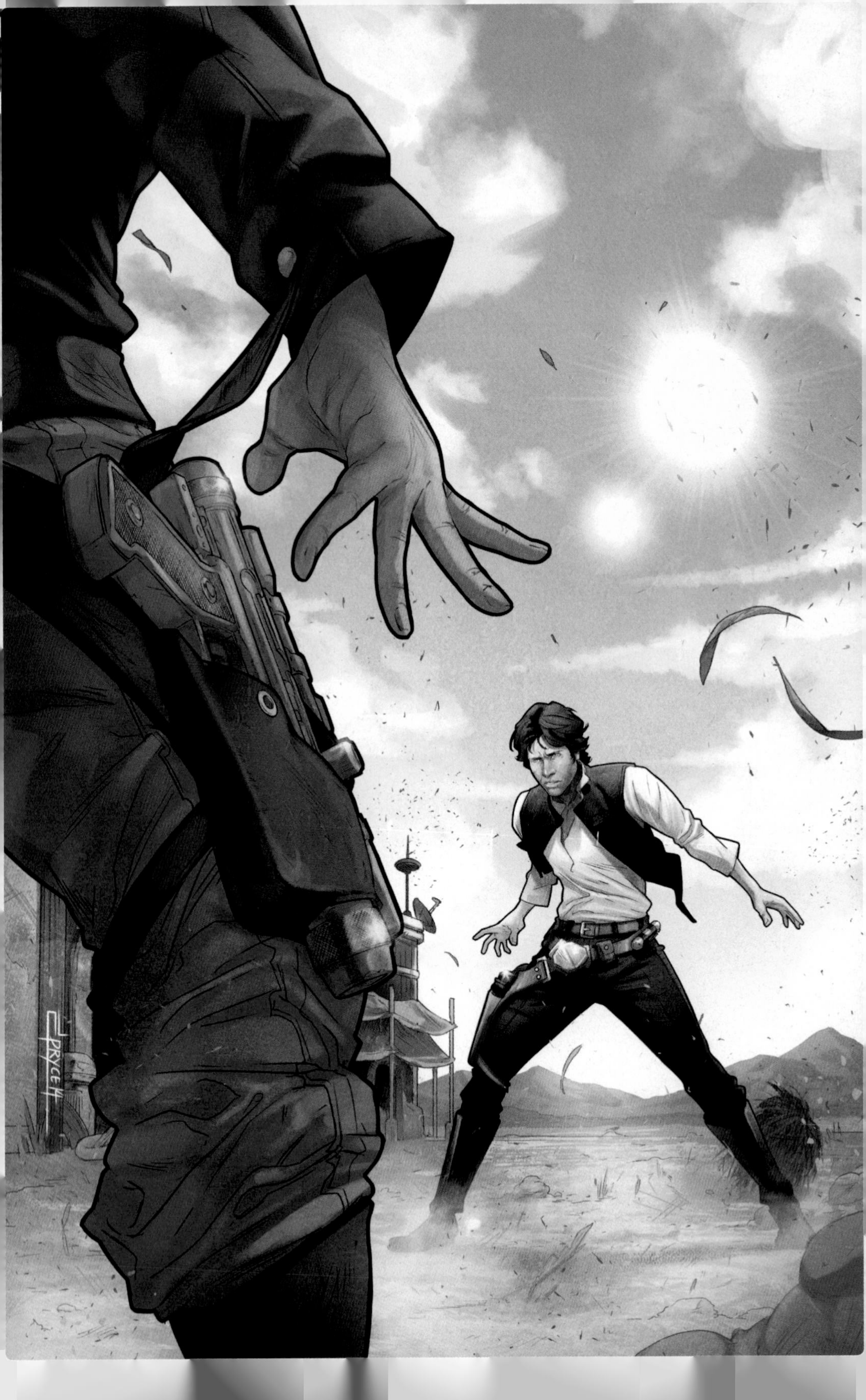

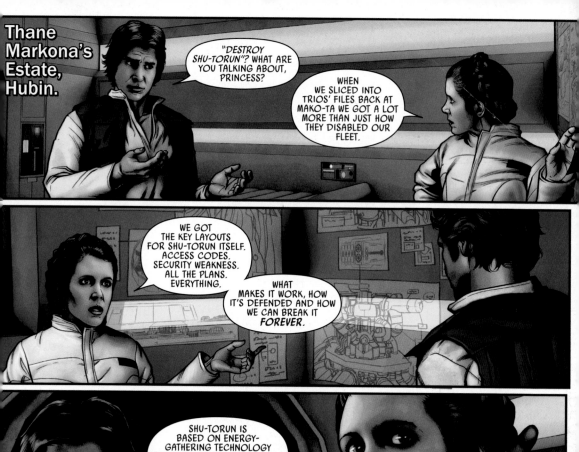

Thane Markona's Estate, Hubin.

"DESTROY SHU-TORUN"? WHAT ARE YOU TALKING ABOUT, PRINCESS?

WHEN WE SLICED INTO TRIOS' FILES BACK AT MAKO-TA WE GOT A LOT MORE THAN JUST HOW THEY DISABLED OUR FLEET.

WE GOT THE KEY LAYOUTS FOR SHU-TORUN ITSELF. ACCESS CODES. SECURITY WEAKNESS. ALL THE PLANS. EVERYTHING.

WHAT MAKES IT WORK, HOW IT'S DEFENDED AND HOW WE CAN BREAK IT FOREVER.

SHU-TORUN IS BASED ON ENERGY-GATHERING TECHNOLOGY THAT'S THOUSANDS OF YEARS OLD AND FRAGILE. WITHOUT IT, THE PLANET JUST WON'T OPERATE.

WHEN WE'RE FINISHED, SHU-TORUN WILL HAVE ALL THE IMPORTANCE TO THE GALACTIC ECONOMY OF TATOOINE.

SO, YOU'VE BEEN UP HERE WORKING OUT HOW BEST TO GIVE QUEEN TRIOS A LITTLE PAYBACK? YOU ROYALS PLAY DIRTY.

YOU SHOULD TELL LUKE. IT'LL HELP THE KID UNDERSTAND WHY YOU'VE BEEN HOLED UP IN HERE.

YES, I... JUST WANTED TO BE SURE THIS COULD ACTUALLY WORK.

I DIDN'T WANT TO GIVE FALSE HOPE.

HEH. FALSE HOPE. OH, I GET THAT.

I MEAN, ALL THESE PLANS ARE VERY IMPRESSIVE, BUT IT'S NOT WHAT I WAS EXPECTING...

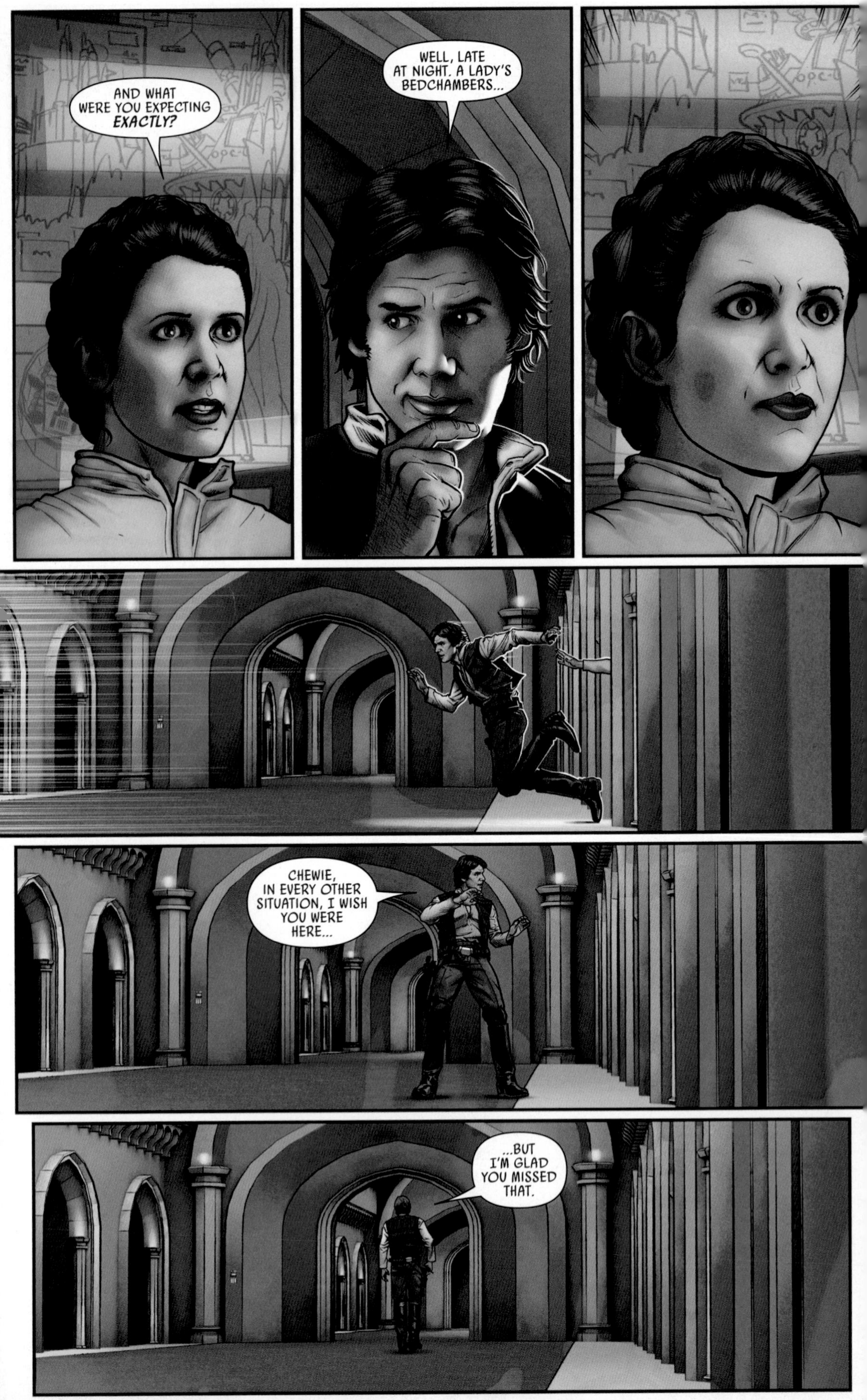
AND WHAT WERE YOU EXPECTING *EXACTLY?*
WELL, LATE AT NIGHT. A LADY'S BEDCHAMBERS...
CHEWIE, IN EVERY OTHER SITUATION, I WISH YOU WERE HERE...
...BUT I'M GLAD YOU MISSED THAT.

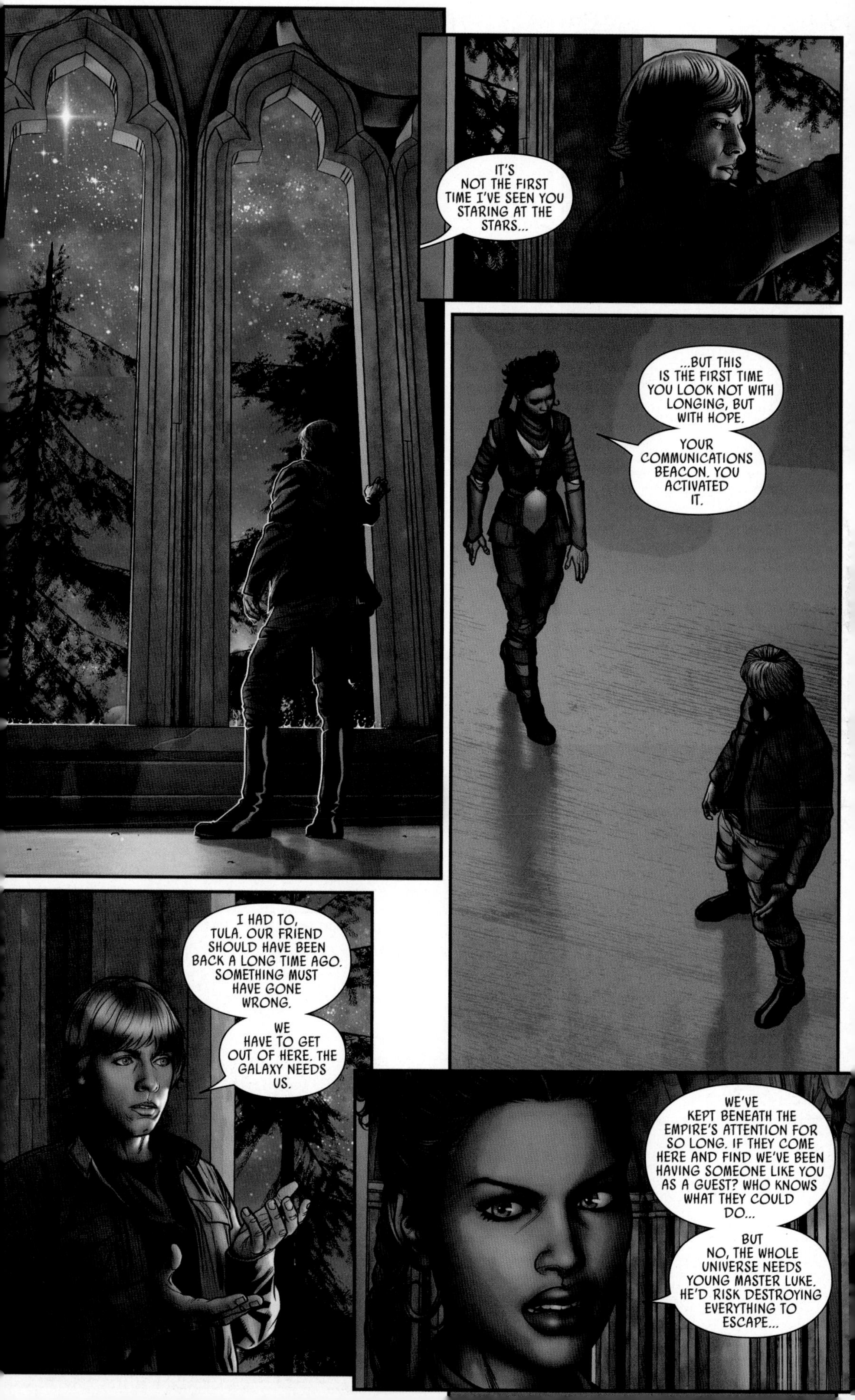
IT'S NOT THE FIRST TIME I'VE SEEN YOU STARING AT THE STARS...
...BUT THIS IS THE FIRST TIME YOU LOOK NOT WITH LONGING, BUT WITH HOPE.
YOUR COMMUNICATIONS BEACON. YOU ACTIVATED IT.
I HAD TO, TULA. OUR FRIEND SHOULD HAVE BEEN BACK A LONG TIME AGO. SOMETHING MUST HAVE GONE WRONG.
WE HAVE TO GET OUT OF HERE. THE GALAXY NEEDS US.
WE'VE KEPT BENEATH THE EMPIRE'S ATTENTION FOR SO LONG. IF THEY COME HERE AND FIND WE'VE BEEN HAVING SOMEONE LIKE YOU AS A GUEST? WHO KNOWS WHAT THEY COULD DO...
BUT NO, THE WHOLE UNIVERSE NEEDS YOUNG MASTER LUKE. HE'D RISK DESTROYING EVERYTHING TO ESCAPE...

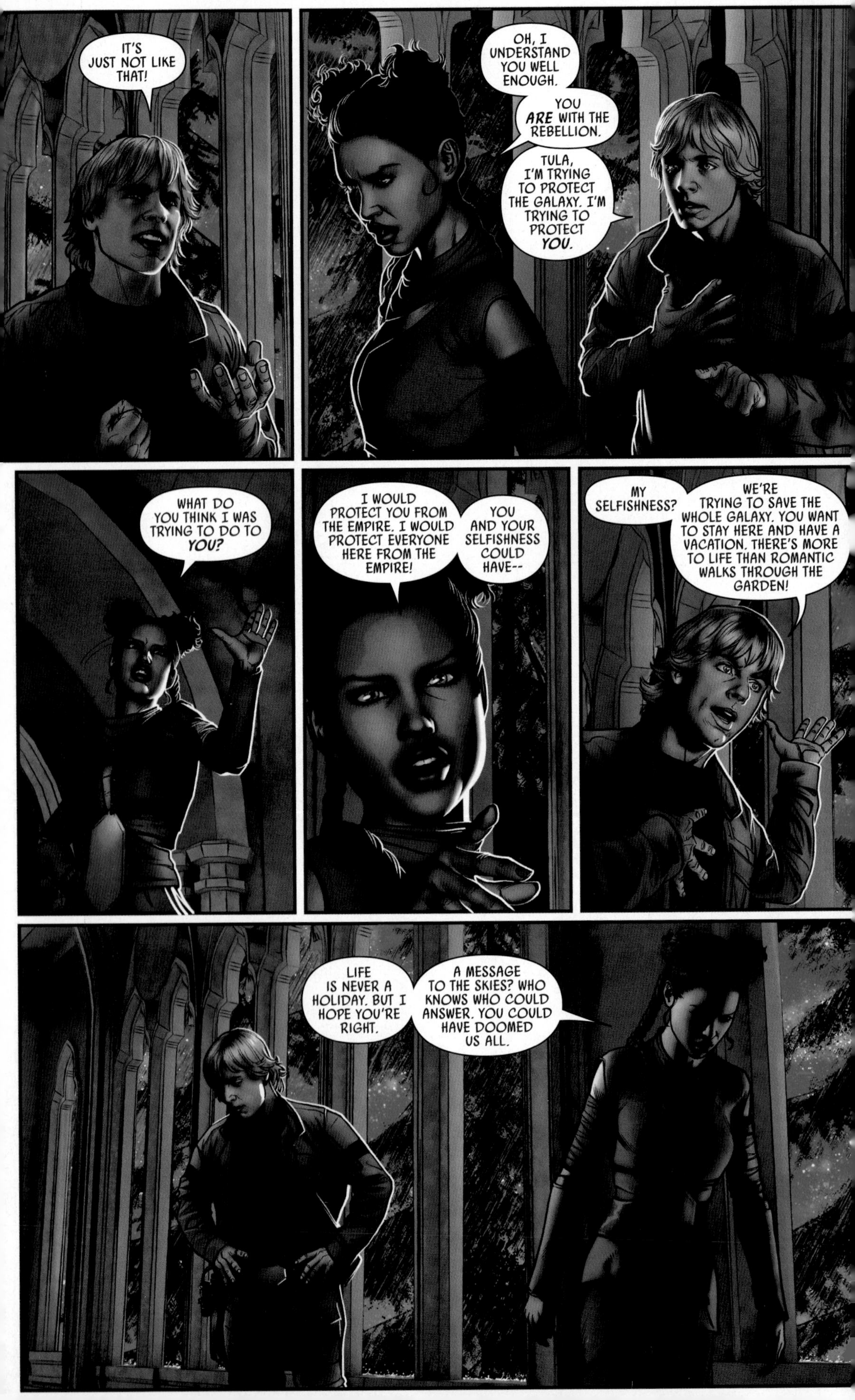
IT'S JUST NOT LIKE THAT!
OH, I UNDERSTAND YOU WELL ENOUGH.
YOU ARE WITH THE REBELLION.
TULA, I'M TRYING TO PROTECT THE GALAXY. I'M TRYING TO PROTECT YOU.
WHAT DO YOU THINK I WAS TRYING TO DO TO YOU?
I WOULD PROTECT YOU FROM THE EMPIRE. I WOULD PROTECT EVERYONE HERE FROM THE EMPIRE!
YOU AND YOUR SELFISHNESS COULD HAVE--
MY SELFISHNESS?
WE'RE TRYING TO SAVE THE WHOLE GALAXY. YOU WANT TO STAY HERE AND HAVE A VACATION. THERE'S MORE TO LIFE THAN ROMANTIC WALKS THROUGH THE GARDEN!
A MESSAGE TO THE SKIES? WHO KNOWS WHO COULD ANSWER. YOU COULD HAVE DOOMED US ALL.
LIFE IS NEVER A HOLIDAY. BUT I HOPE YOU'RE RIGHT.

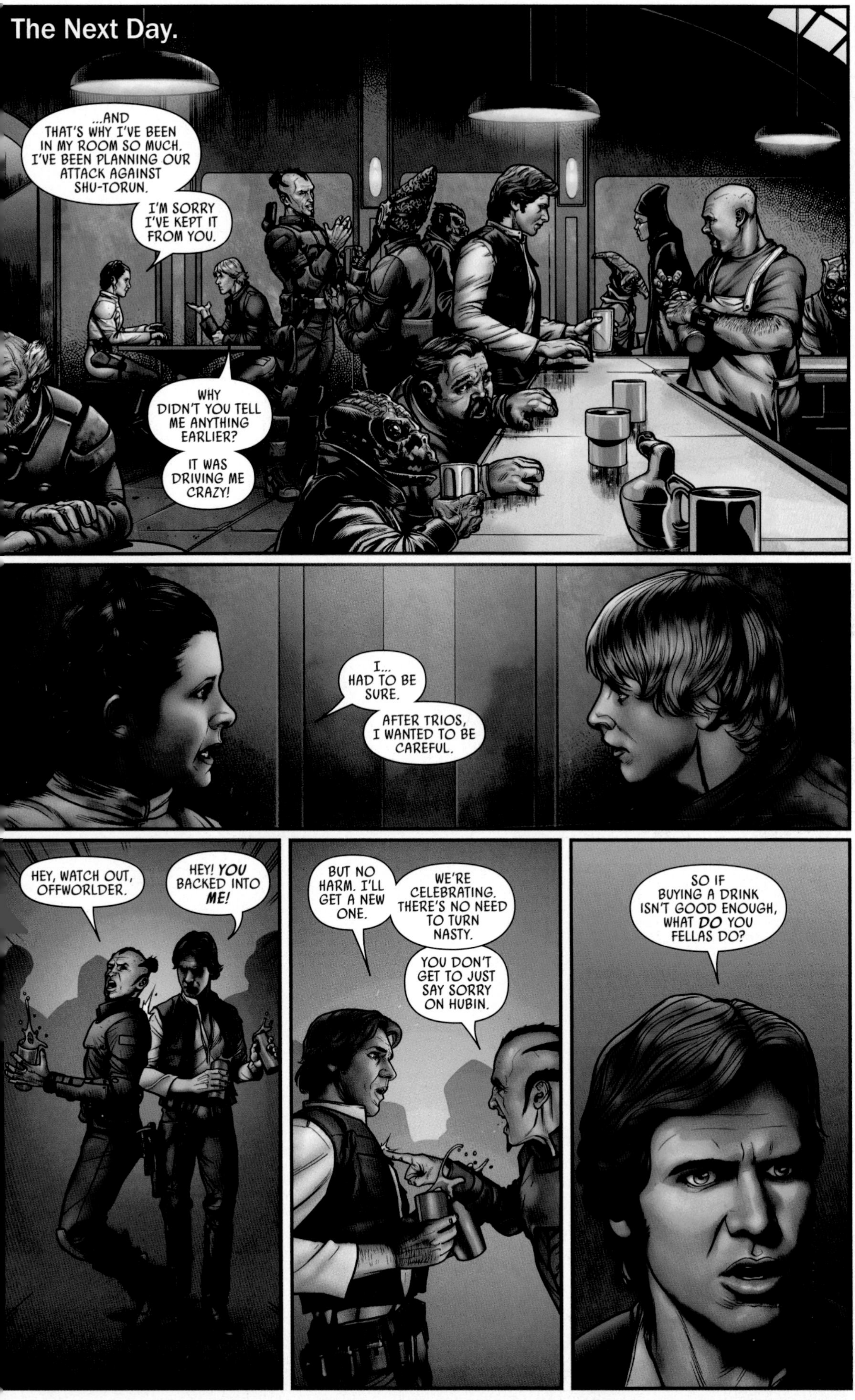
The Next Day.
...AND THAT'S WHY I'VE BEEN IN MY ROOM SO MUCH. I'VE BEEN PLANNING OUR ATTACK AGAINST SHU-TORUN.
I'M SORRY I'VE KEPT IT FROM YOU.
WHY DIDN'T YOU TELL ME ANYTHING EARLIER?
IT WAS DRIVING ME CRAZY!
I... HAD TO BE SURE.
AFTER TRIOS, I WANTED TO BE CAREFUL.
HEY, WATCH OUT, OFFWORLDER.
HEY! YOU BACKED INTO ME!
BUT NO HARM. I'LL GET A NEW ONE.
WE'RE CELEBRATING. THERE'S NO NEED TO TURN NASTY.
YOU DON'T GET TO JUST SAY SORRY ON HUBIN.
SO IF BUYING A DRINK ISN'T GOOD ENOUGH, WHAT DO YOU FELLAS DO?

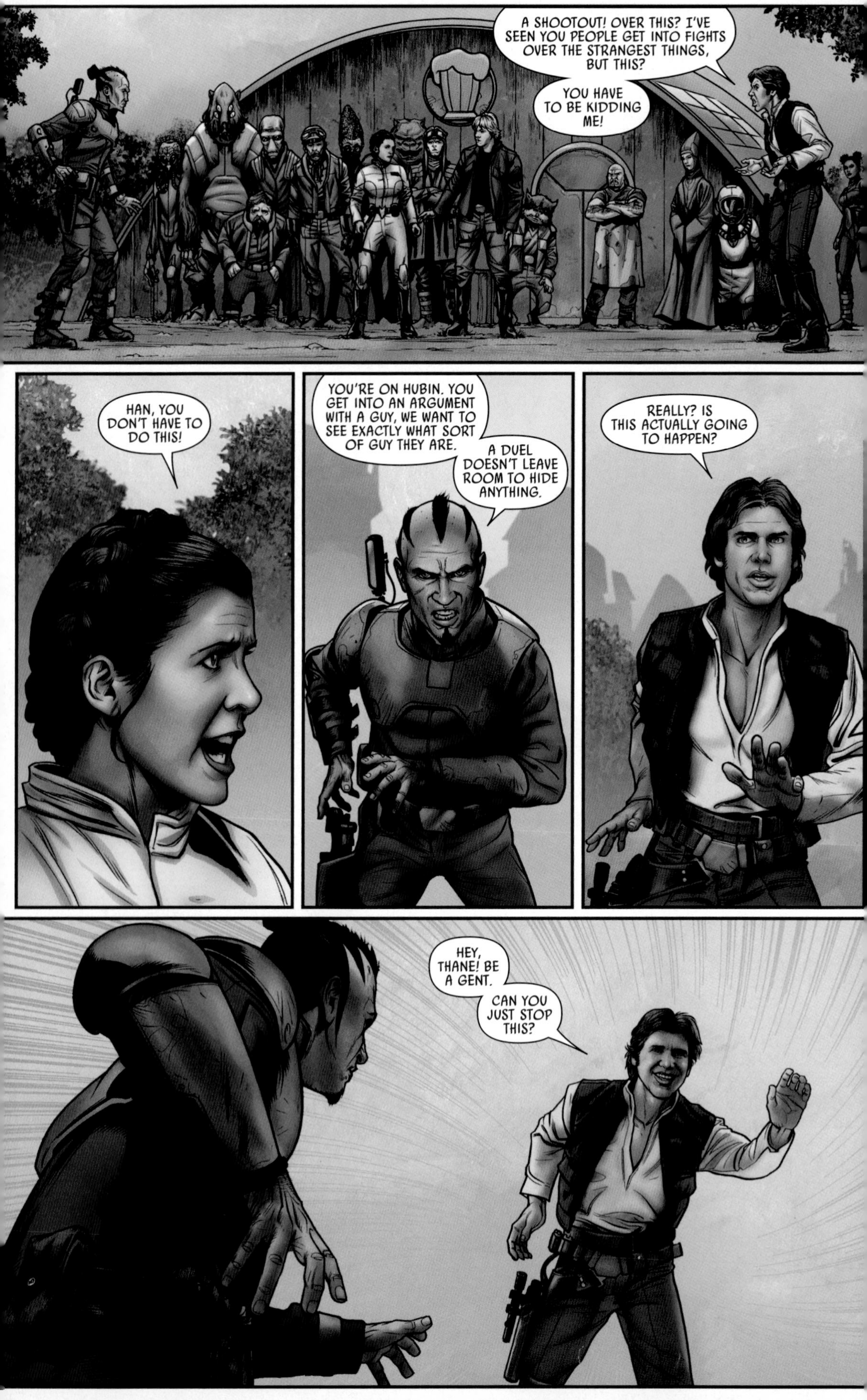
A SHOOTOUT! OVER THIS? I'VE SEEN YOU PEOPLE GET INTO FIGHTS OVER THE STRANGEST THINGS, BUT THIS?
YOU HAVE TO BE KIDDING ME!
HAN, YOU DON'T HAVE TO DO THIS!
YOU'RE ON HUBIN. YOU GET INTO AN ARGUMENT WITH A GUY, WE WANT TO SEE EXACTLY WHAT SORT OF GUY THEY ARE.
A DUEL DOESN'T LEAVE ROOM TO HIDE ANYTHING.
REALLY? IS THIS ACTUALLY GOING TO HAPPEN?
HEY, THANE! BE A GENT.
CAN YOU JUST STOP THIS?

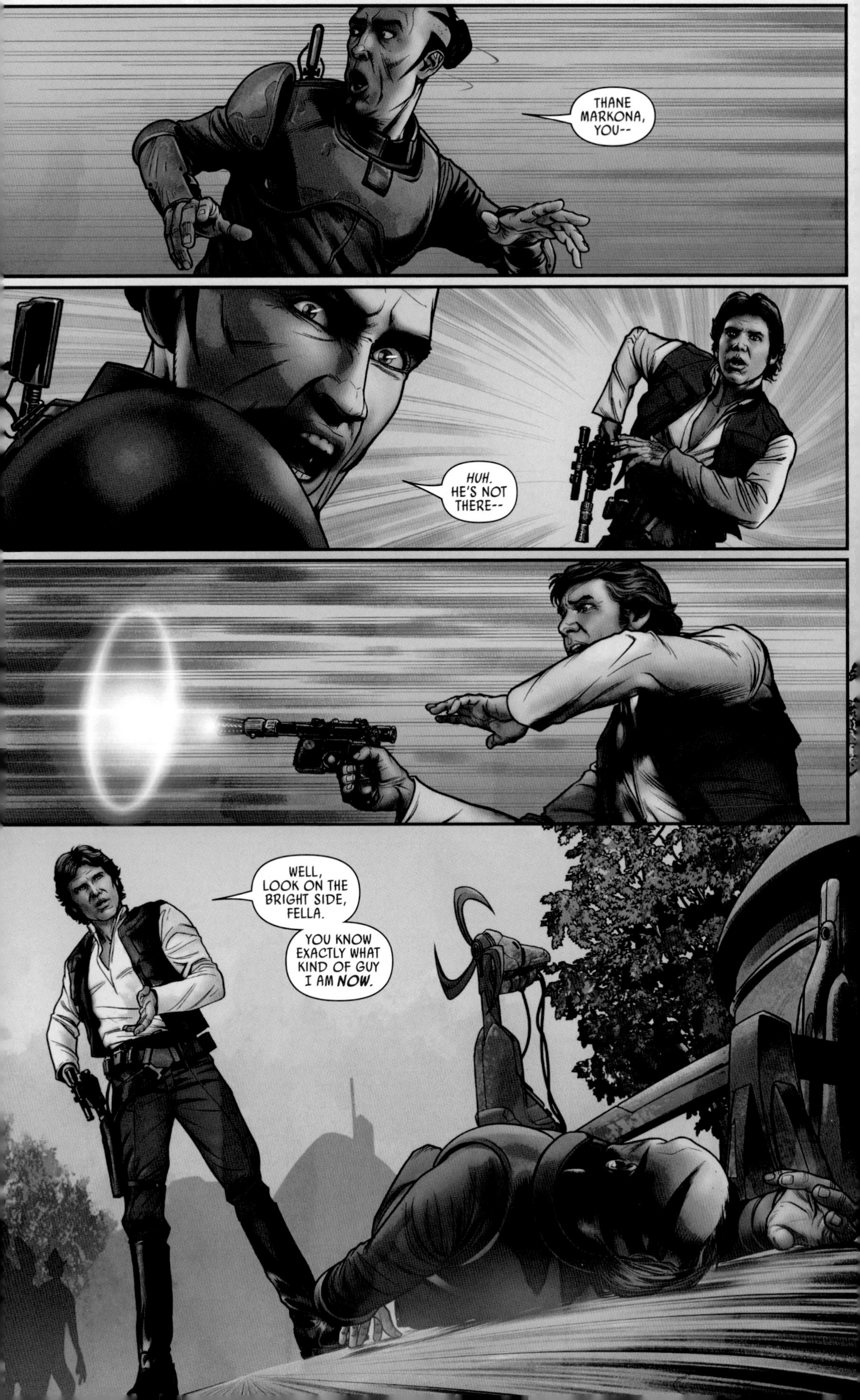

THANE MARKONA, YOU--
HUH. HE'S NOT THERE--
WELL, LOOK ON THE BRIGHT SIDE, FELLA.
YOU KNOW EXACTLY WHAT KIND OF GUY I AM **NOW**.

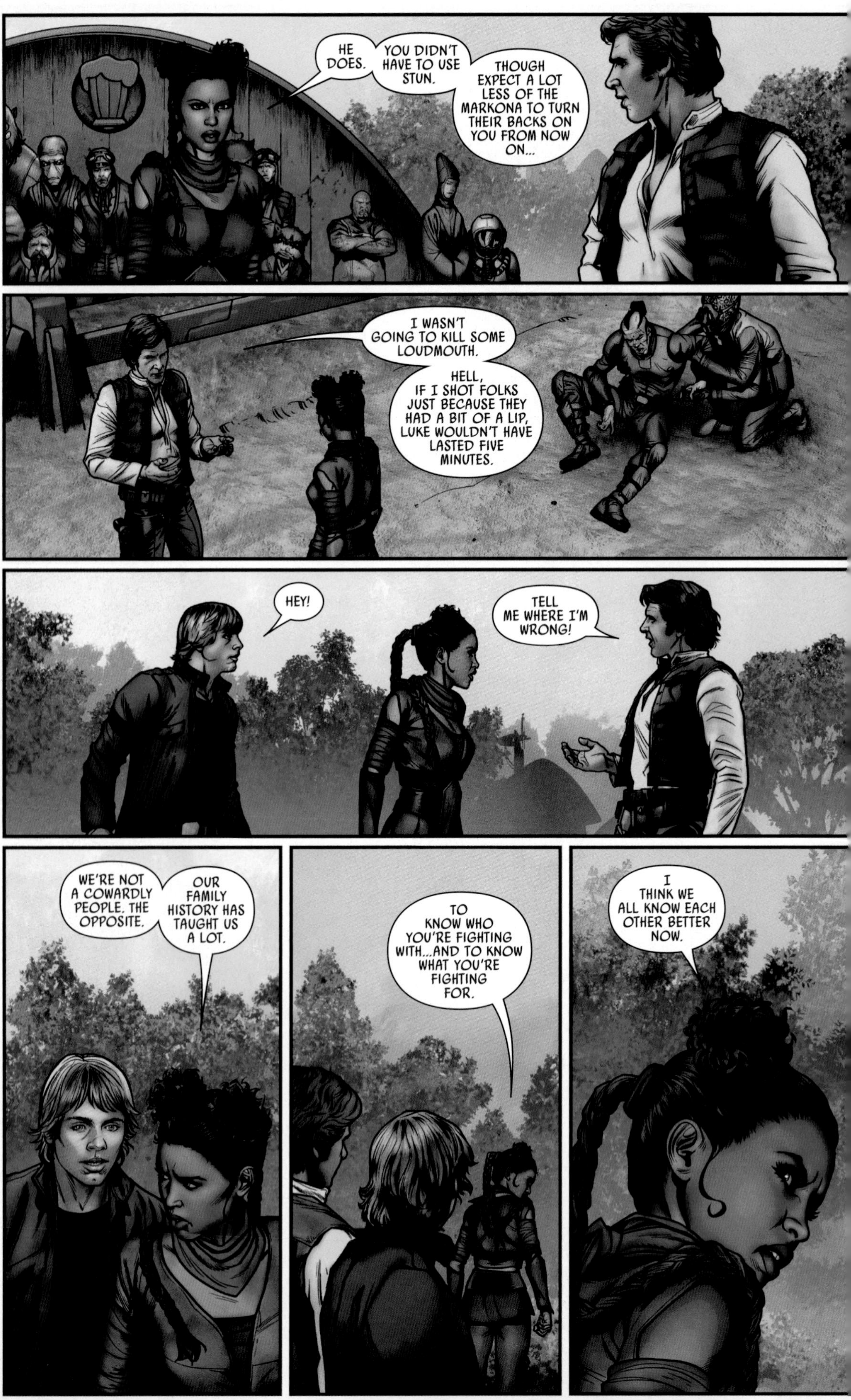
HE DOES.
YOU DIDN'T HAVE TO USE STUN.
THOUGH EXPECT A LOT LESS OF THE MARKONA TO TURN THEIR BACKS ON YOU FROM NOW ON...
I WASN'T GOING TO KILL SOME LOUDMOUTH.
HELL, IF I SHOT FOLKS JUST BECAUSE THEY HAD A BIT OF A LIP, LUKE WOULDN'T HAVE LASTED FIVE MINUTES.
HEY!
TELL ME WHERE I'M WRONG!
WE'RE NOT A COWARDLY PEOPLE. THE OPPOSITE.
OUR FAMILY HISTORY HAS TAUGHT US A LOT.
TO KNOW WHO YOU'RE FIGHTING WITH...AND TO KNOW WHAT YOU'RE FIGHTING FOR.
I THINK WE ALL KNOW EACH OTHER BETTER NOW.

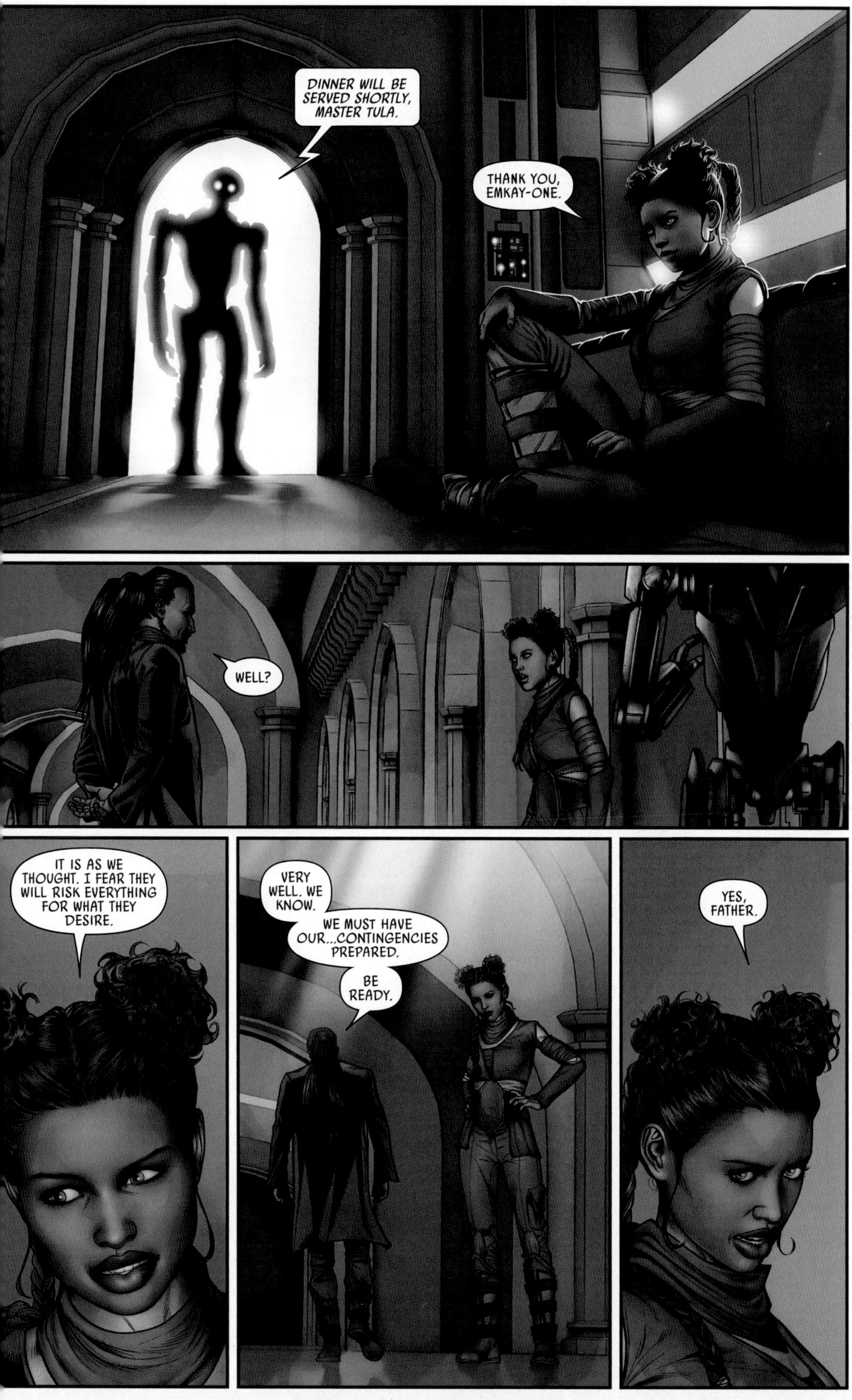
DINNER WILL BE SERVED SHORTLY, MASTER TULA.
THANK YOU, EMKAY-ONE.
WELL?
IT IS AS WE THOUGHT. I FEAR THEY WILL RISK EVERYTHING FOR WHAT THEY DESIRE.
VERY WELL. WE KNOW.
WE MUST HAVE OUR...CONTINGENCIES PREPARED.
BE READY.
YES, FATHER.

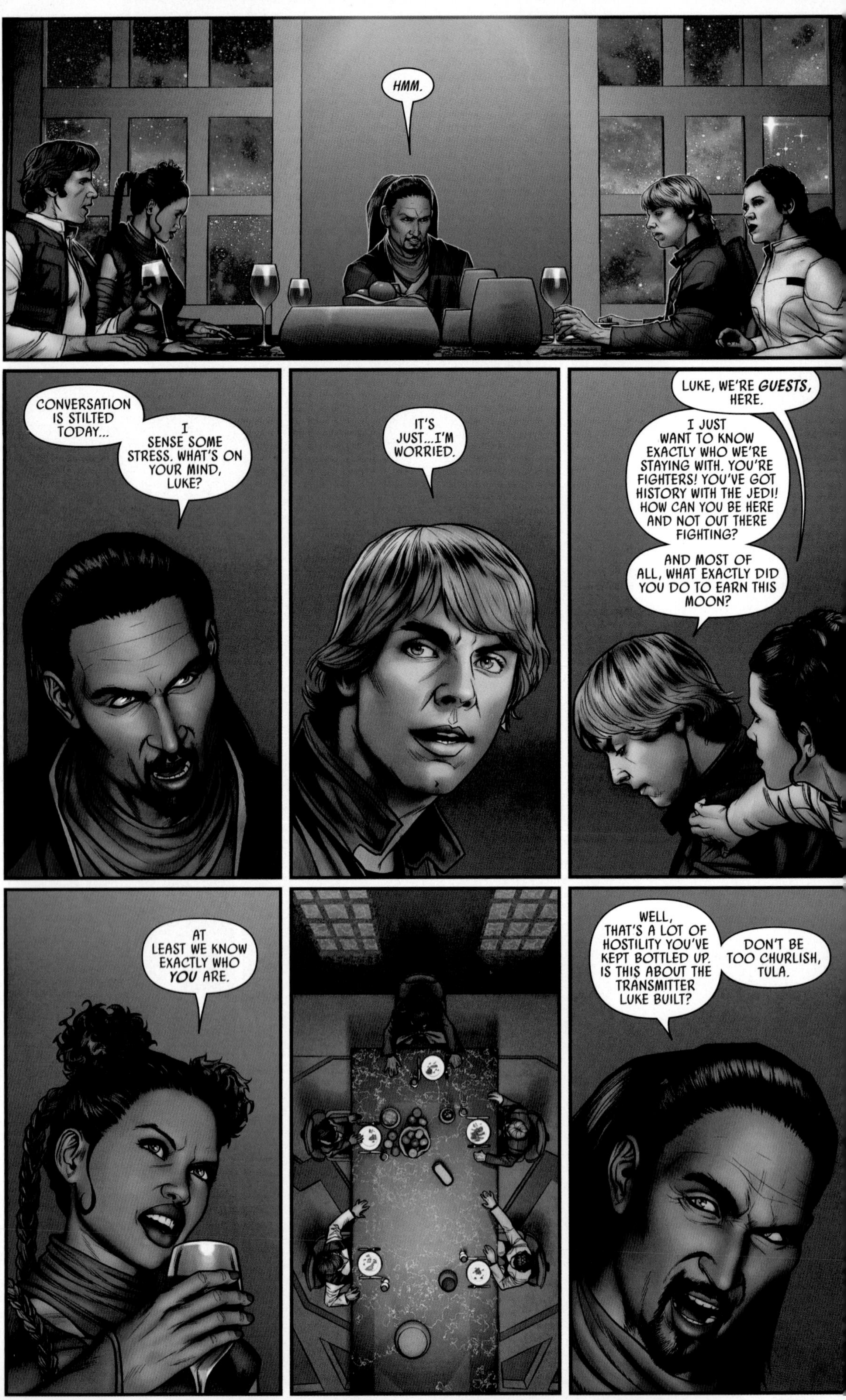
HMM.
CONVERSATION IS STILTED TODAY...
I SENSE SOME STRESS. WHAT'S ON YOUR MIND, LUKE?
IT'S JUST...I'M WORRIED.
LUKE, WE'RE GUESTS, HERE.
I JUST WANT TO KNOW EXACTLY WHO WE'RE STAYING WITH. YOU'RE FIGHTERS! YOU'VE GOT HISTORY WITH THE JEDI! HOW CAN YOU BE HERE AND NOT OUT THERE FIGHTING?
AND MOST OF ALL, WHAT EXACTLY DID YOU DO TO EARN THIS MOON?
AT LEAST WE KNOW EXACTLY WHO YOU ARE.
WELL, THAT'S A LOT OF HOSTILITY YOU'VE KEPT BOTTLED UP. IS THIS ABOUT THE TRANSMITTER LUKE BUILT?
DON'T BE TOO CHURLISH, TULA.

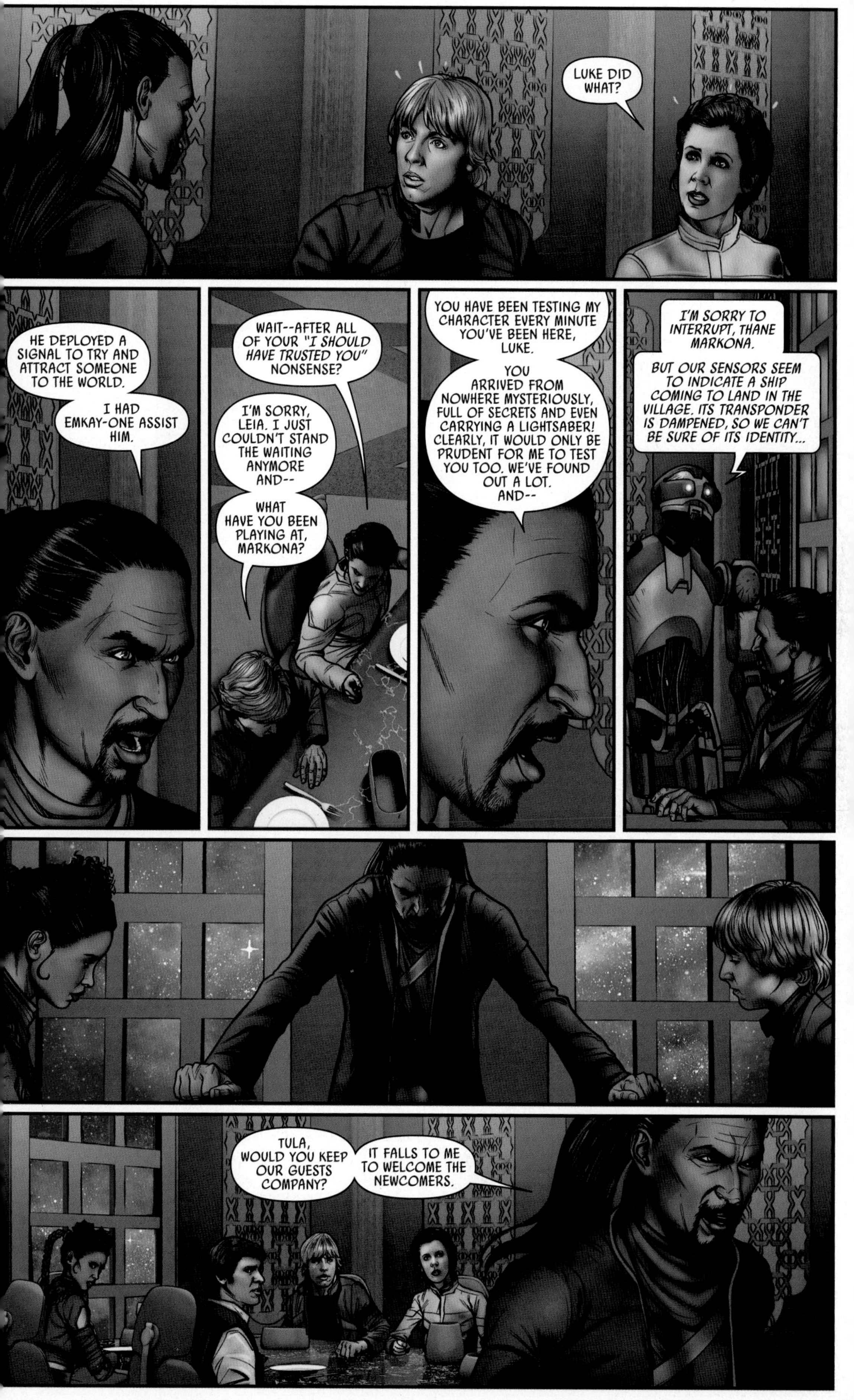

LUKE DID WHAT?
HE DEPLOYED A SIGNAL TO TRY AND ATTRACT SOMEONE TO THE WORLD.
I HAD EMKAY-ONE ASSIST HIM.
WAIT--AFTER ALL OF YOUR "I SHOULD HAVE TRUSTED YOU" NONSENSE?
I'M SORRY, LEIA. I JUST COULDN'T STAND THE WAITING ANYMORE AND--
WHAT HAVE YOU BEEN PLAYING AT, MARKONA?
YOU HAVE BEEN TESTING MY CHARACTER EVERY MINUTE YOU'VE BEEN HERE, LUKE.
YOU ARRIVED FROM NOWHERE MYSTERIOUSLY, FULL OF SECRETS AND EVEN CARRYING A LIGHTSABER! CLEARLY, IT WOULD ONLY BE PRUDENT FOR ME TO TEST YOU TOO. WE'VE FOUND OUT A LOT. AND--
I'M SORRY TO INTERRUPT, THANE MARKONA.
BUT OUR SENSORS SEEM TO INDICATE A SHIP COMING TO LAND IN THE VILLAGE. ITS TRANSPONDER IS DAMPENED, SO WE CAN'T BE SURE OF ITS IDENTITY...
TULA, WOULD YOU KEEP OUR GUESTS COMPANY?
IT FALLS TO ME TO WELCOME THE NEWCOMERS.

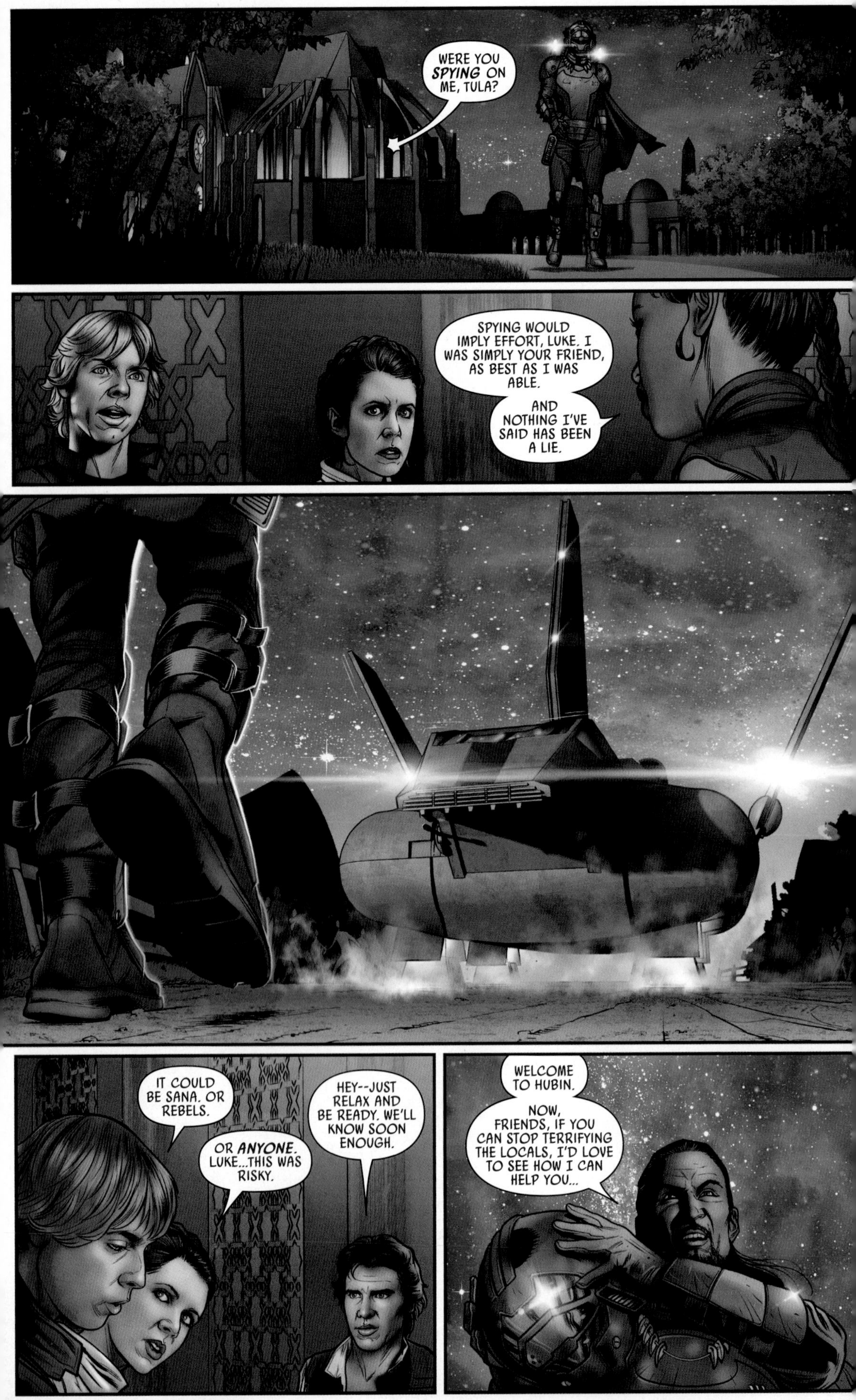

WERE YOU SPYING ON ME, TULA?
SPYING WOULD IMPLY EFFORT, LUKE. I WAS SIMPLY YOUR FRIEND, AS BEST AS I WAS ABLE.
AND NOTHING I'VE SAID HAS BEEN A LIE.
IT COULD BE SANA. OR REBELS.
OR ANYONE. LUKE...THIS WAS RISKY.
HEY--JUST RELAX AND BE READY. WE'LL KNOW SOON ENOUGH.
WELCOME TO HUBIN.
NOW, FRIENDS, IF YOU CAN STOP TERRIFYING THE LOCALS, I'D LOVE TO SEE HOW I CAN HELP YOU...

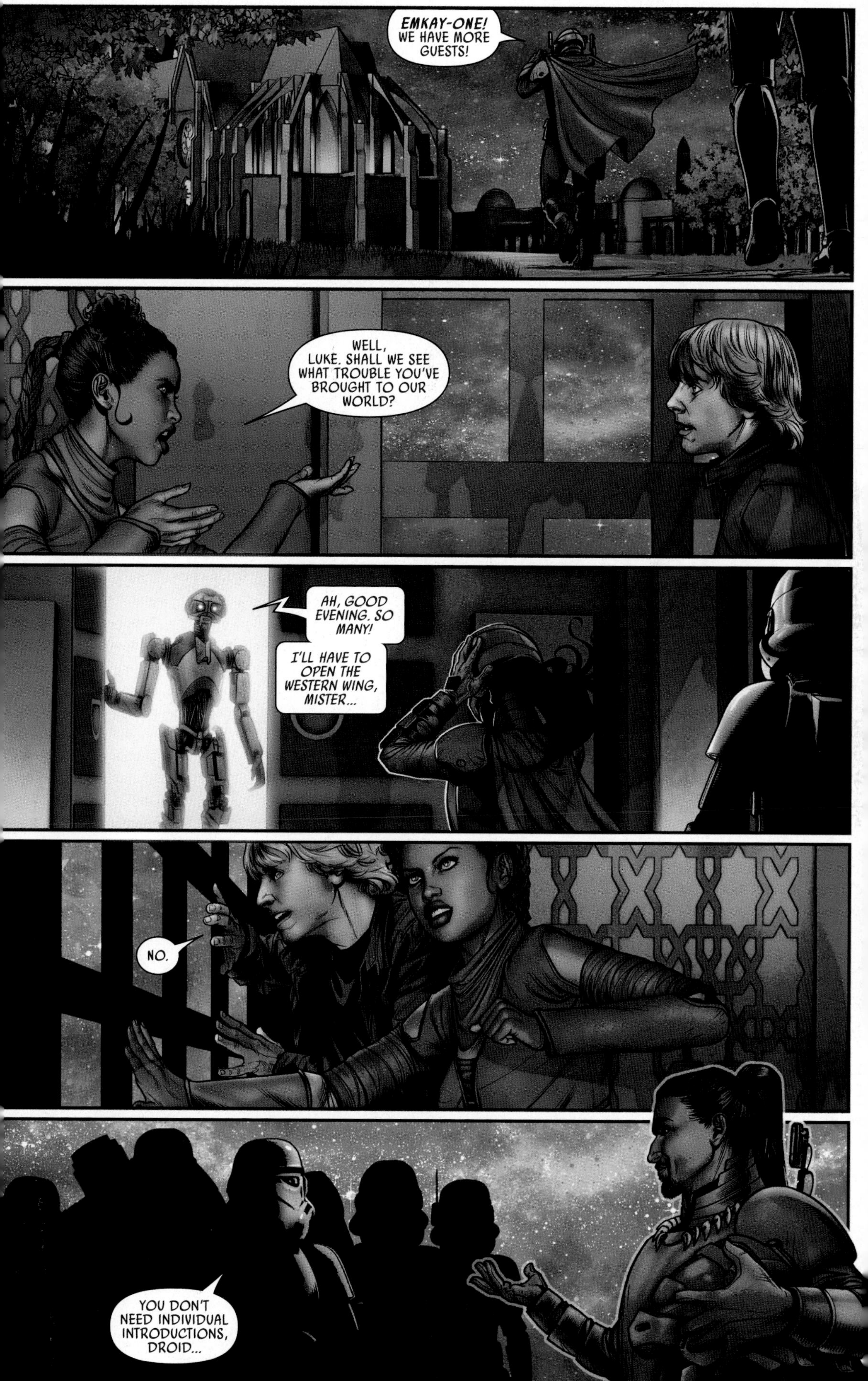
EMKAY-ONE! WE HAVE MORE GUESTS!
WELL, LUKE. SHALL WE SEE WHAT TROUBLE YOU'VE BROUGHT TO OUR WORLD?
AH, GOOD EVENING. SO MANY!
I'LL HAVE TO OPEN THE WESTERN WING, MISTER...
NO.
YOU DON'T NEED INDIVIDUAL INTRODUCTIONS, DROID...

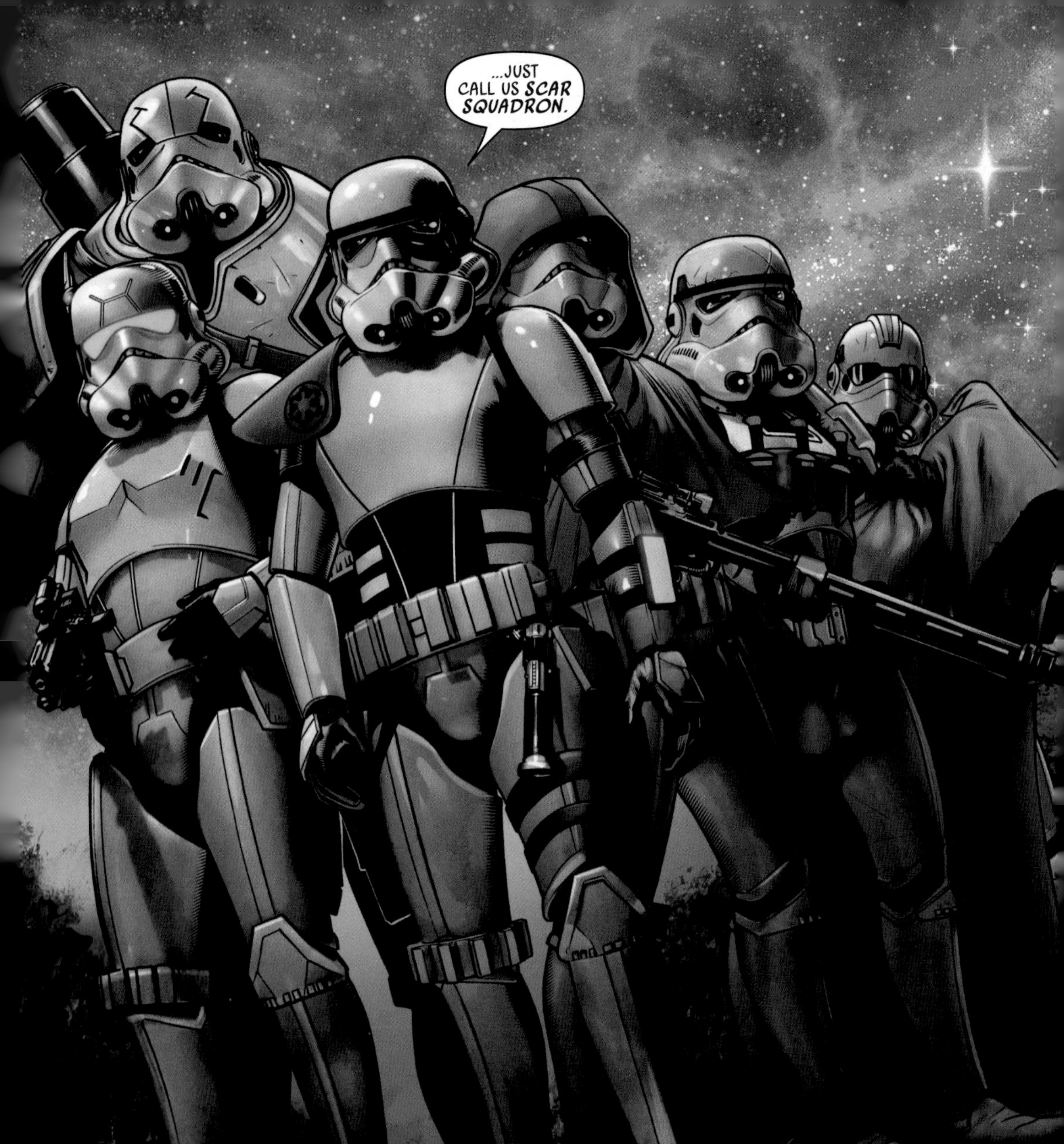
...JUST CALL US SCAR SQUADRON.

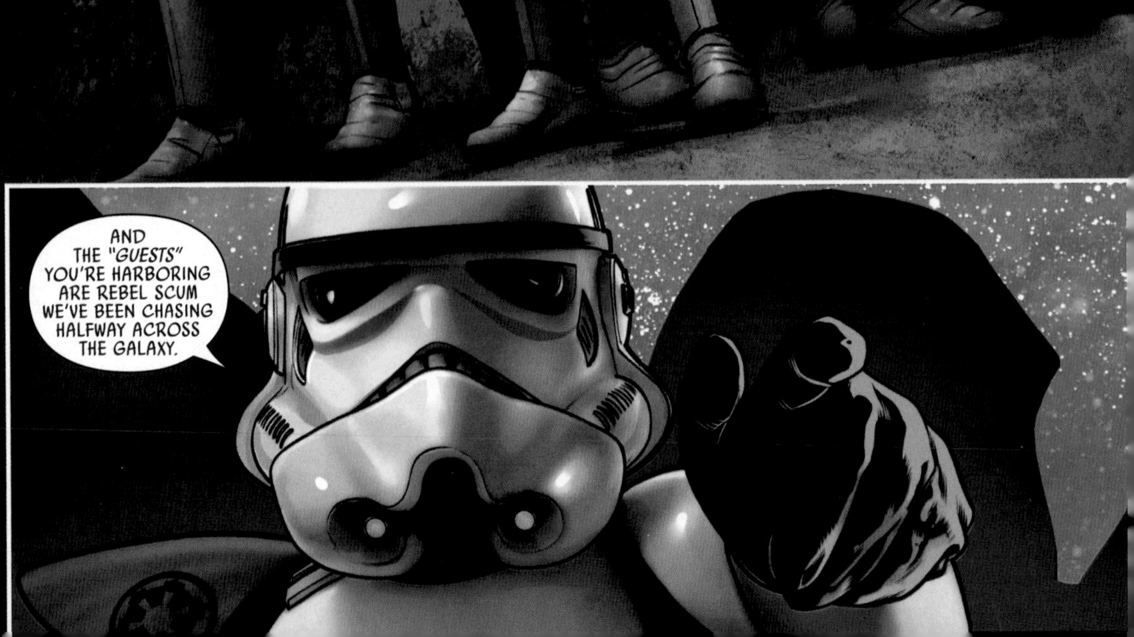
AND THE "GUESTS" YOU'RE HARBORING ARE REBEL SCUM WE'VE BEEN CHASING HALFWAY ACROSS THE GALAXY.

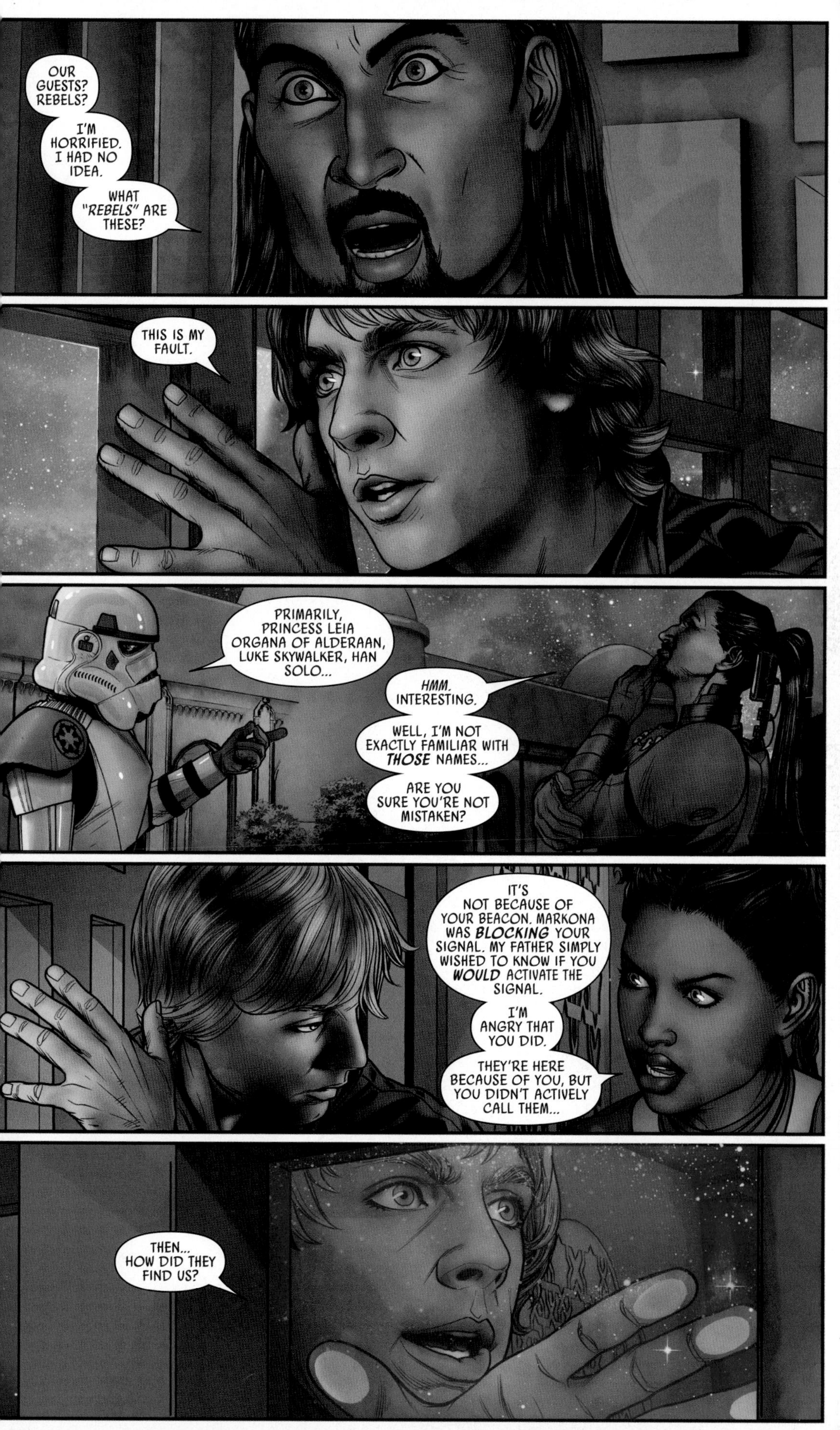
OUR GUESTS? REBELS?
I'M HORRIFIED. I HAD NO IDEA.
WHAT "*REBELS*" ARE THESE?
THIS IS MY FAULT.
PRIMARILY, PRINCESS LEIA ORGANA OF ALDERAAN, LUKE SKYWALKER, HAN SOLO...
HMM. INTERESTING.
WELL, I'M NOT EXACTLY FAMILIAR WITH ***THOSE*** NAMES...
ARE YOU SURE YOU'RE NOT MISTAKEN?
IT'S NOT BECAUSE OF YOUR BEACON. MARKONA WAS ***BLOCKING*** YOUR SIGNAL. MY FATHER SIMPLY WISHED TO KNOW IF YOU ***WOULD*** ACTIVATE THE SIGNAL.
I'M ANGRY THAT YOU DID.
THEY'RE HERE BECAUSE OF YOU, BUT YOU DIDN'T ACTIVELY CALL THEM...
THEN... HOW DID THEY FIND US?

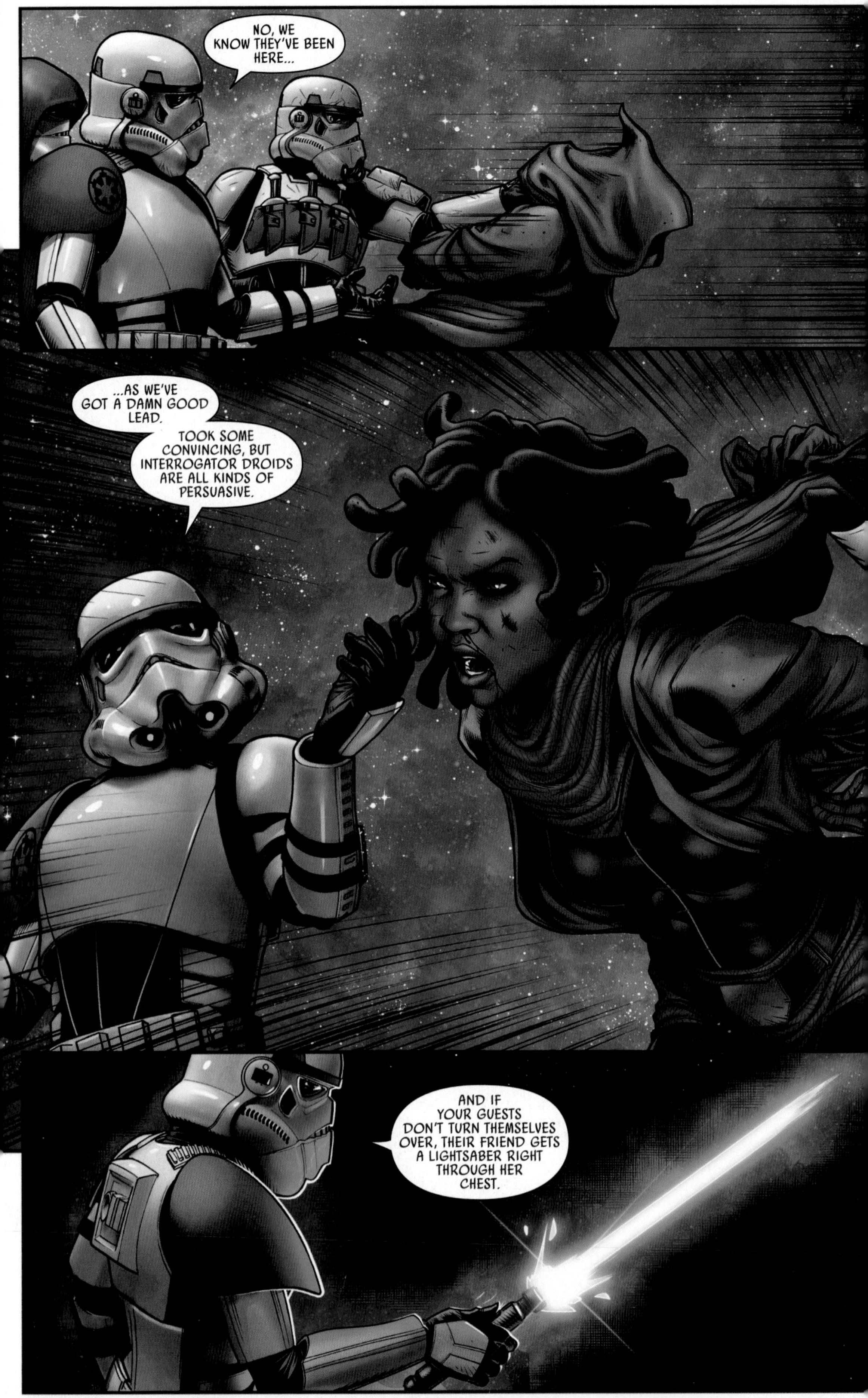
NO, WE KNOW THEY'VE BEEN HERE...
...AS WE'VE GOT A DAMN GOOD LEAD.
TOOK SOME CONVINCING, BUT INTERROGATOR DROIDS ARE ALL KINDS OF PERSUASIVE.
AND IF YOUR GUESTS DON'T TURN THEMSELVES OVER, THEIR FRIEND GETS A LIGHTSABER RIGHT THROUGH HER CHEST.

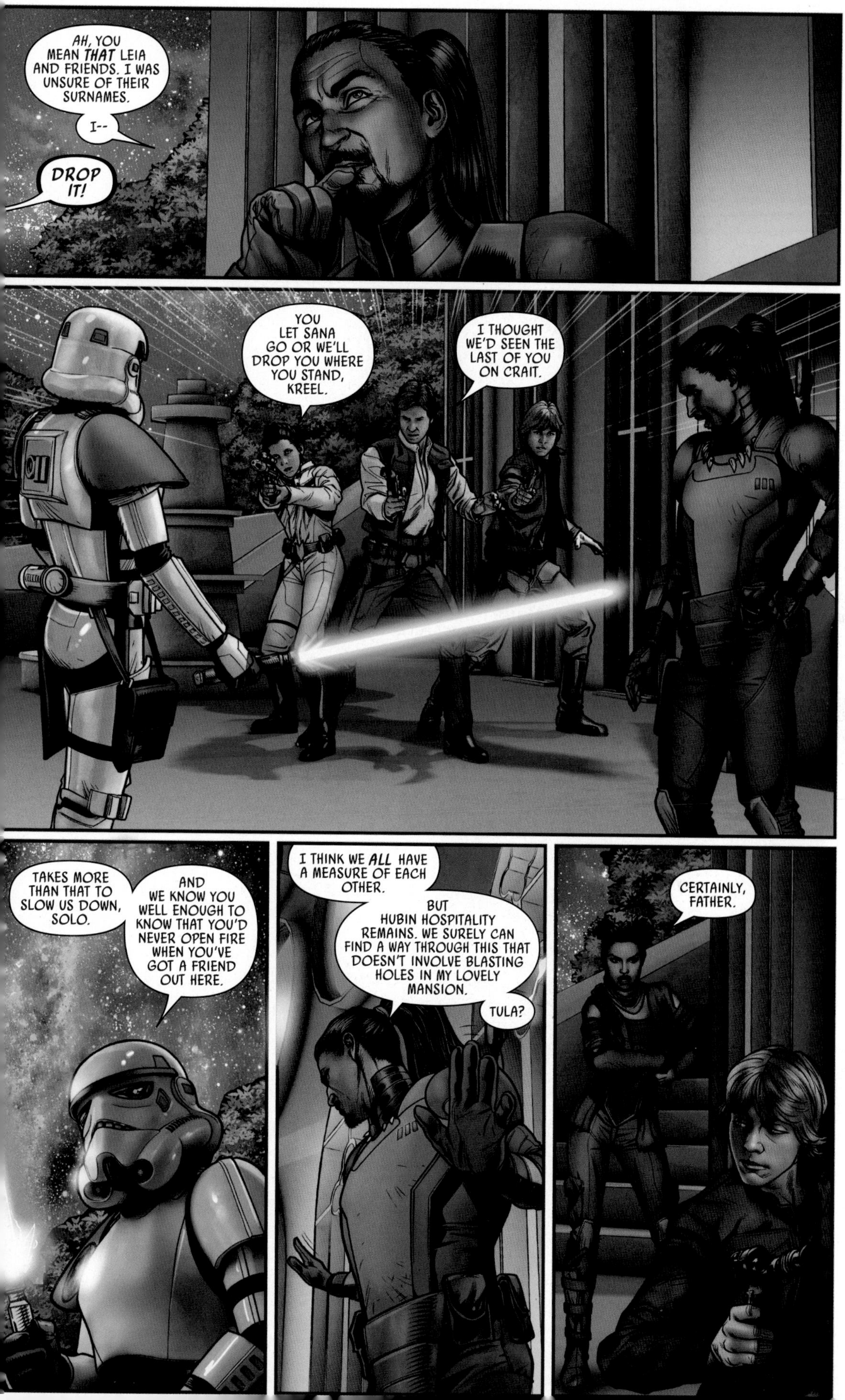

AH, YOU MEAN THAT LEIA AND FRIENDS. I WAS UNSURE OF THEIR SURNAMES.
I--
DROP IT!
YOU LET SANA GO OR WE'LL DROP YOU WHERE YOU STAND, KREEL.
I THOUGHT WE'D SEEN THE LAST OF YOU ON CRAIT.
TAKES MORE THAN THAT TO SLOW US DOWN, SOLO.
AND WE KNOW YOU WELL ENOUGH TO KNOW THAT YOU'D NEVER OPEN FIRE WHEN YOU'VE GOT A FRIEND OUT HERE.
I THINK WE ALL HAVE A MEASURE OF EACH OTHER.
BUT HUBIN HOSPITALITY REMAINS. WE SURELY CAN FIND A WAY THROUGH THIS THAT DOESN'T INVOLVE BLASTING HOLES IN MY LOVELY MANSION.
TULA?
CERTAINLY, FATHER.

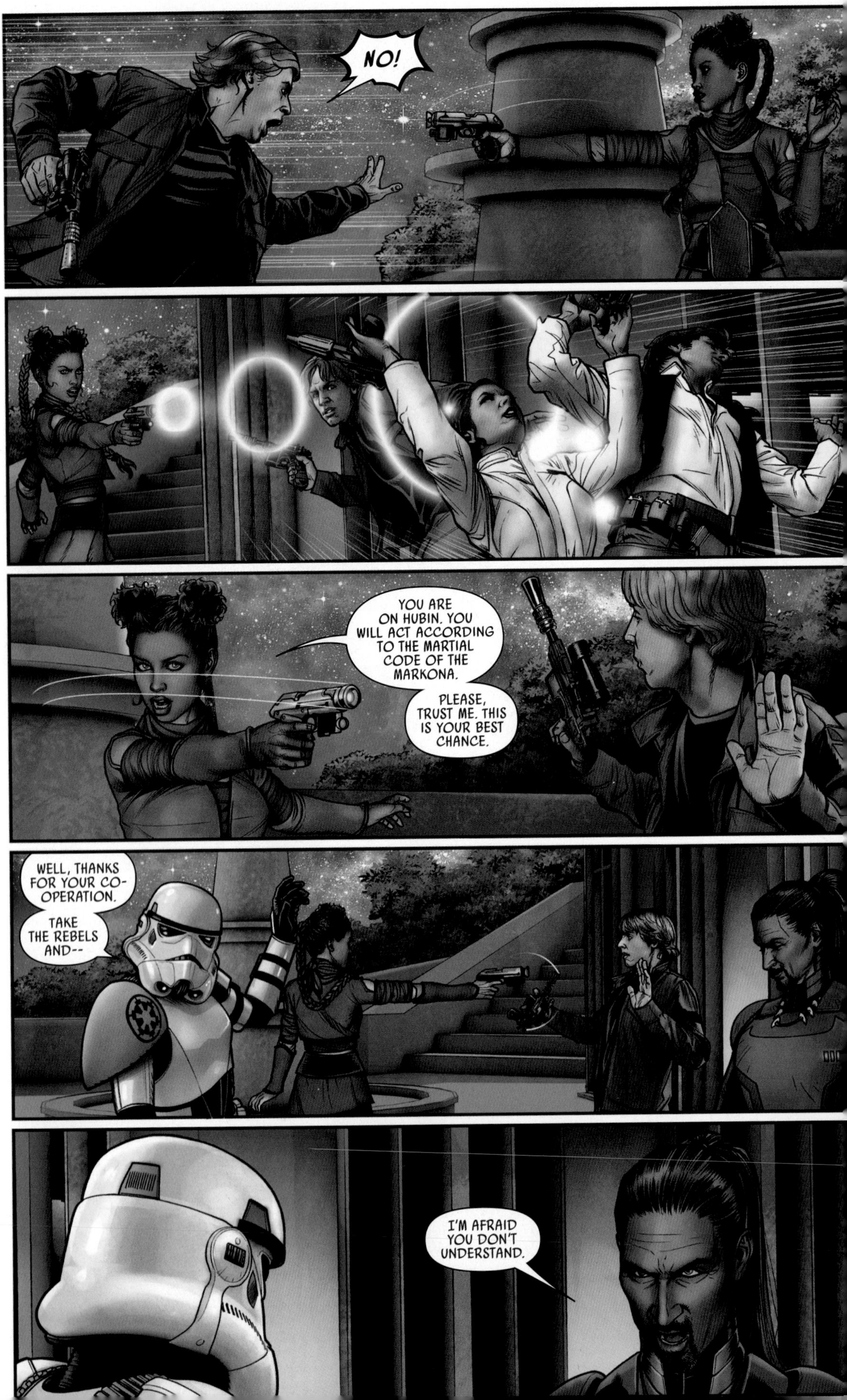
NO!
YOU ARE ON HUBIN. YOU WILL ACT ACCORDING TO THE MARTIAL CODE OF THE MARKONA.
PLEASE, TRUST ME. THIS IS YOUR BEST CHANCE.
WELL, THANKS FOR YOUR CO-OPERATION.
TAKE THE REBELS AND--
I'M AFRAID YOU DON'T UNDERSTAND.

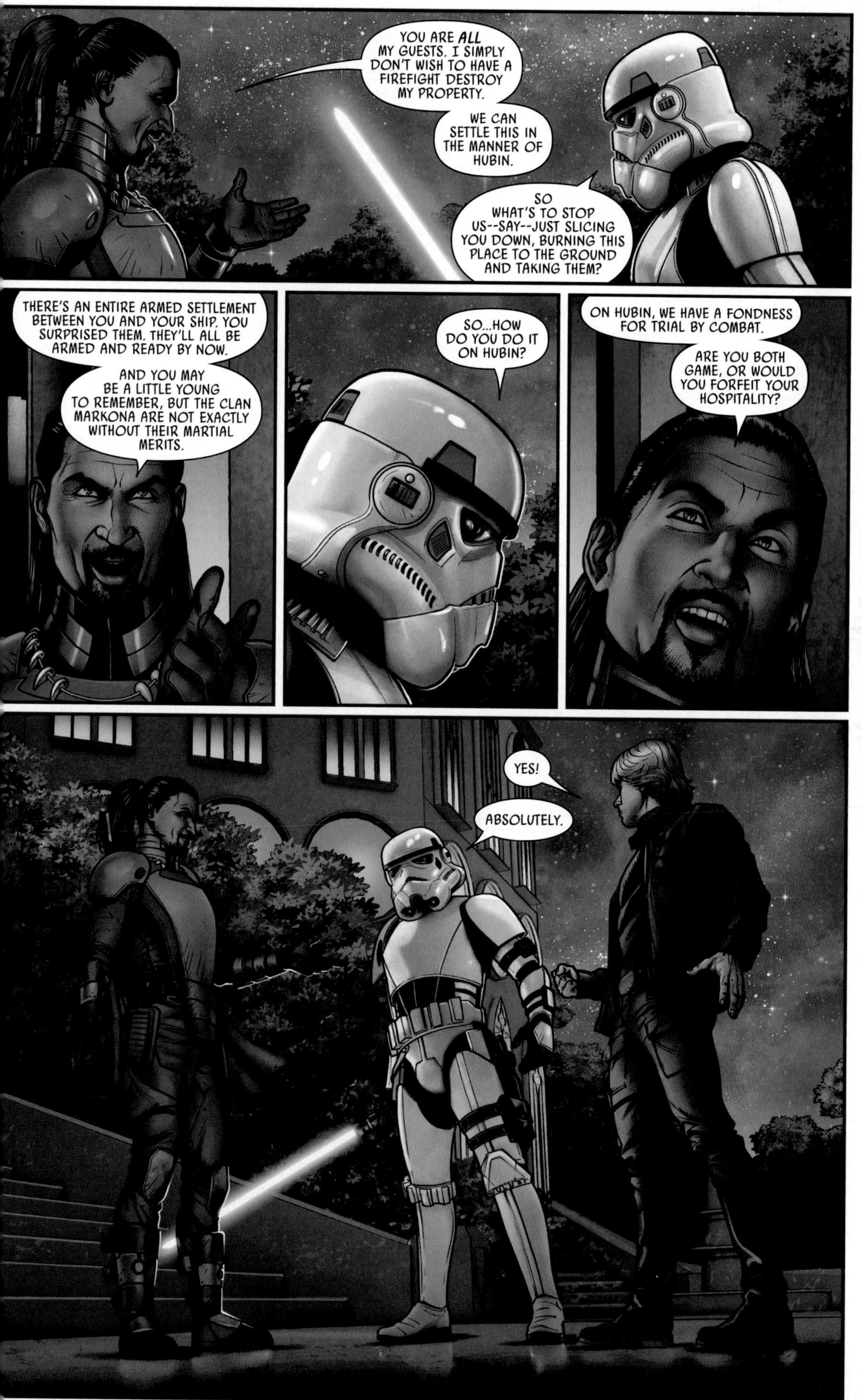
YOU ARE ALL MY GUESTS. I SIMPLY DON'T WISH TO HAVE A FIREFIGHT DESTROY MY PROPERTY.
WE CAN SETTLE THIS IN THE MANNER OF HUBIN.
SO WHAT'S TO STOP US--SAY--JUST SLICING YOU DOWN, BURNING THIS PLACE TO THE GROUND AND TAKING THEM?
THERE'S AN ENTIRE ARMED SETTLEMENT BETWEEN YOU AND YOUR SHIP. YOU SURPRISED THEM. THEY'LL ALL BE ARMED AND READY BY NOW.
AND YOU MAY BE A LITTLE YOUNG TO REMEMBER, BUT THE CLAN MARKONA ARE NOT EXACTLY WITHOUT THEIR MARTIAL MERITS.
SO...HOW DO YOU DO IT ON HUBIN?
ON HUBIN, WE HAVE A FONDNESS FOR TRIAL BY COMBAT.
ARE YOU BOTH GAME, OR WOULD YOU FORFEIT YOUR HOSPITALITY?
YES!
ABSOLUTELY.

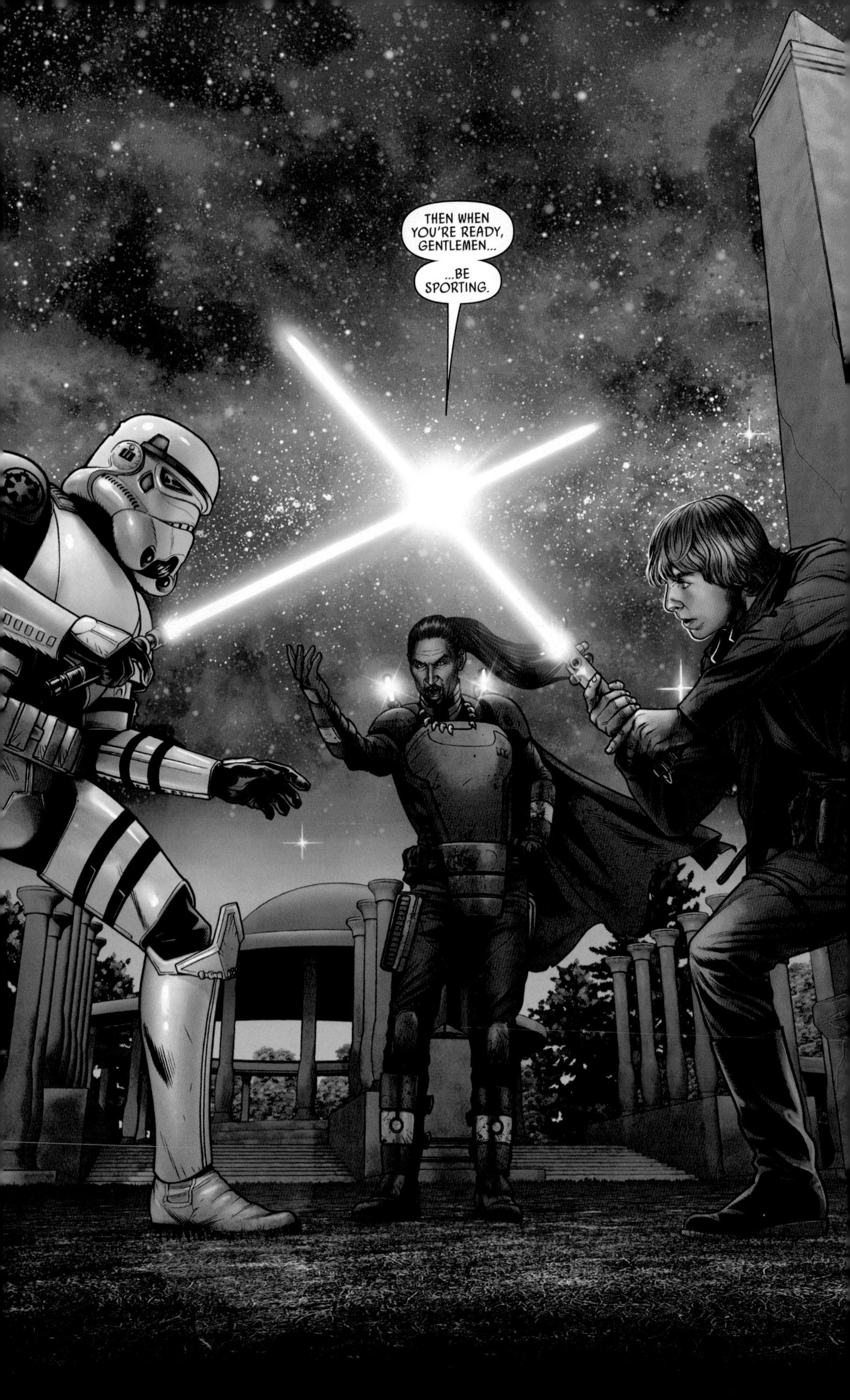
THEN WHEN YOU'RE READY, GENTLEMEN...
...BE SPORTING.

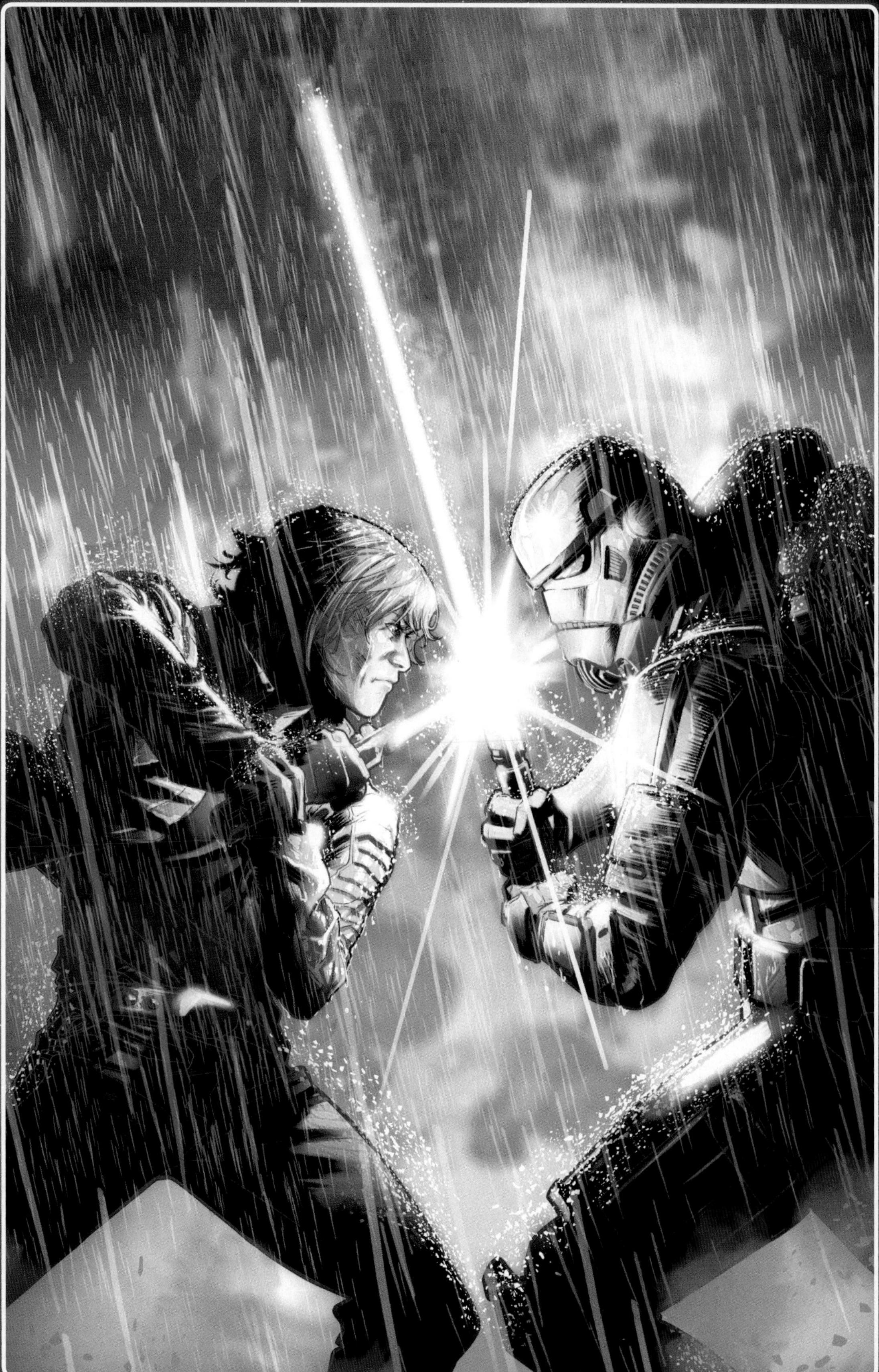

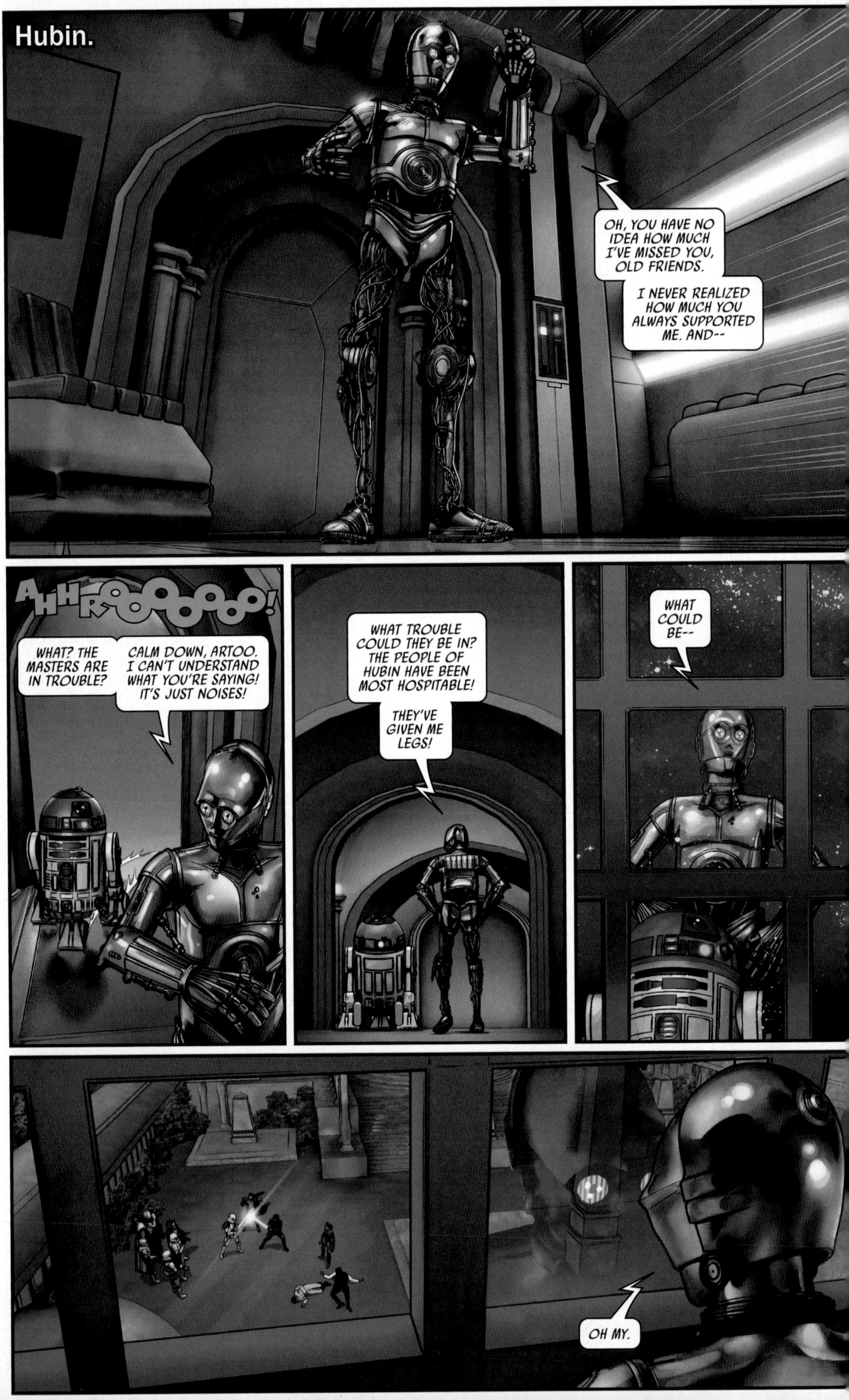
Hubin.
OH, YOU HAVE NO IDEA HOW MUCH I'VE MISSED YOU, OLD FRIENDS.
I NEVER REALIZED HOW MUCH YOU ALWAYS SUPPORTED ME. AND--
AHHROOOOOOO!
WHAT? THE MASTERS ARE IN TROUBLE?
CALM DOWN, ARTOO. I CAN'T UNDERSTAND WHAT YOU'RE SAYING! IT'S JUST NOISES!
WHAT TROUBLE COULD THEY BE IN? THE PEOPLE OF HUBIN HAVE BEEN MOST HOSPITABLE!
THEY'VE GIVEN ME LEGS!
WHAT COULD BE--
OH MY.

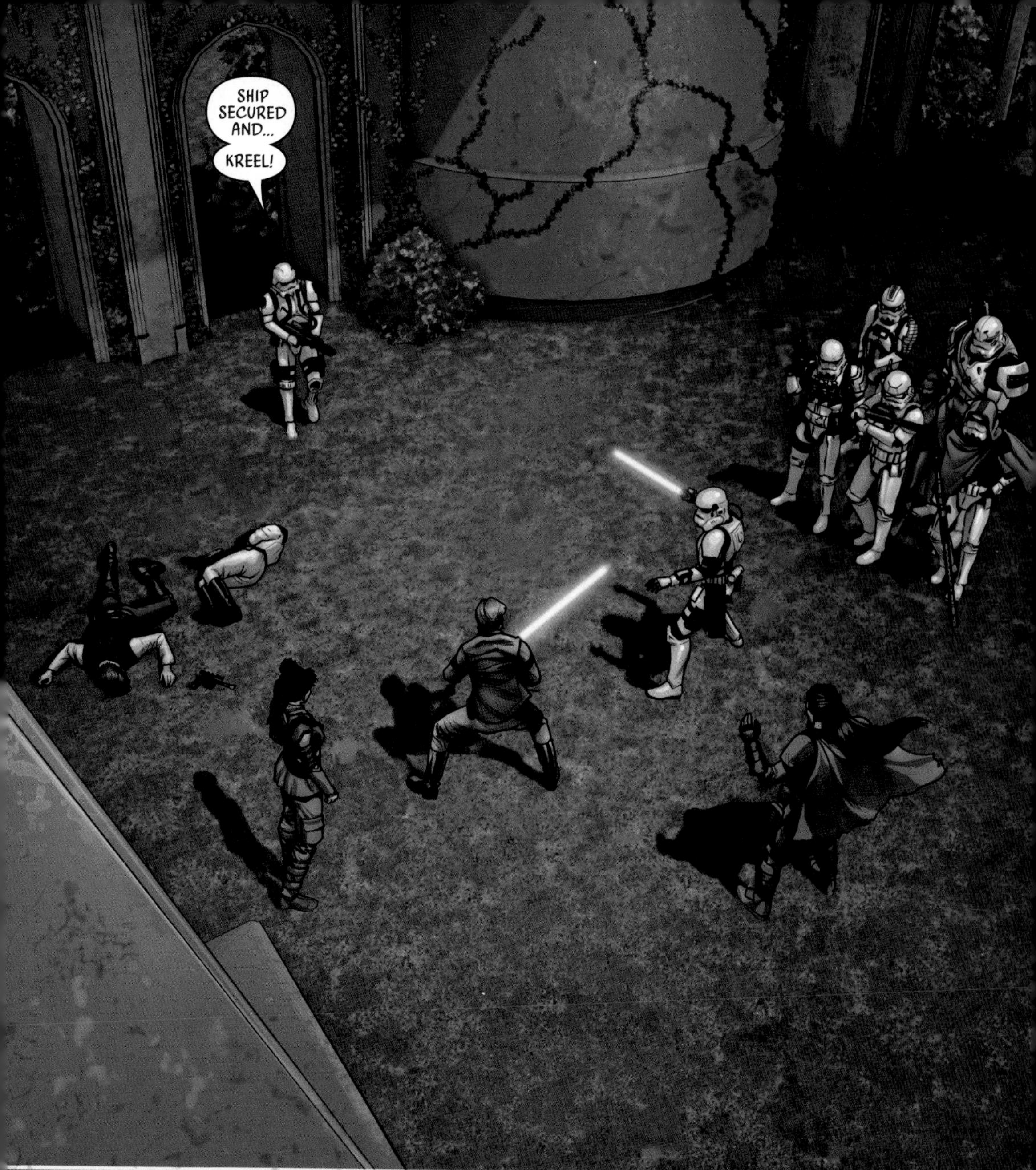
SHIP SECURED AND...
KREEL!

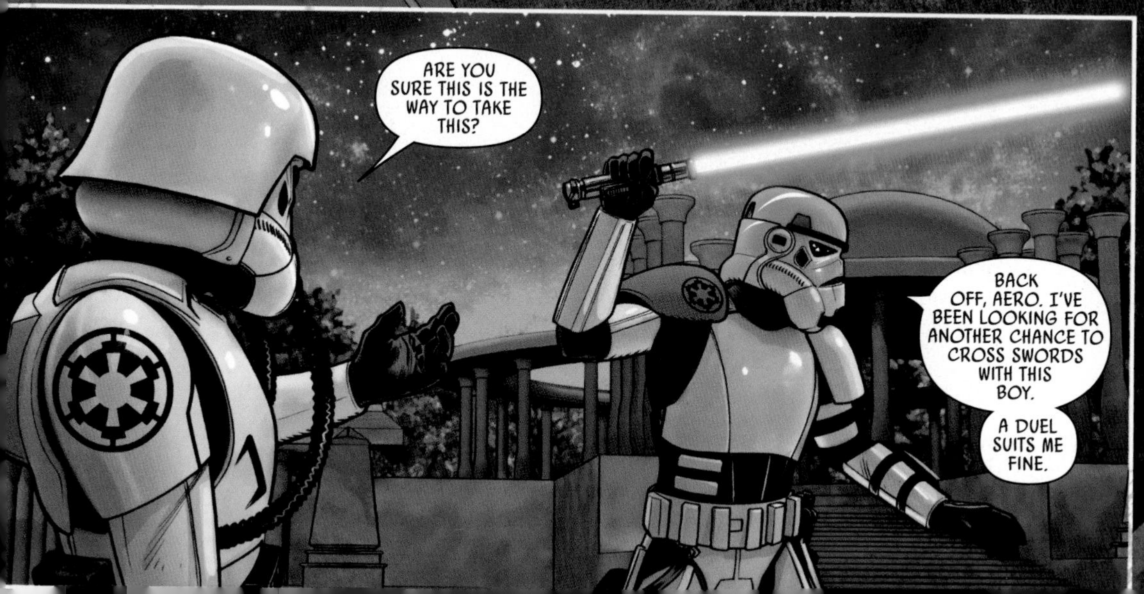
ARE YOU SURE THIS IS THE WAY TO TAKE THIS?
BACK OFF, AERO. I'VE BEEN LOOKING FOR ANOTHER CHANCE TO CROSS SWORDS WITH THIS BOY.
A DUEL SUITS ME FINE.

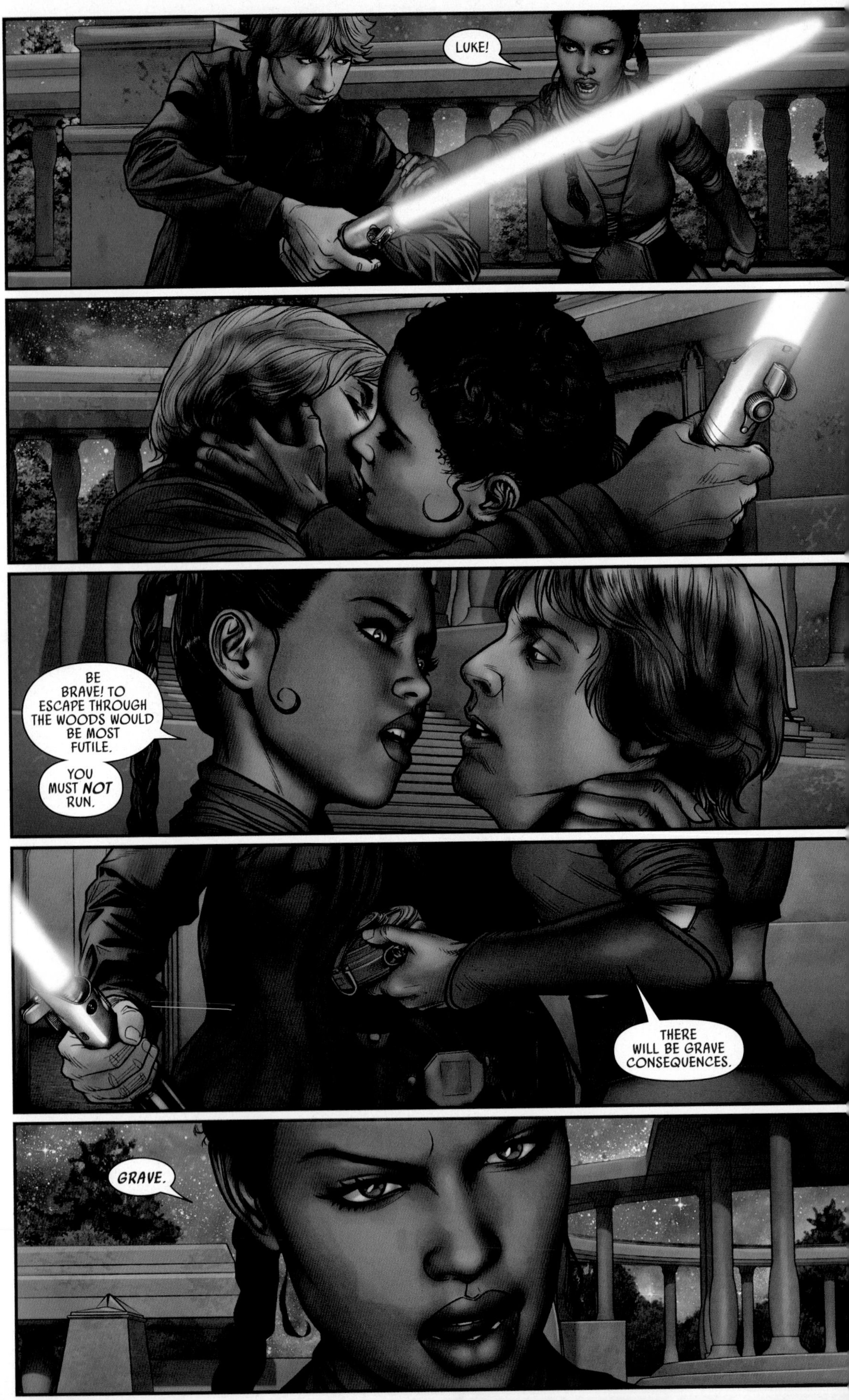
LUKE!
BE BRAVE! TO ESCAPE THROUGH THE WOODS WOULD BE MOST FUTILE.
YOU MUST NOT RUN.
THERE WILL BE GRAVE CONSEQUENCES.
GRAVE.

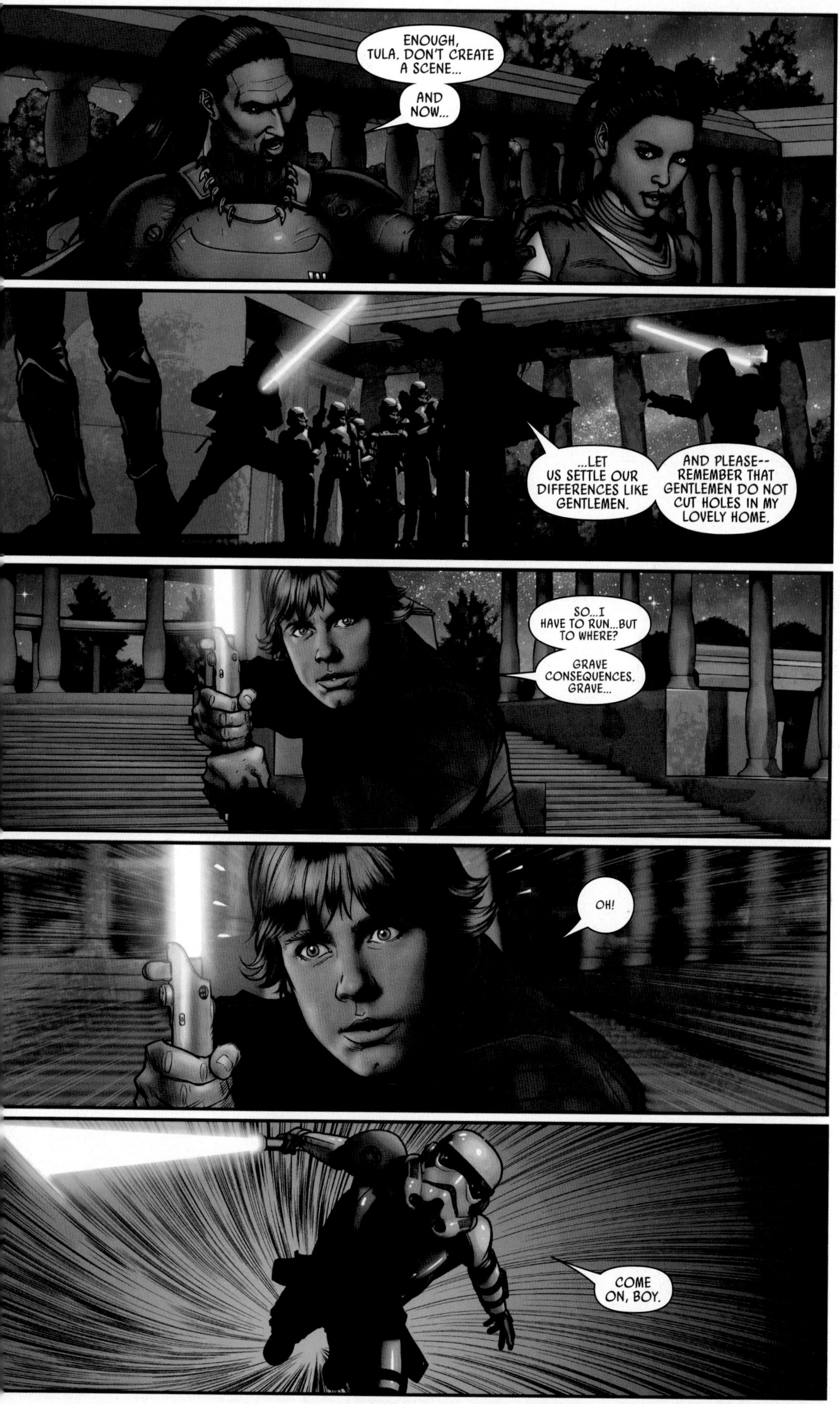
ENOUGH, TULA. DON'T CREATE A SCENE...
AND NOW...
...LET US SETTLE OUR DIFFERENCES LIKE GENTLEMEN.
AND PLEASE-- REMEMBER THAT GENTLEMEN DO NOT CUT HOLES IN MY LOVELY HOME.
SO...I HAVE TO RUN...BUT TO WHERE?
GRAVE CONSEQUENCES. GRAVE...
OH!
COME ON, BOY.

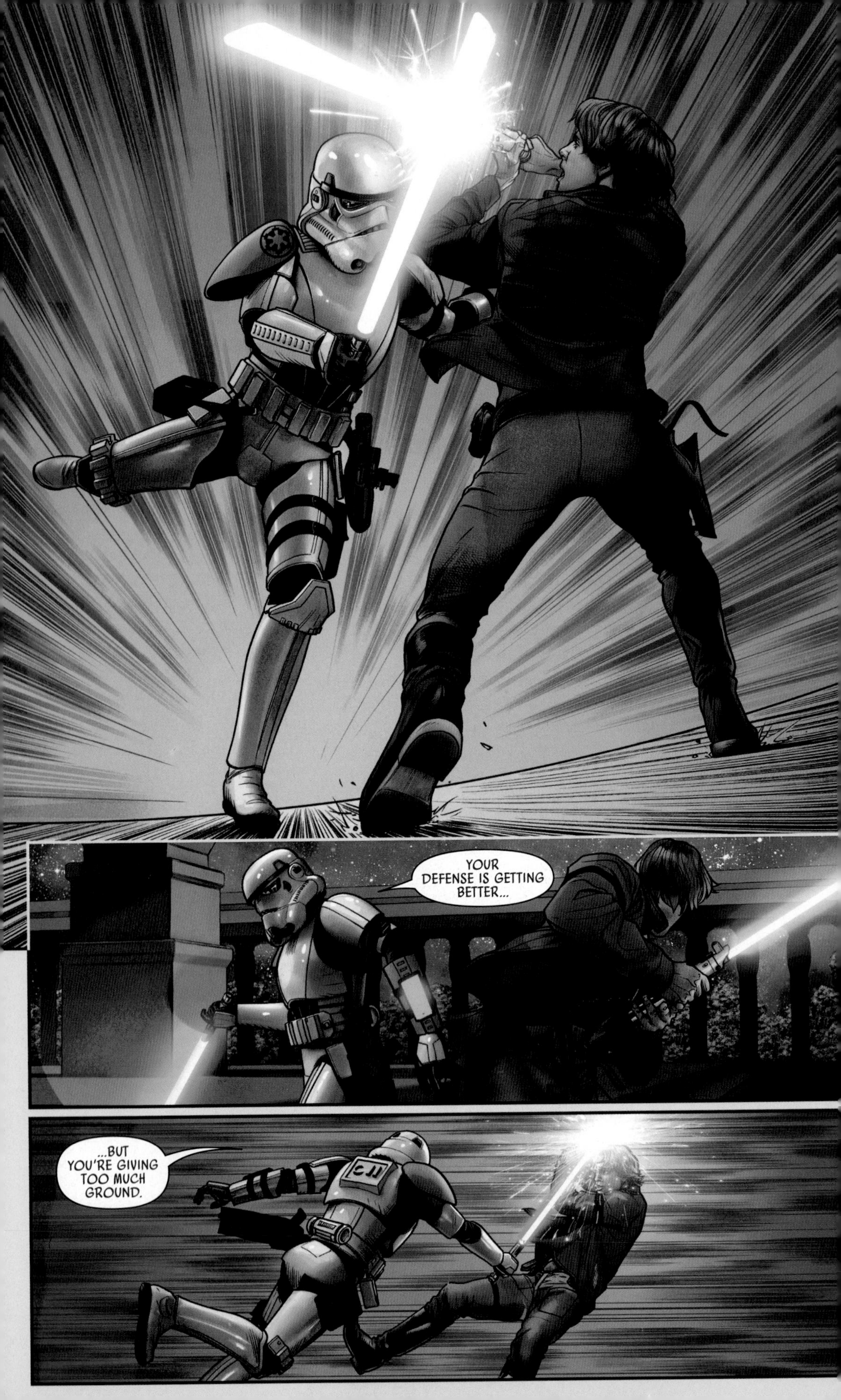
YOUR DEFENSE IS GETTING BETTER...
...BUT YOU'RE GIVING TOO MUCH GROUND.

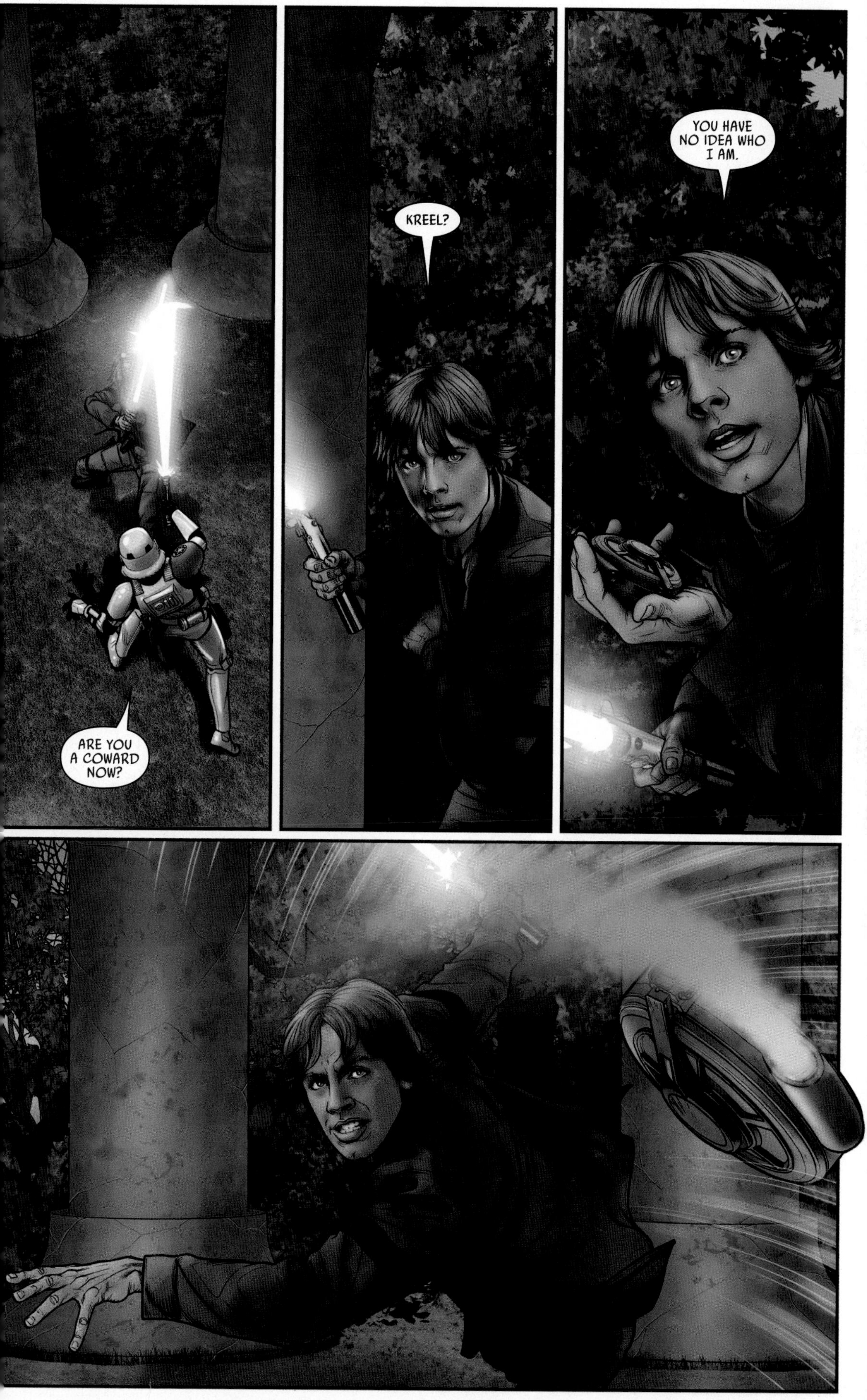
ARE YOU A COWARD NOW?
KREEL?
YOU HAVE NO IDEA WHO I AM.

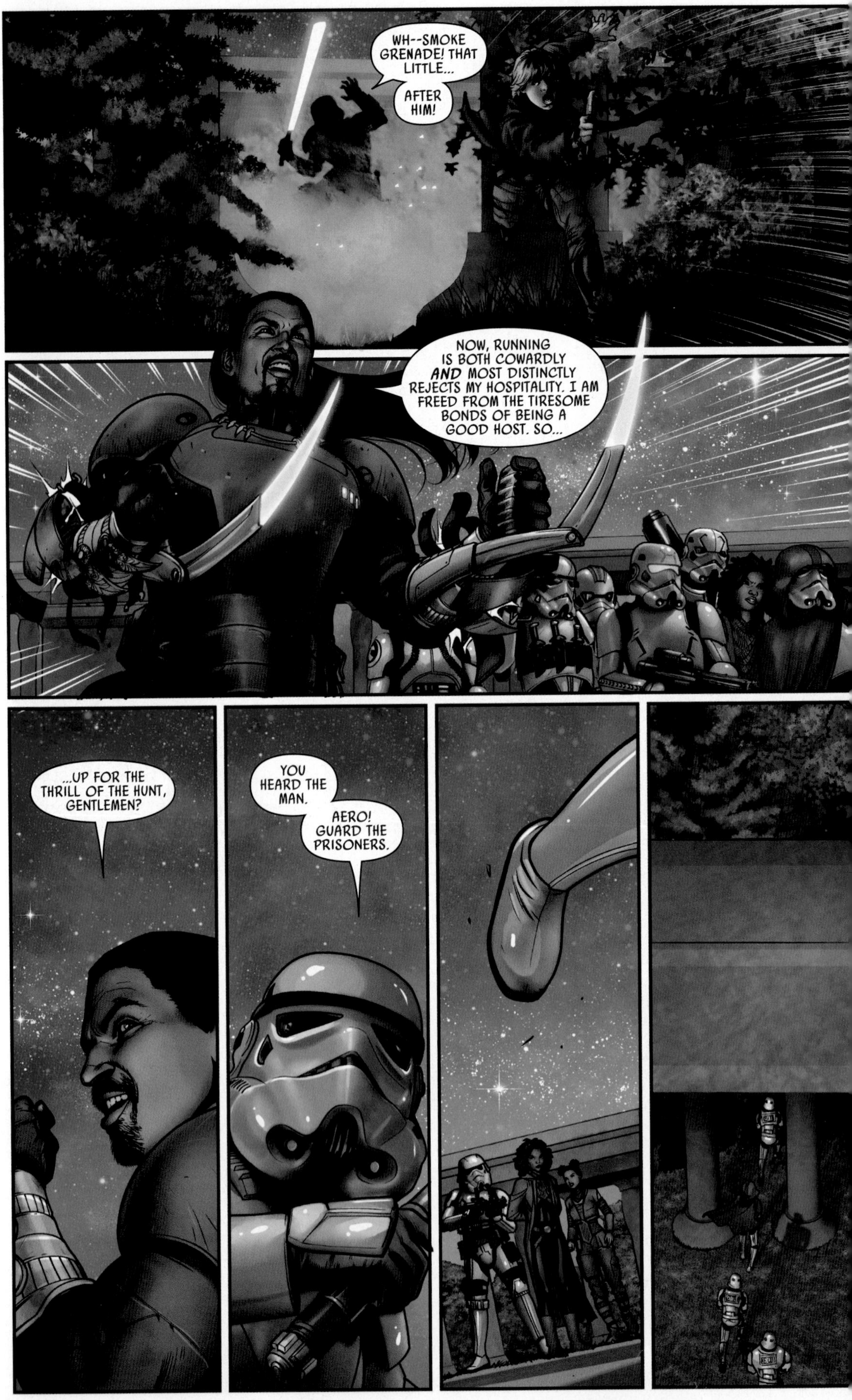
WH--SMOKE GRENADE! THAT LITTLE...
AFTER HIM!
NOW, RUNNING IS BOTH COWARDLY AND MOST DISTINCTLY REJECTS MY HOSPITALITY. I AM FREED FROM THE TIRESOME BONDS OF BEING A GOOD HOST. SO...
...UP FOR THE THRILL OF THE HUNT, GENTLEMEN?
YOU HEARD THE MAN.
AERO! GUARD THE PRISONERS.

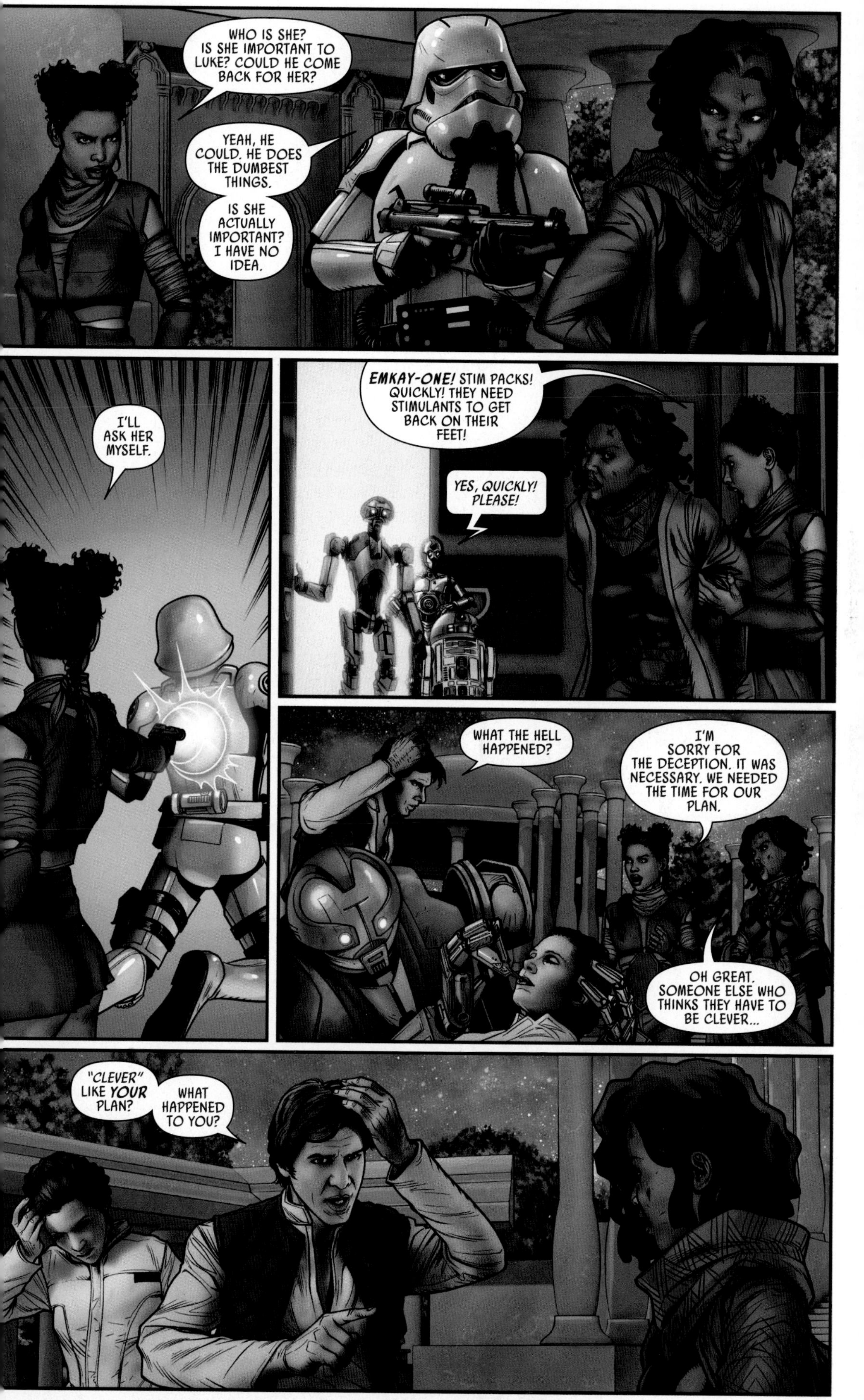

WHO IS SHE? IS SHE IMPORTANT TO LUKE? COULD HE COME BACK FOR HER?
YEAH, HE COULD. HE DOES THE DUMBEST THINGS.
IS SHE ACTUALLY IMPORTANT? I HAVE NO IDEA.
I'LL ASK HER MYSELF.
EMKAY-ONE! STIM PACKS! QUICKLY! THEY NEED STIMULANTS TO GET BACK ON THEIR FEET!
YES, QUICKLY! PLEASE!
WHAT THE HELL HAPPENED?
I'M SORRY FOR THE DECEPTION. IT WAS NECESSARY. WE NEEDED THE TIME FOR OUR PLAN.
OH GREAT. SOMEONE ELSE WHO THINKS THEY HAVE TO BE CLEVER...
"CLEVER" LIKE YOUR PLAN?
WHAT HAPPENED TO YOU?

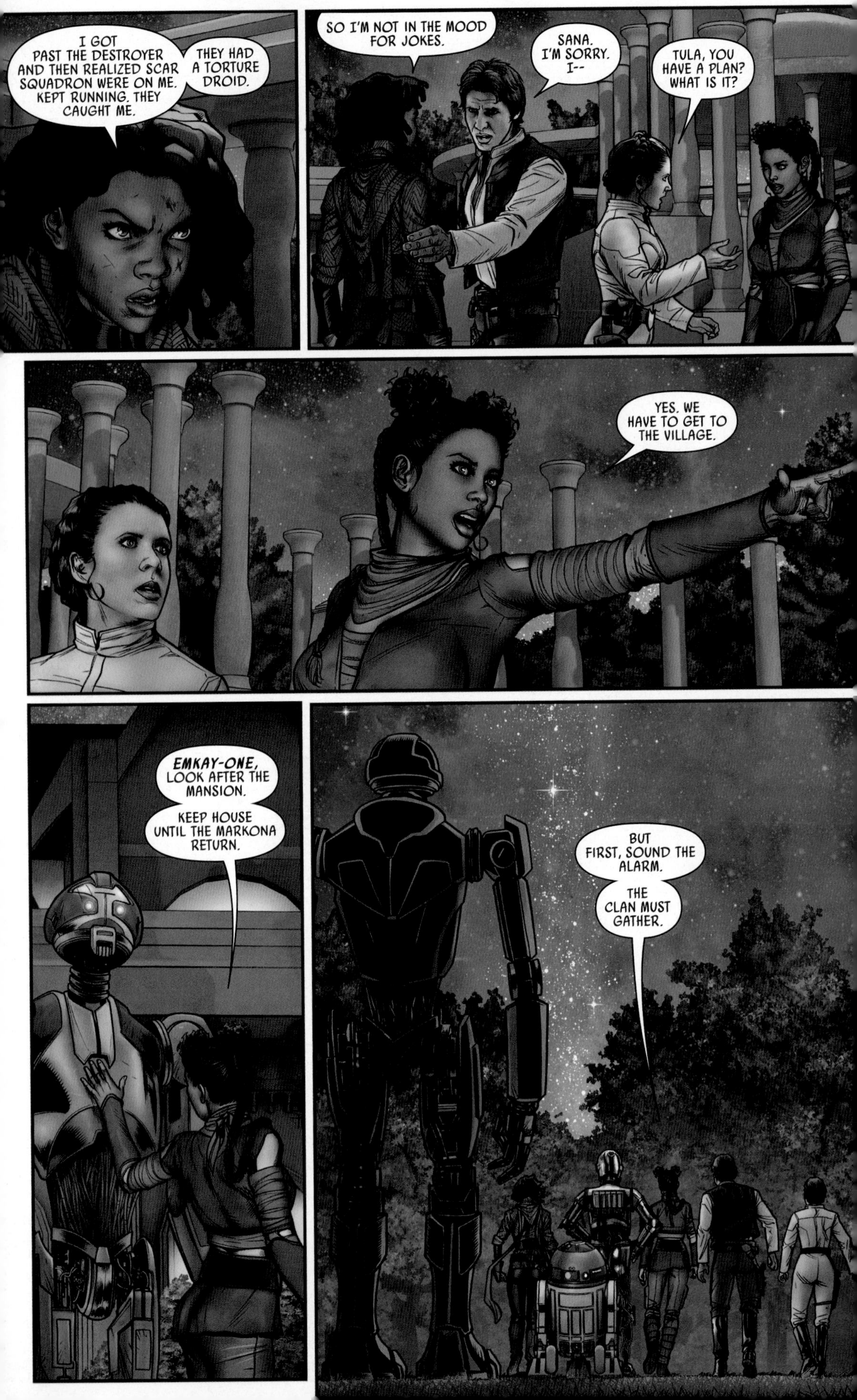
I GOT PAST THE DESTROYER AND THEN REALIZED SCAR SQUADRON WERE ON ME. KEPT RUNNING. THEY CAUGHT ME.
THEY HAD A TORTURE DROID.
SO I'M NOT IN THE MOOD FOR JOKES.
SANA. I'M SORRY. I--
TULA, YOU HAVE A PLAN? WHAT IS IT?
YES. WE HAVE TO GET TO THE VILLAGE.
EMKAY-ONE, LOOK AFTER THE MANSION.
KEEP HOUSE UNTIL THE MARKONA RETURN.
BUT FIRST, SOUND THE ALARM.
THE CLAN MUST GATHER.

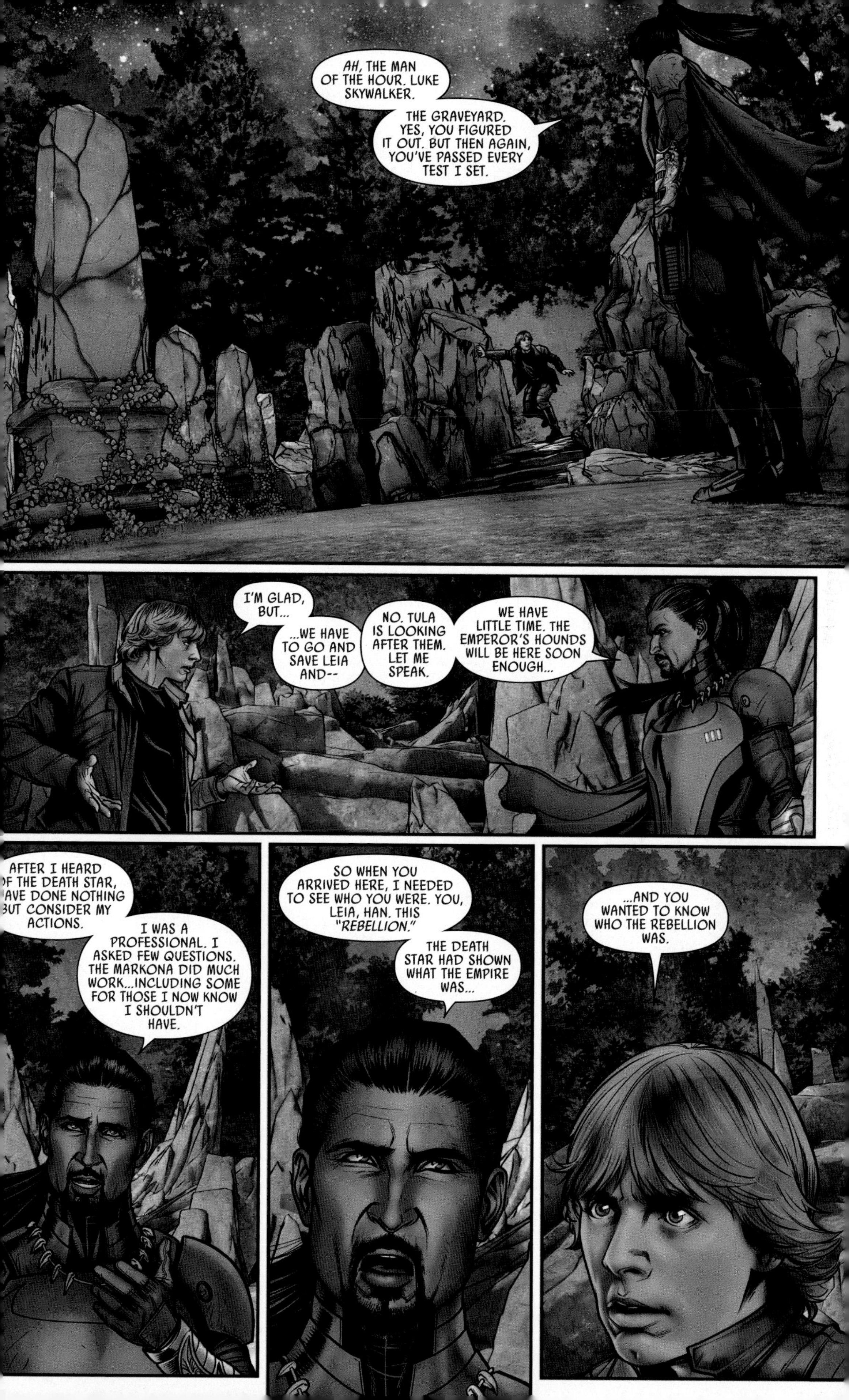
AH, THE MAN OF THE HOUR. LUKE SKYWALKER.
THE GRAVEYARD. YES, YOU FIGURED IT OUT. BUT THEN AGAIN, YOU'VE PASSED EVERY TEST I SET.
I'M GLAD, BUT...
...WE HAVE TO GO AND SAVE LEIA AND--
NO. TULA IS LOOKING AFTER THEM. LET ME SPEAK.
WE HAVE LITTLE TIME. THE EMPEROR'S HOUNDS WILL BE HERE SOON ENOUGH...
AFTER I HEARD OF THE DEATH STAR, I HAVE DONE NOTHING BUT CONSIDER MY ACTIONS.
I WAS A PROFESSIONAL. I ASKED FEW QUESTIONS. THE MARKONA DID MUCH WORK...INCLUDING SOME FOR THOSE I NOW KNOW I SHOULDN'T HAVE.
SO WHEN YOU ARRIVED HERE, I NEEDED TO SEE WHO YOU WERE. YOU, LEIA, HAN. THIS "REBELLION."
THE DEATH STAR HAD SHOWN WHAT THE EMPIRE WAS...
...AND YOU WANTED TO KNOW WHO THE REBELLION WAS.

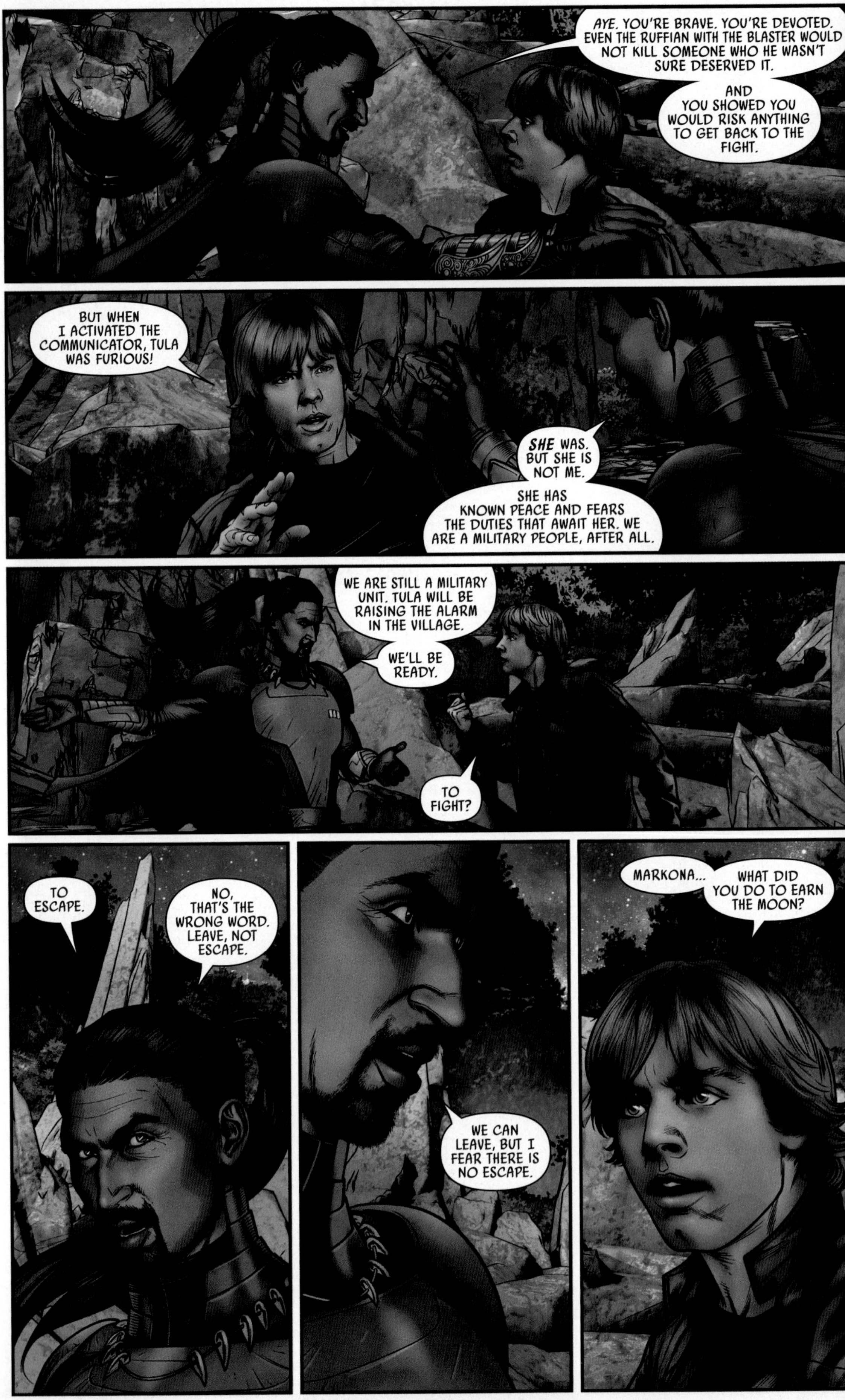
AYE. YOU'RE BRAVE. YOU'RE DEVOTED. EVEN THE RUFFIAN WITH THE BLASTER WOULD NOT KILL SOMEONE WHO HE WASN'T SURE DESERVED IT.
AND YOU SHOWED YOU WOULD RISK ANYTHING TO GET BACK TO THE FIGHT.
BUT WHEN I ACTIVATED THE COMMUNICATOR, TULA WAS FURIOUS!
SHE WAS. BUT SHE IS NOT ME.
SHE HAS KNOWN PEACE AND FEARS THE DUTIES THAT AWAIT HER. WE ARE A MILITARY PEOPLE, AFTER ALL.
WE ARE STILL A MILITARY UNIT. TULA WILL BE RAISING THE ALARM IN THE VILLAGE.
WE'LL BE READY.
TO FIGHT?
TO ESCAPE.
NO, THAT'S THE WRONG WORD. LEAVE, NOT ESCAPE.
WE CAN LEAVE, BUT I FEAR THERE IS NO ESCAPE.
MARKONA...
WHAT DID YOU DO TO EARN THE MOON?

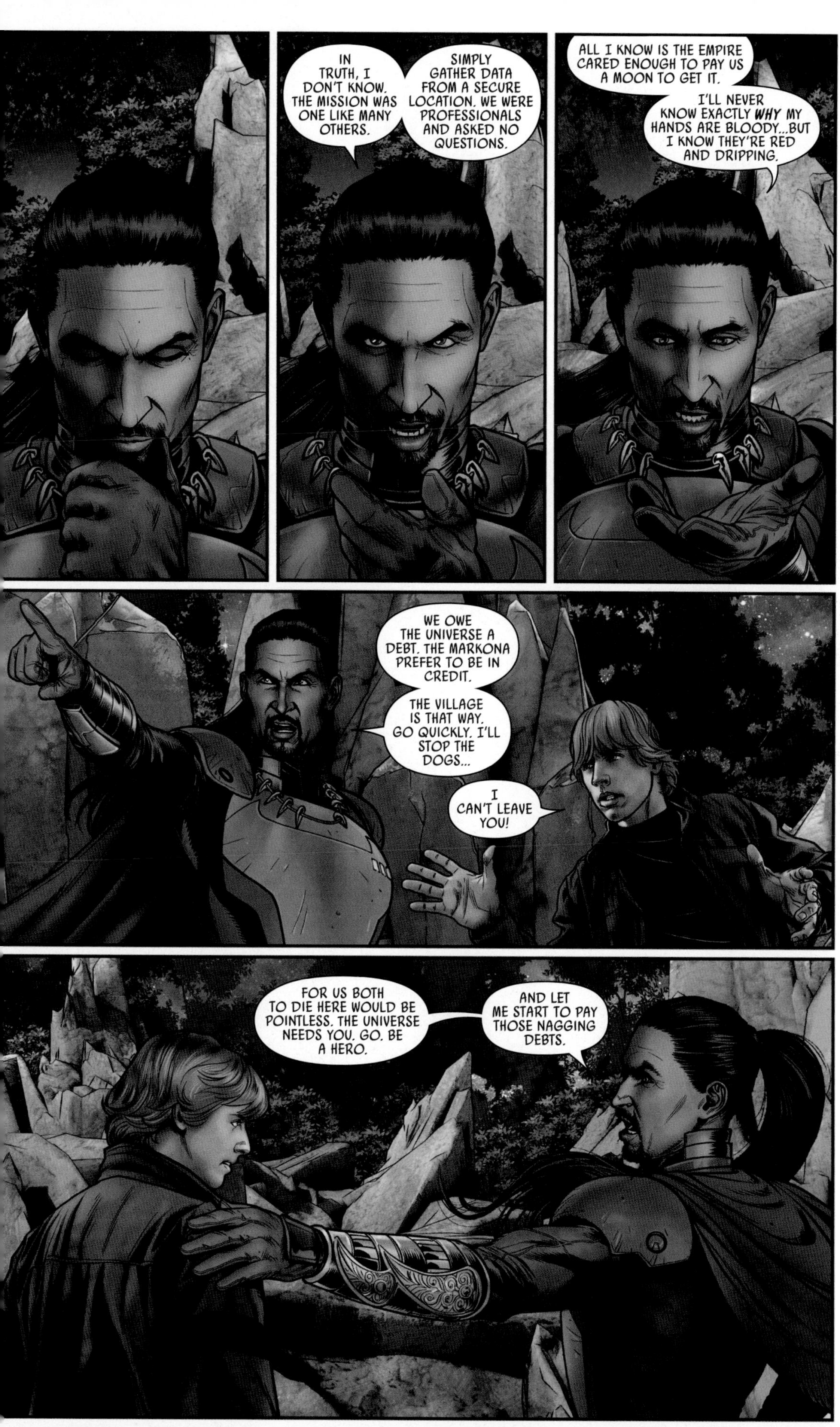
IN TRUTH, I DON'T KNOW. THE MISSION WAS ONE LIKE MANY OTHERS.
SIMPLY GATHER DATA FROM A SECURE LOCATION. WE WERE PROFESSIONALS AND ASKED NO QUESTIONS.
ALL I KNOW IS THE EMPIRE CARED ENOUGH TO PAY US A MOON TO GET IT.
I'LL NEVER KNOW EXACTLY WHY MY HANDS ARE BLOODY...BUT I KNOW THEY'RE RED AND DRIPPING.
WE OWE THE UNIVERSE A DEBT. THE MARKONA PREFER TO BE IN CREDIT.
THE VILLAGE IS THAT WAY. GO QUICKLY. I'LL STOP THE DOGS...
I CAN'T LEAVE YOU!
FOR US BOTH TO DIE HERE WOULD BE POINTLESS. THE UNIVERSE NEEDS YOU. GO. BE A HERO.
AND LET ME START TO PAY THOSE NAGGING DEBTS.

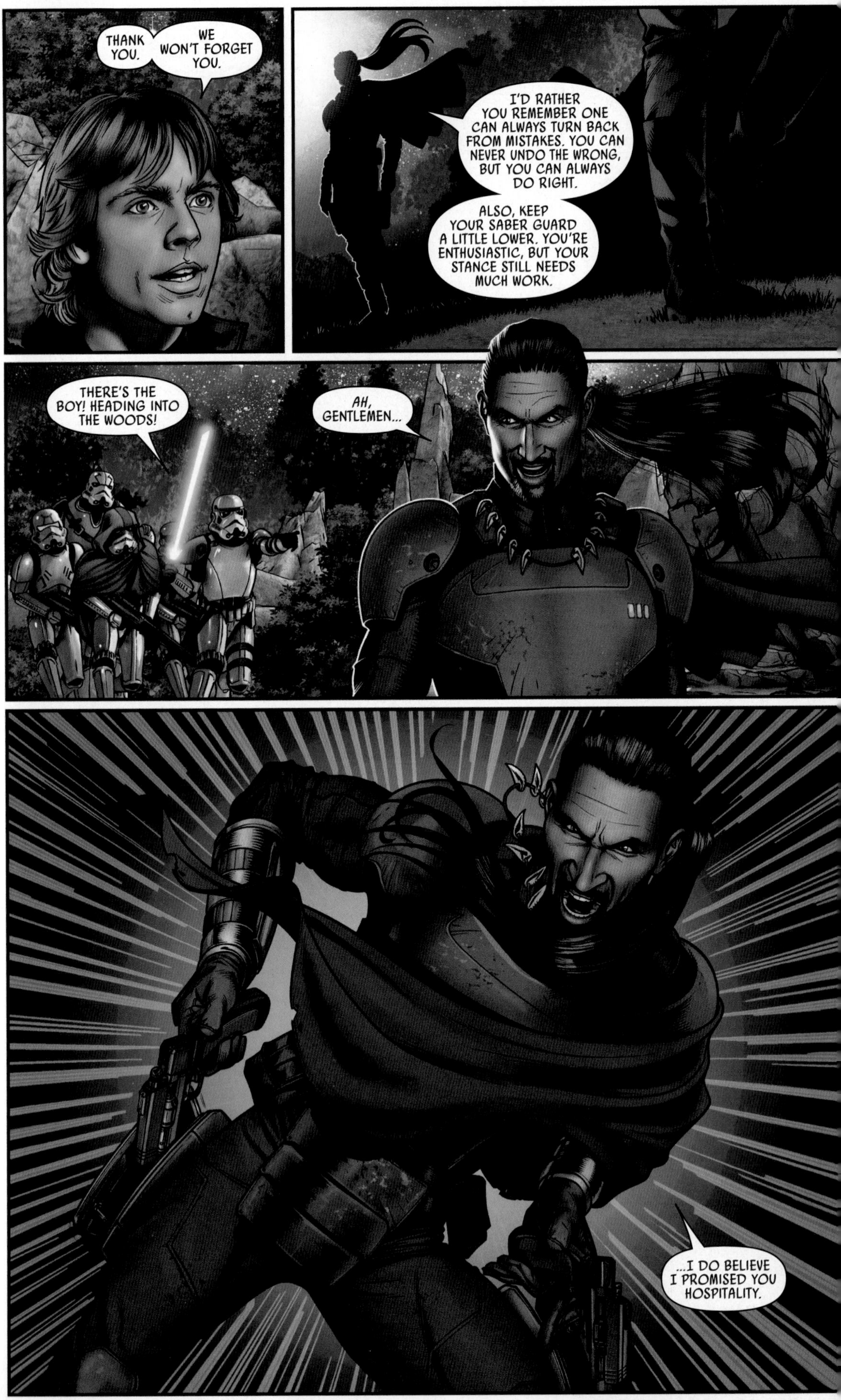
THANK YOU.
WE WON'T FORGET YOU.
I'D RATHER YOU REMEMBER ONE CAN ALWAYS TURN BACK FROM MISTAKES. YOU CAN NEVER UNDO THE WRONG, BUT YOU CAN ALWAYS DO RIGHT.
ALSO, KEEP YOUR SABER GUARD A LITTLE LOWER. YOU'RE ENTHUSIASTIC, BUT YOUR STANCE STILL NEEDS MUCH WORK.
THERE'S THE BOY! HEADING INTO THE WOODS!
AH, GENTLEMEN...
...I DO BELIEVE I PROMISED YOU HOSPITALITY.

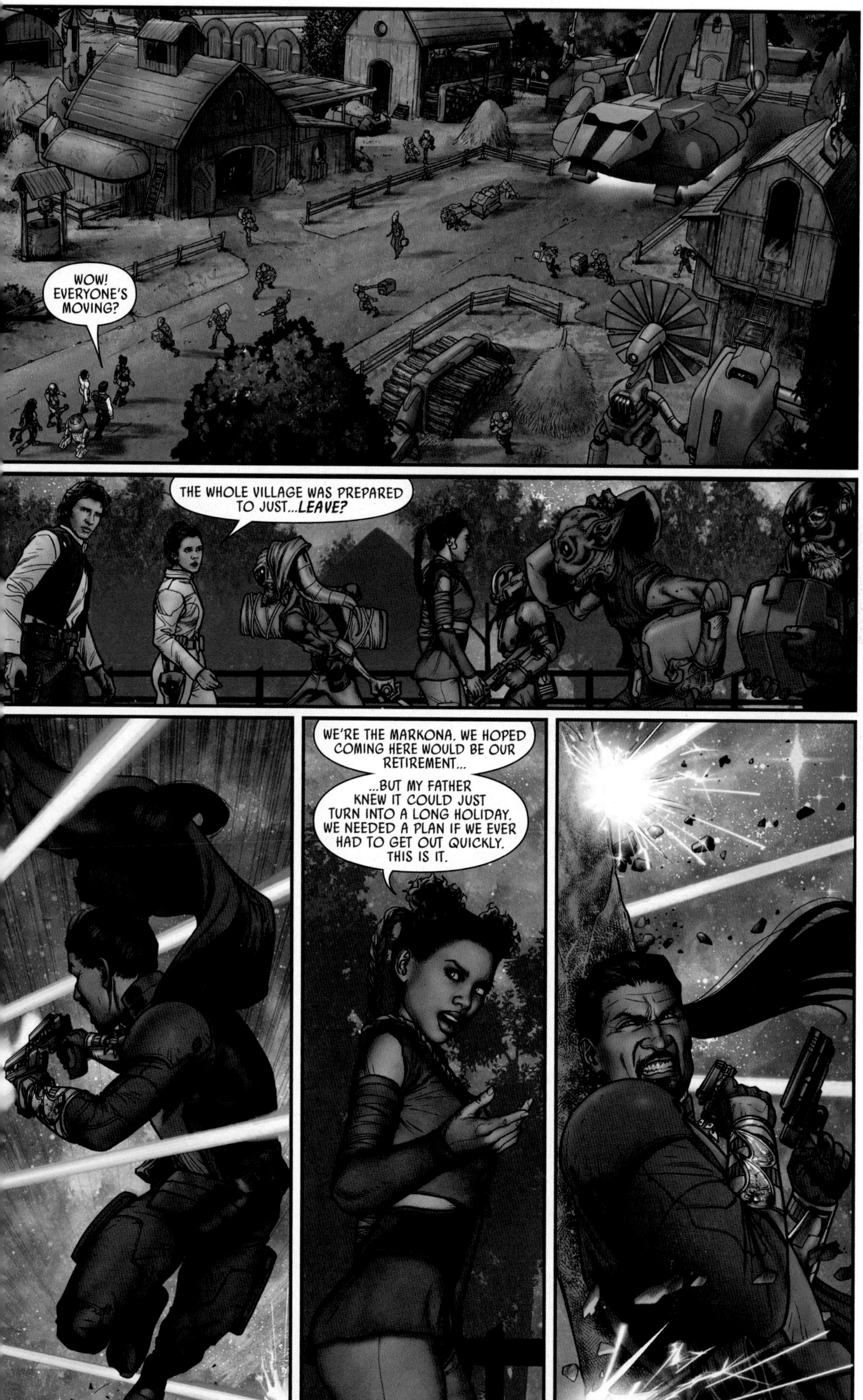

WOW! EVERYONE'S MOVING?
THE WHOLE VILLAGE WAS PREPARED TO JUST...LEAVE?
WE'RE THE MARKONA. WE HOPED COMING HERE WOULD BE OUR RETIREMENT...
...BUT MY FATHER KNEW IT COULD JUST TURN INTO A LONG HOLIDAY. WE NEEDED A PLAN IF WE EVER HAD TO GET OUT QUICKLY. THIS IS IT.

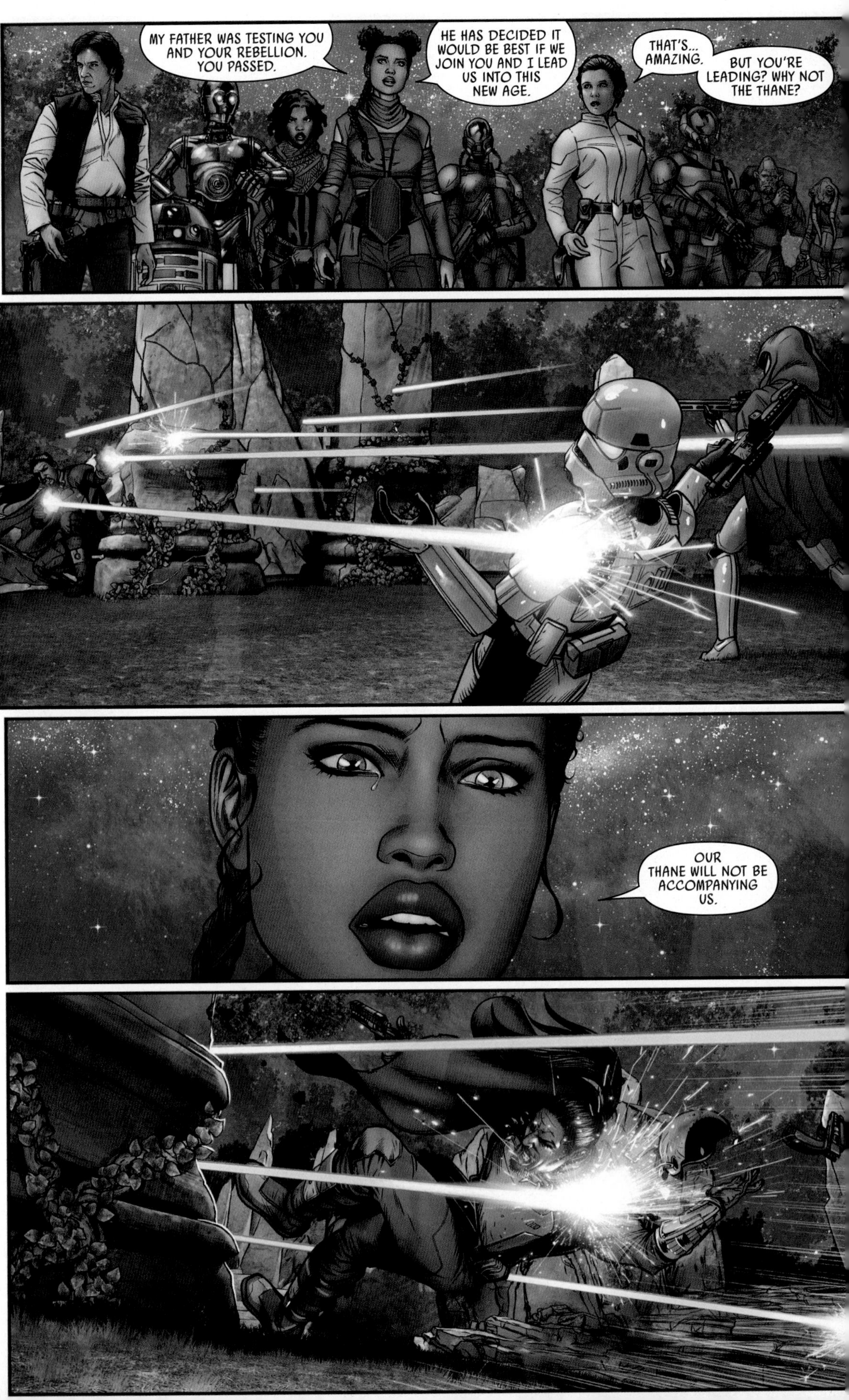
MY FATHER WAS TESTING YOU AND YOUR REBELLION. YOU PASSED.
HE HAS DECIDED IT WOULD BE BEST IF WE JOIN YOU AND I LEAD US INTO THIS NEW AGE.
THAT'S... AMAZING.
BUT YOU'RE LEADING? WHY NOT THE THANE?
OUR THANE WILL NOT BE ACCOMPANYING US.

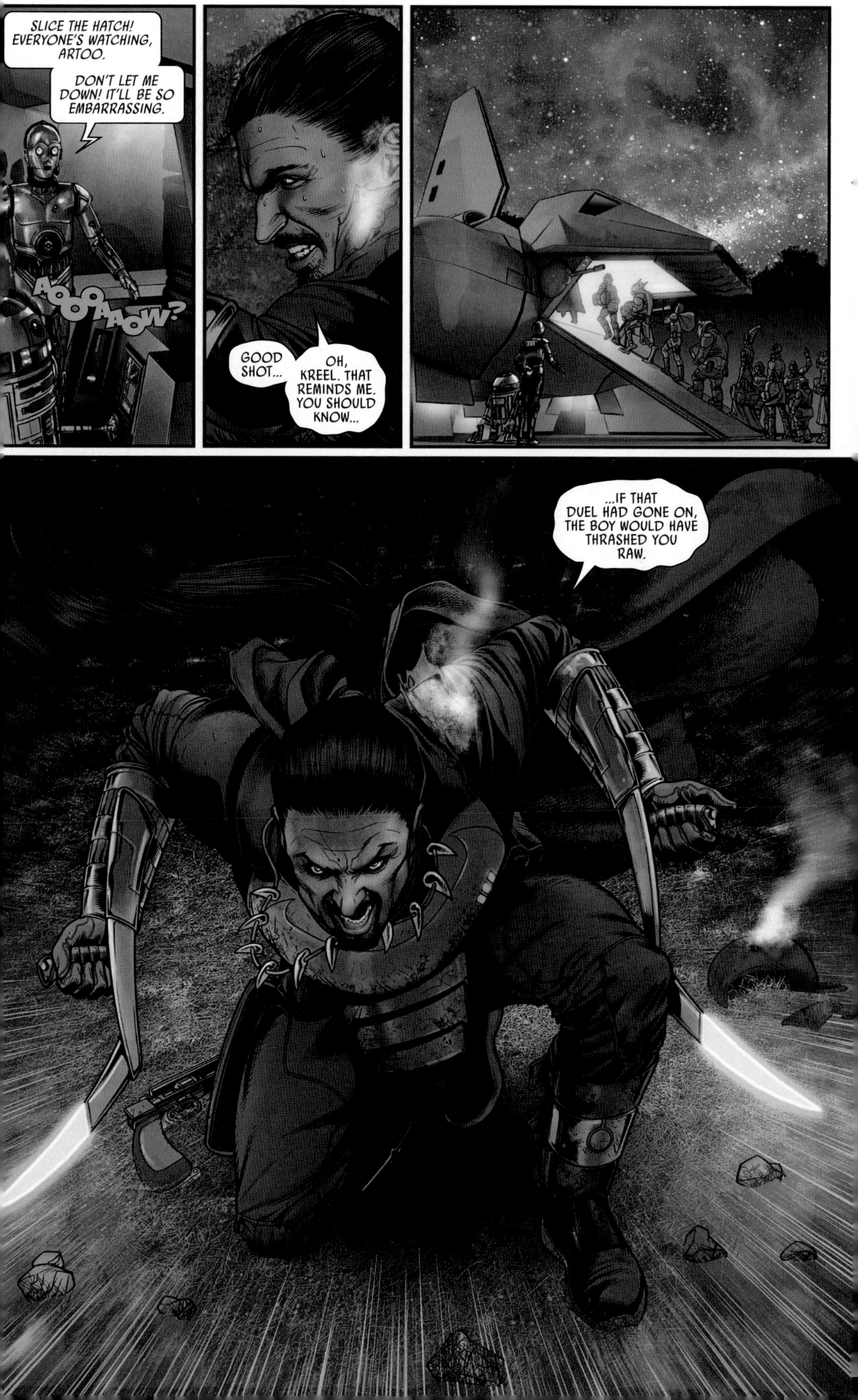
SLICE THE HATCH! EVERYONE'S WATCHING, ARTOO.
DON'T LET ME DOWN! IT'LL BE SO EMBARRASSING.
AOOOAAOW?
GOOD SHOT...
OH, KREEL. THAT REMINDS ME. YOU SHOULD KNOW...
...IF THAT DUEL HAD GONE ON, THE BOY WOULD HAVE THRASHED YOU RAW.

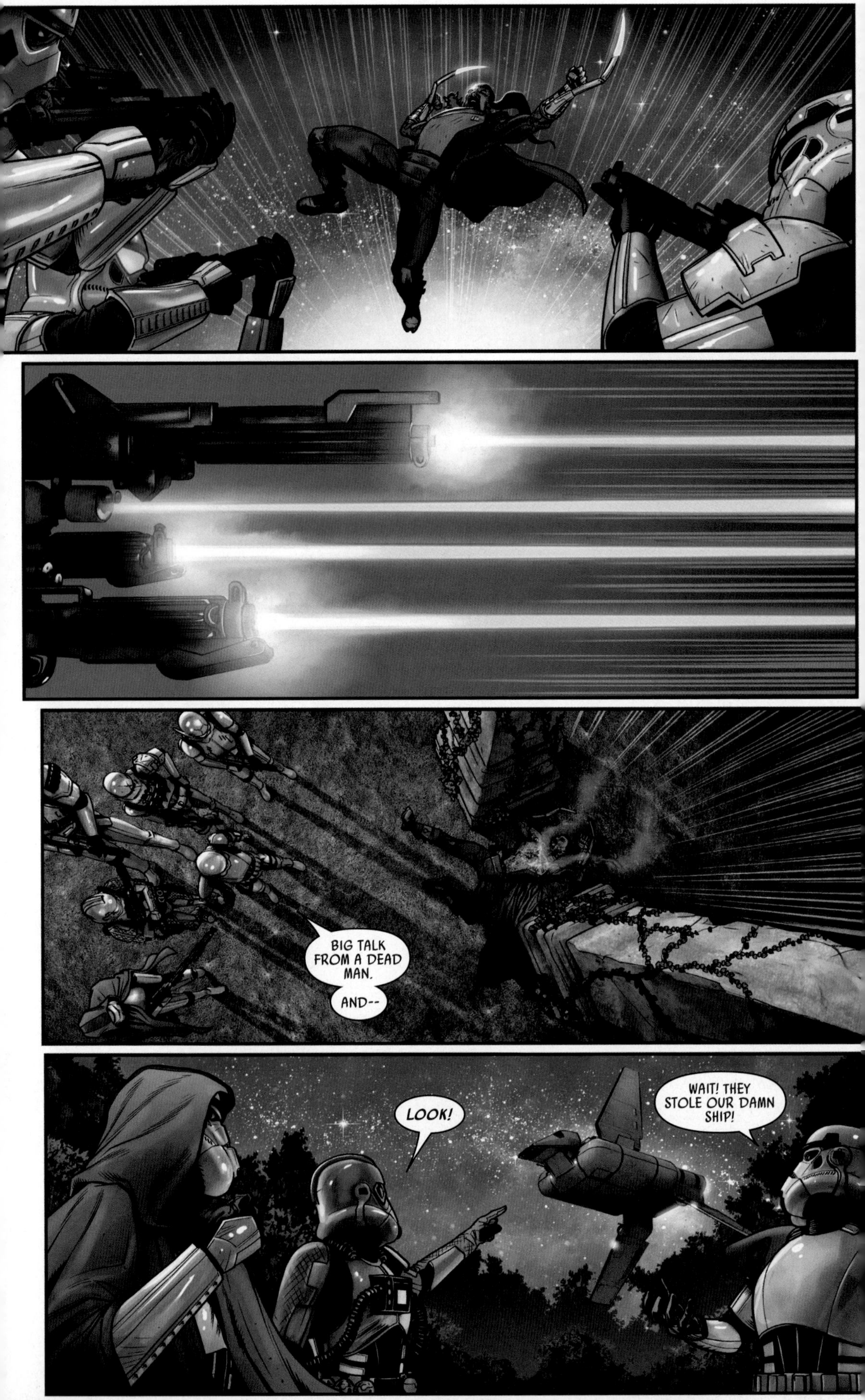
BIG TALK FROM A DEAD MAN.
AND--
LOOK!
WAIT! THEY STOLE OUR DAMN SHIP!

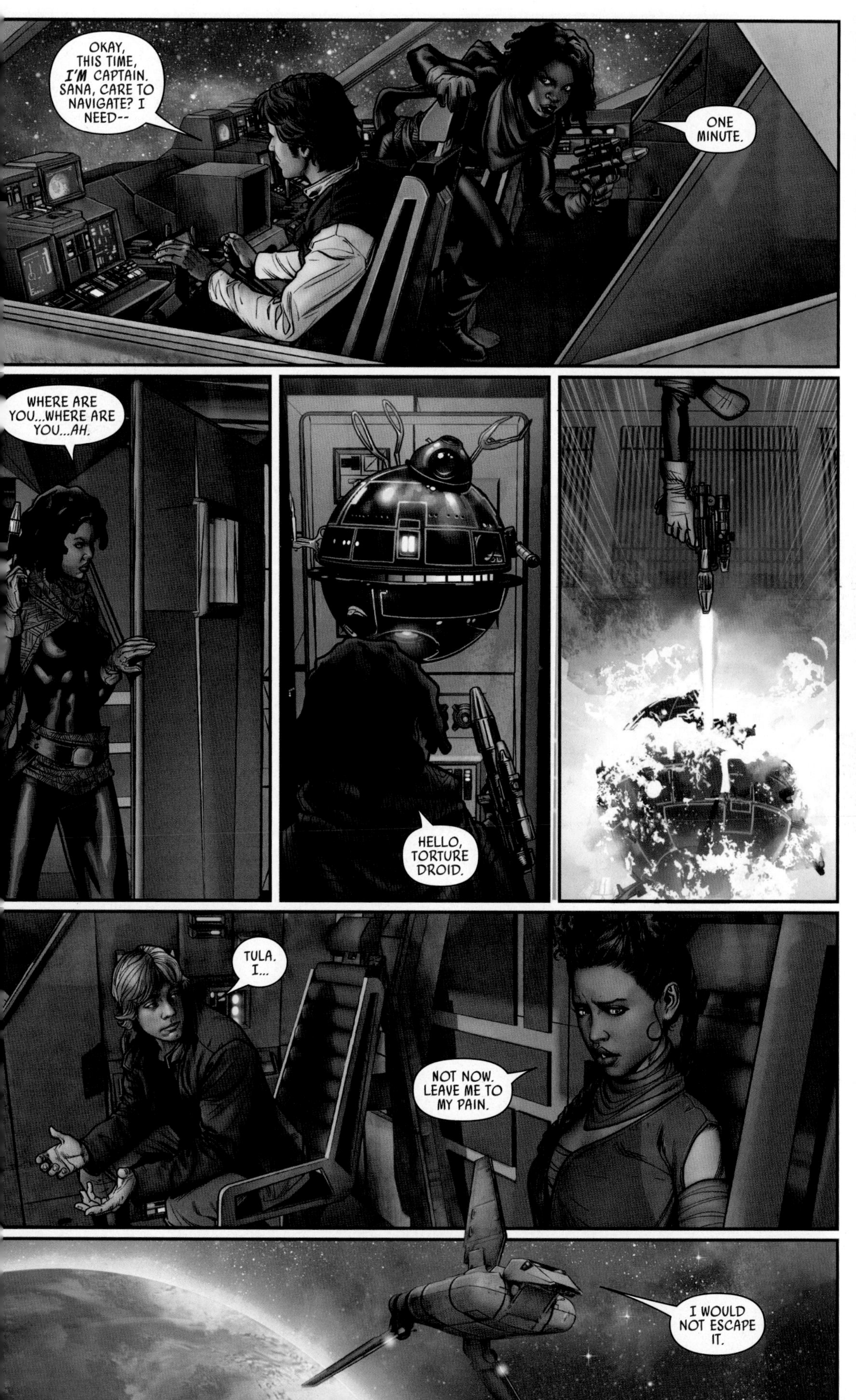

OKAY, THIS TIME, *I'M* CAPTAIN. SANA, CARE TO NAVIGATE? I NEED--
ONE MINUTE.
WHERE ARE YOU...WHERE ARE YOU...*AH.*
HELLO, TORTURE DROID.
TULA. I...
NOT NOW. LEAVE ME TO MY PAIN.
I WOULD NOT ESCAPE IT.

NO TRANSMITTERS IN THE VILLAGE?

LET'S TRY THE MANSION.

HELLO, SIRS. MAY I BE OF SOME ASSISTANCE?

THE MASTER OF THE HOUSE IS ABSENT, BUT I AM TO PROVIDE HOSPITALITY--

TRANSMITTER. NOW.

I'M SORRY, THAT'LL BE IMPOSSIBLE. WE HAVE NO SUCH THING.

THE NEXT SCHEDULED CONTACT WITH THE OUTER WORLD WILL BE IN FOUR MONTHS' TIME.

OR THEREABOUTS. OF COURSE, WE HAVE PLENTY OF ROOM NOW THAT OUR OTHER GUESTS HAVE DEPARTED. I'LL PREPARE ROOMS...

FOUR MONTHS?!

LOOK!

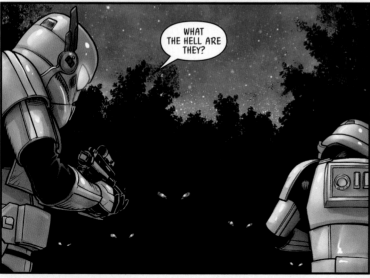

WHAT THE HELL ARE THEY?

AH, THE THANRAX. HOSTILE PREDATORS.

DON'T WORRY--THEY RARELY ATTACK THE LOCALS. THEY'VE LEARNED TO BE WARY AROUND THE MARKONA CLAN...

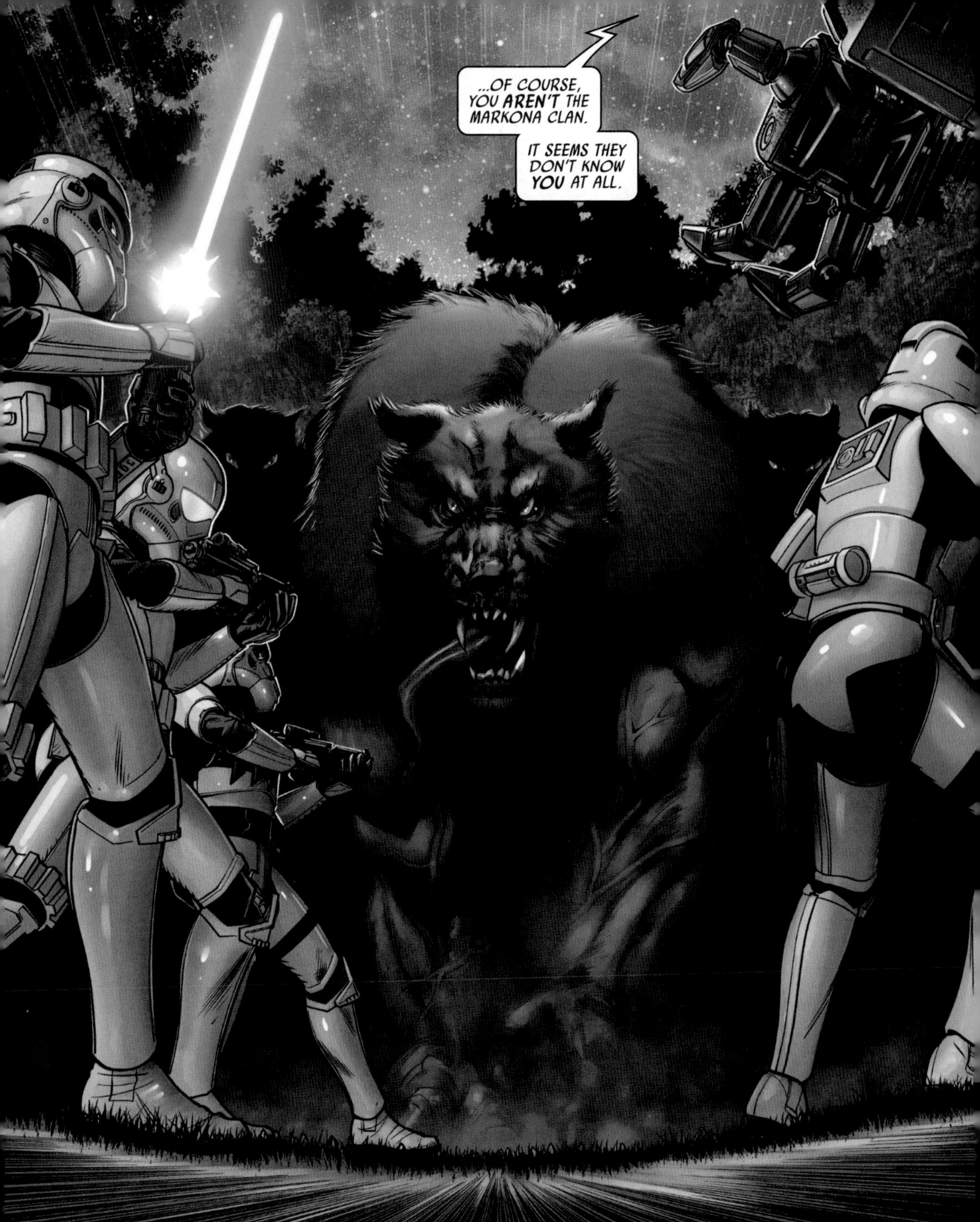
...OF COURSE, YOU AREN'T THE MARKONA CLAN.
IT SEEMS THEY DON'T KNOW YOU AT ALL.

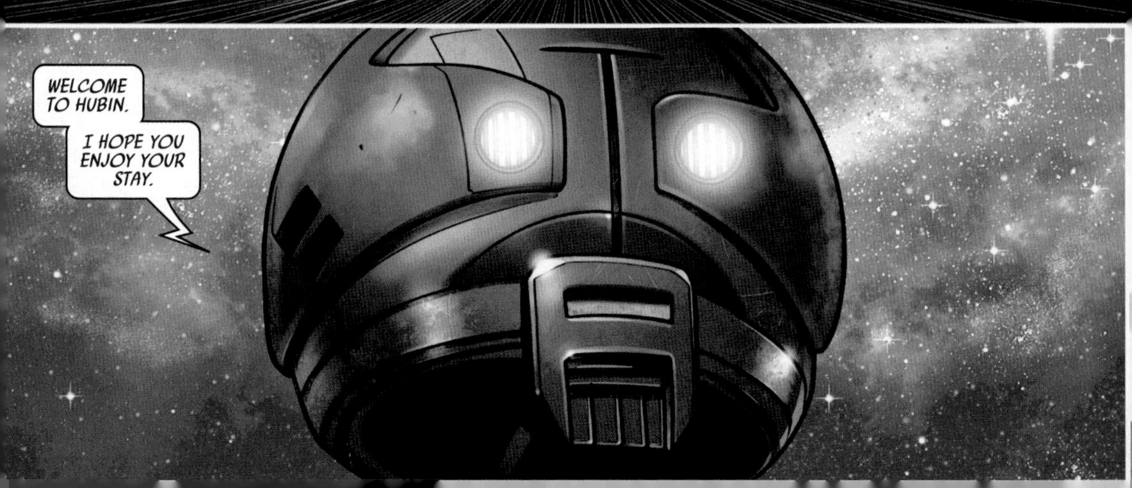
WELCOME TO HUBIN.
I HOPE YOU ENJOY YOUR STAY.

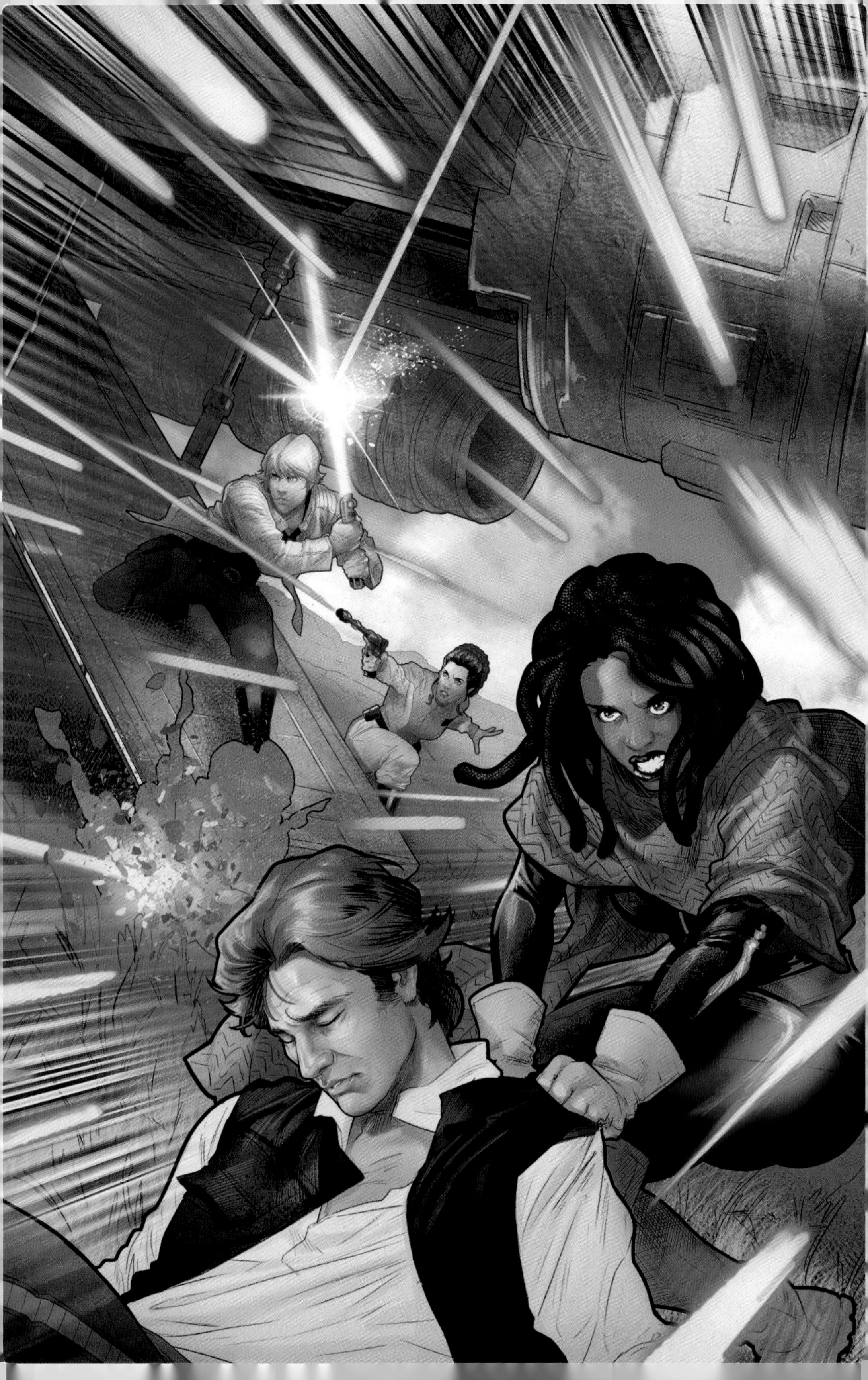

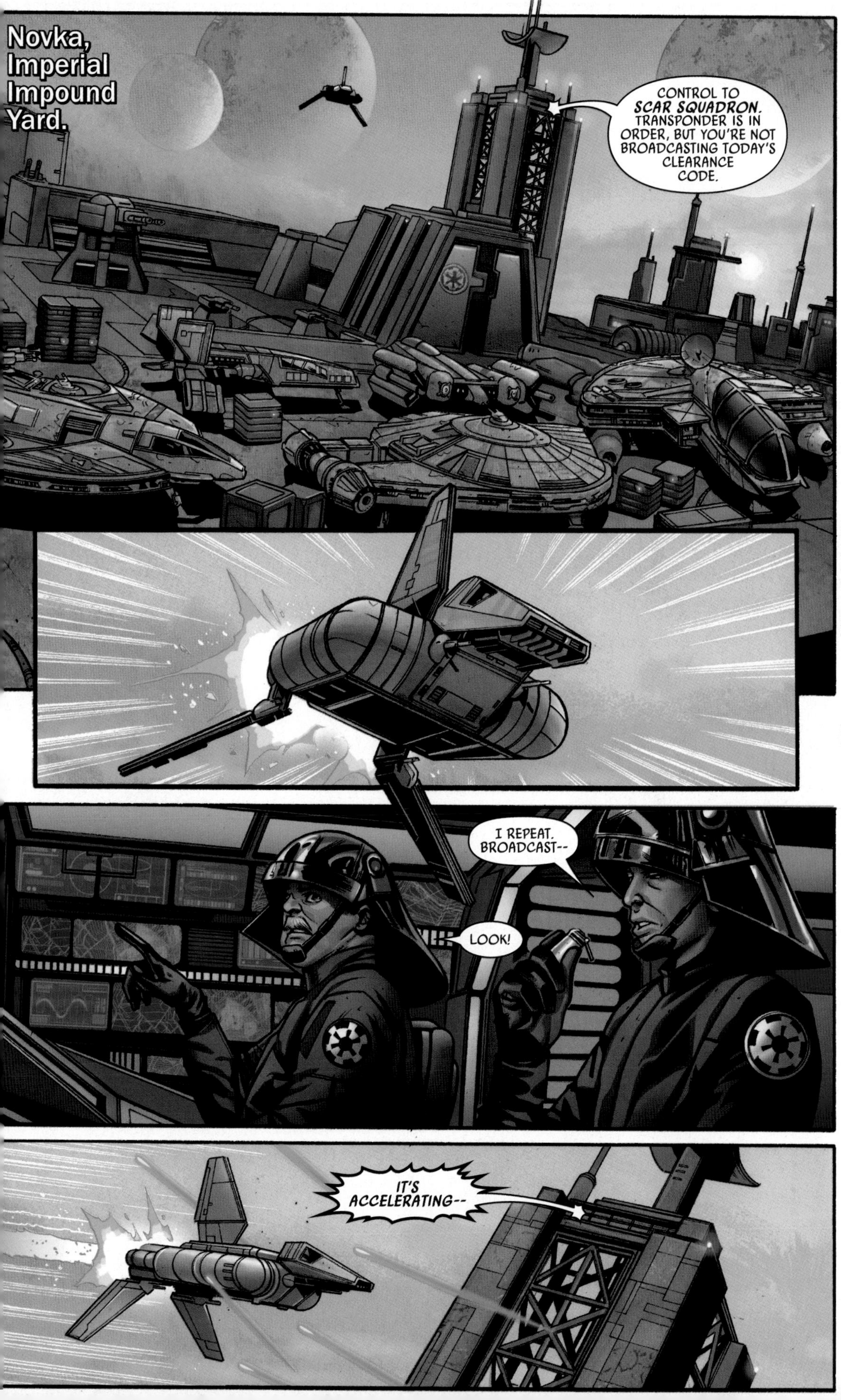
Novka, Imperial Impound Yard.
CONTROL TO SCAR SQUADRON. TRANSPONDER IS IN ORDER, BUT YOU'RE NOT BROADCASTING TODAY'S CLEARANCE CODE.
I REPEAT. BROADCAST--
LOOK!
IT'S ACCELERATING--

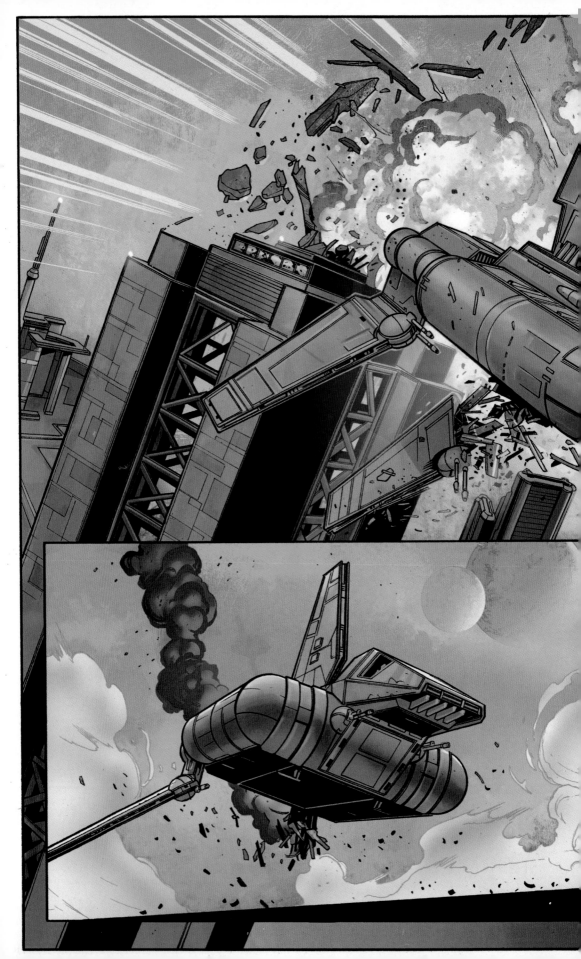

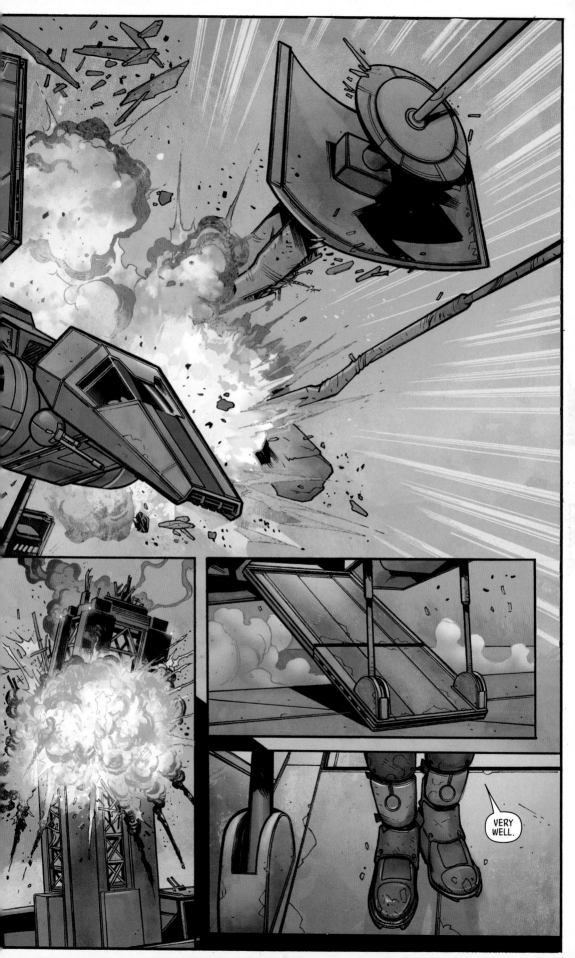

VERY WELL.

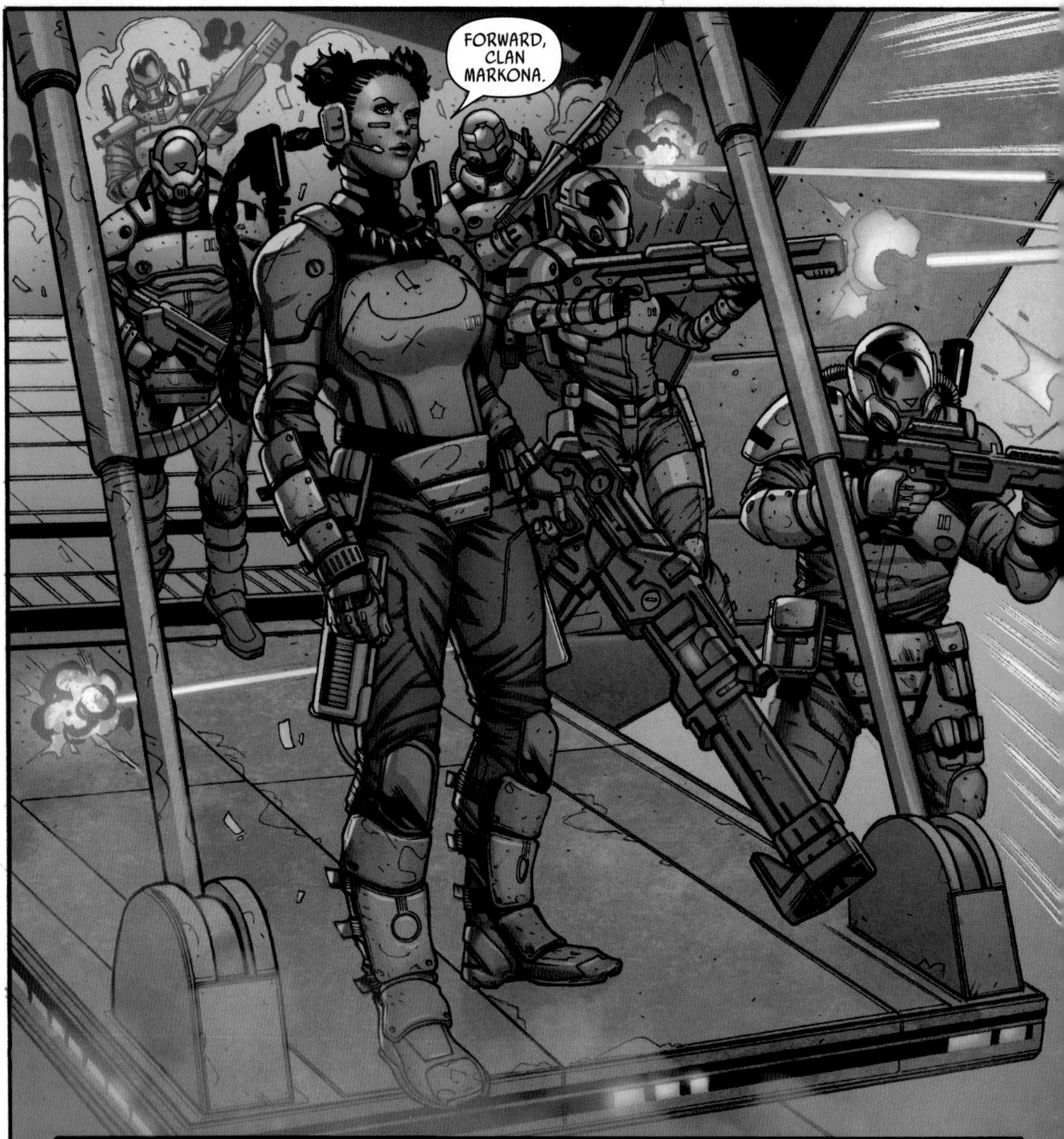
FORWARD, CLAN MARKONA.

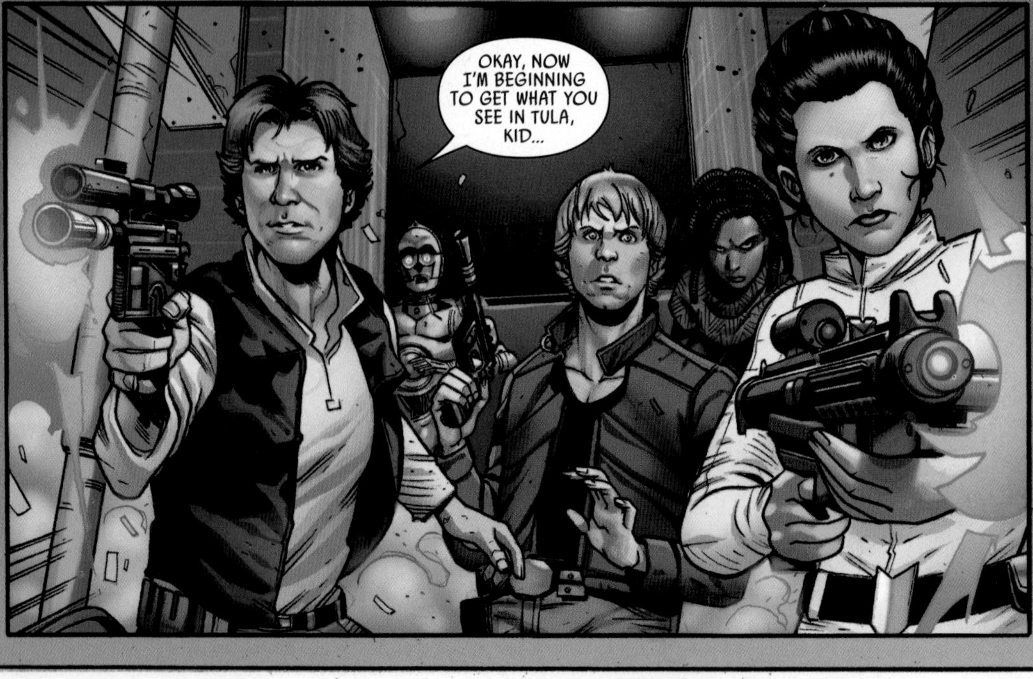
OKAY, NOW I'M BEGINNING TO GET WHAT YOU SEE IN TULA, KID...

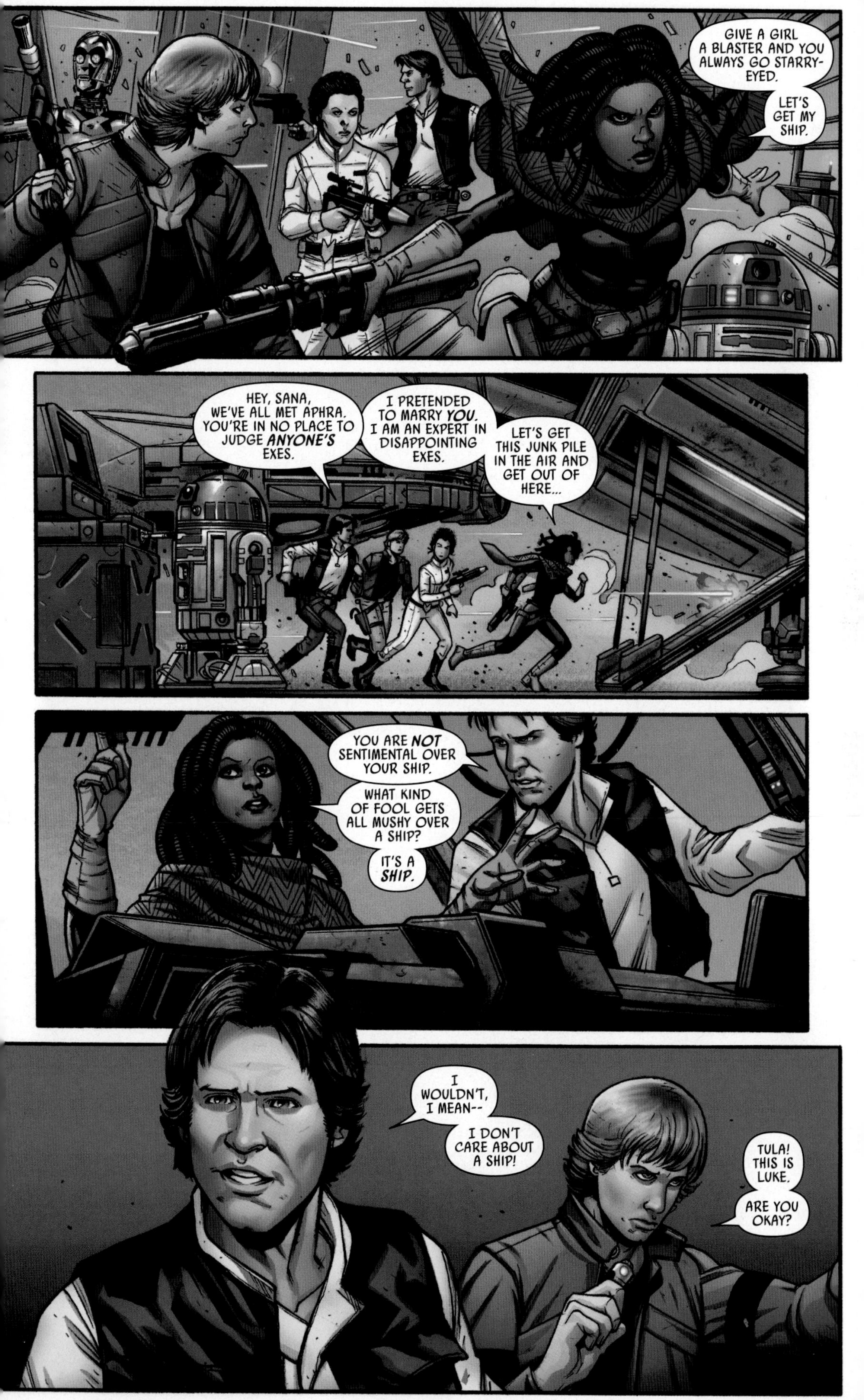
GIVE A GIRL A BLASTER AND YOU ALWAYS GO STARRY-EYED.
LET'S GET MY SHIP.
HEY, SANA, WE'VE ALL MET APHRA. YOU'RE IN NO PLACE TO JUDGE ANYONE'S EXES.
I PRETENDED TO MARRY YOU. I AM AN EXPERT IN DISAPPOINTING EXES.
LET'S GET THIS JUNK PILE IN THE AIR AND GET OUT OF HERE...
YOU ARE NOT SENTIMENTAL OVER YOUR SHIP.
WHAT KIND OF FOOL GETS ALL MUSHY OVER A SHIP?
IT'S A SHIP.
I WOULDN'T, I MEAN--
I DON'T CARE ABOUT A SHIP!
TULA! THIS IS LUKE.
ARE YOU OKAY?

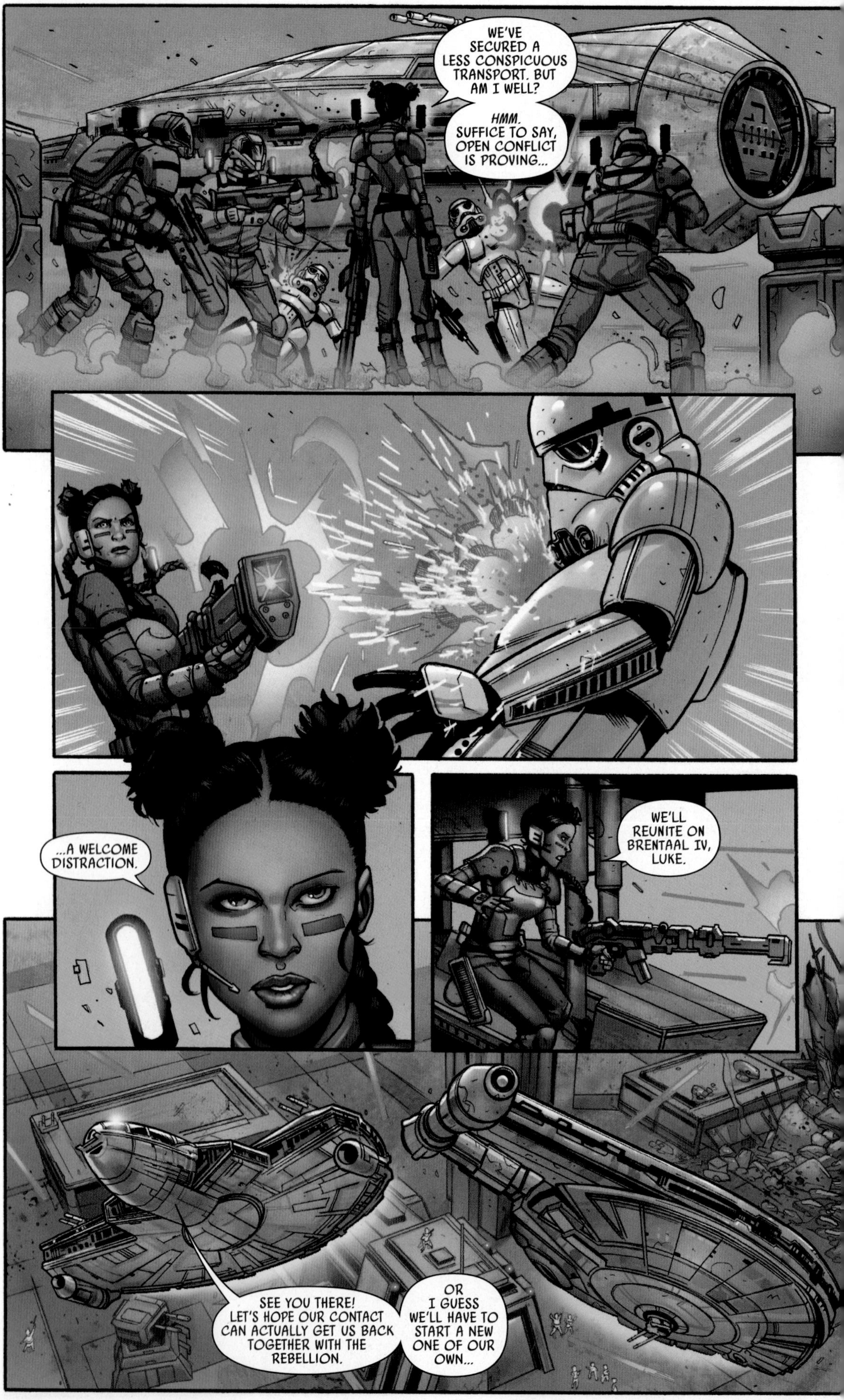
WE'VE SECURED A LESS CONSPICUOUS TRANSPORT. BUT AM I WELL?
HMM. SUFFICE TO SAY, OPEN CONFLICT IS PROVING...
...A WELCOME DISTRACTION.
WE'LL REUNITE ON BRENTAAL IV, LUKE.
SEE YOU THERE! LET'S HOPE OUR CONTACT CAN ACTUALLY GET US BACK TOGETHER WITH THE REBELLION.
OR I GUESS WE'LL HAVE TO START A NEW ONE OF OUR OWN...

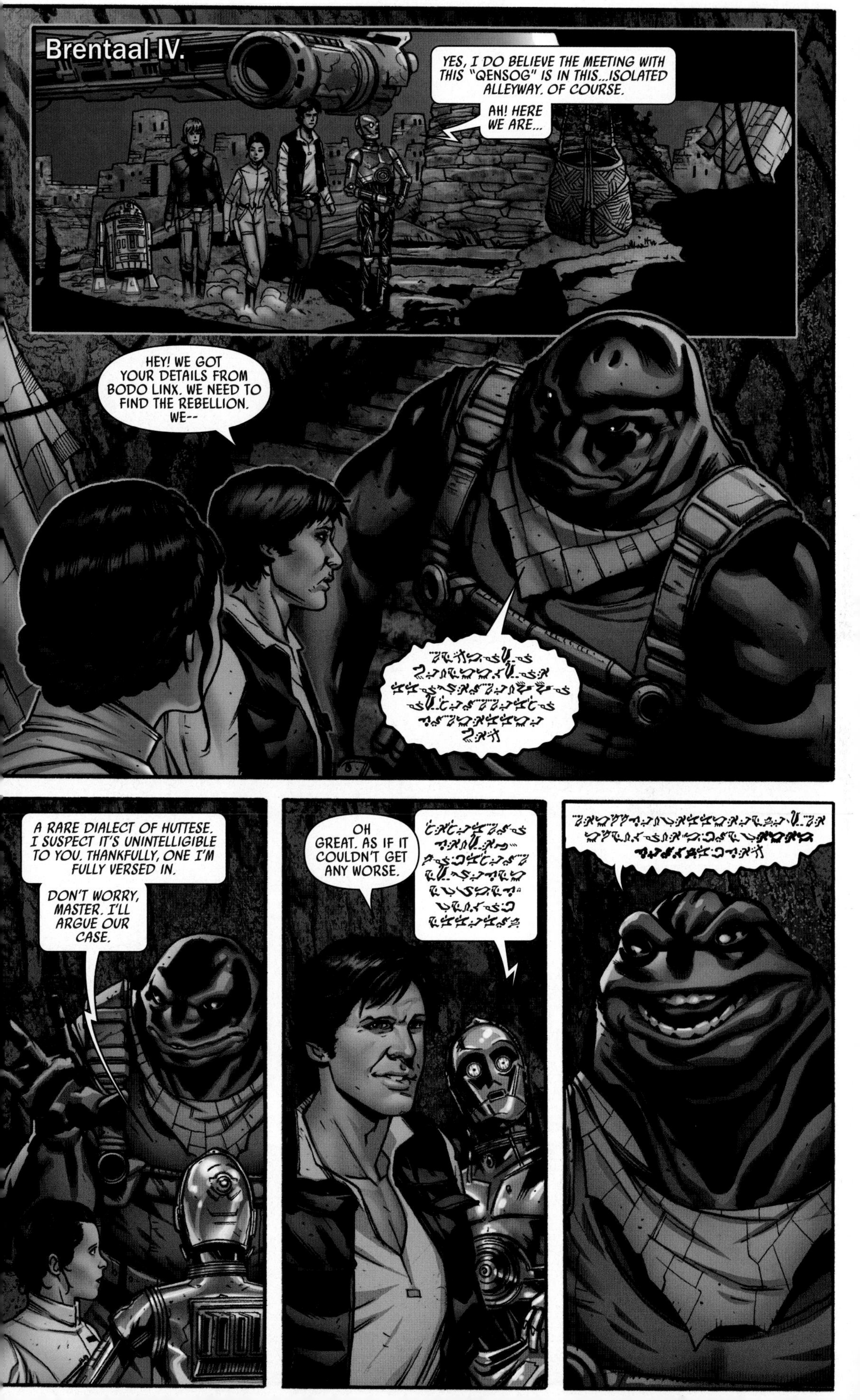
Brentaal IV.
YES, I DO BELIEVE THE MEETING WITH THIS "QENSOG" IS IN THIS...ISOLATED ALLEYWAY. OF COURSE.
AH! HERE WE ARE...
HEY! WE GOT YOUR DETAILS FROM BODO LINX. WE NEED TO FIND THE REBELLION. WE--
A RARE DIALECT OF HUTTESE. I SUSPECT IT'S UNINTELLIGIBLE TO YOU. THANKFULLY, ONE I'M FULLY VERSED IN.
DON'T WORRY, MASTER. I'LL ARGUE OUR CASE.
OH GREAT. AS IF IT COULDN'T GET ANY WORSE.

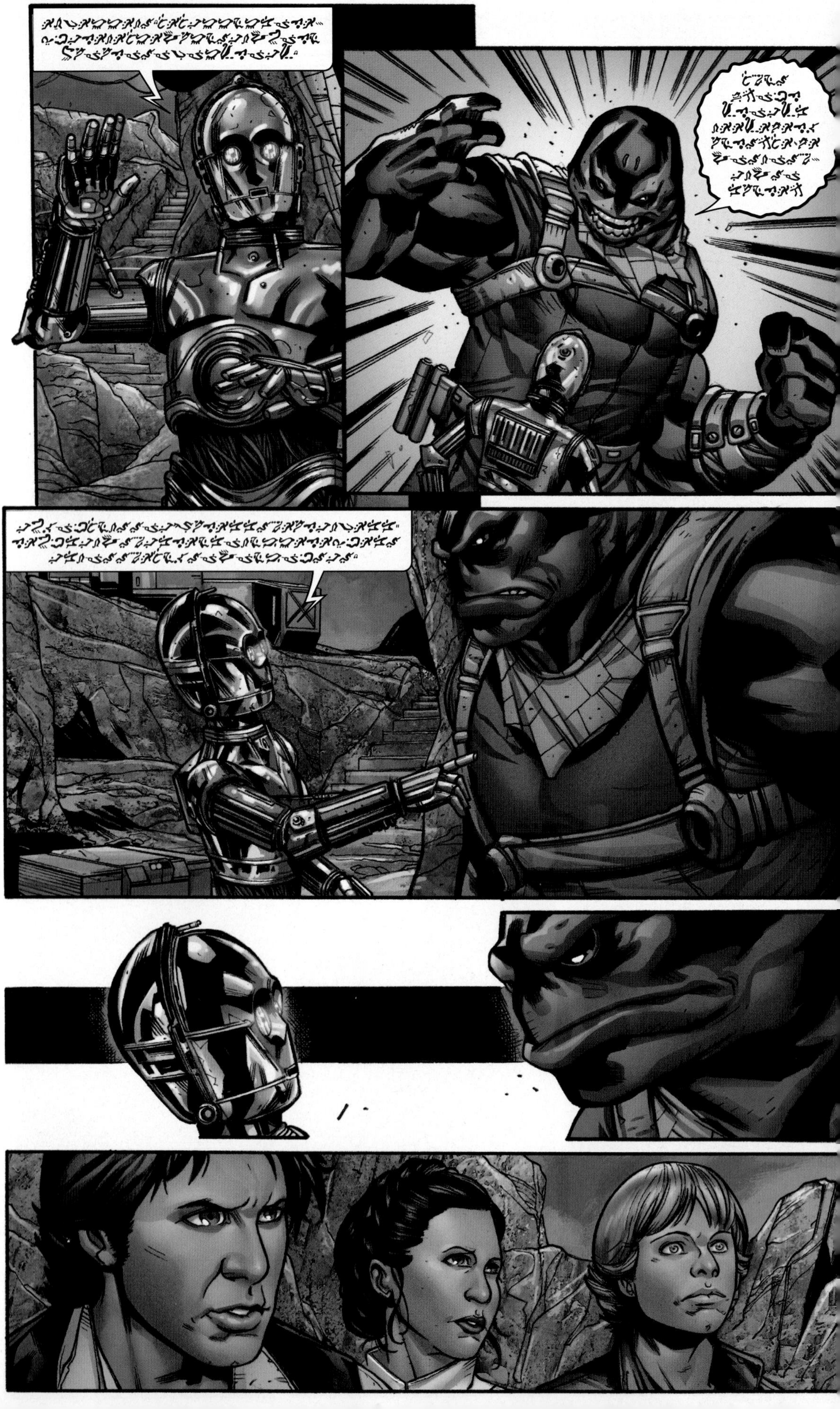

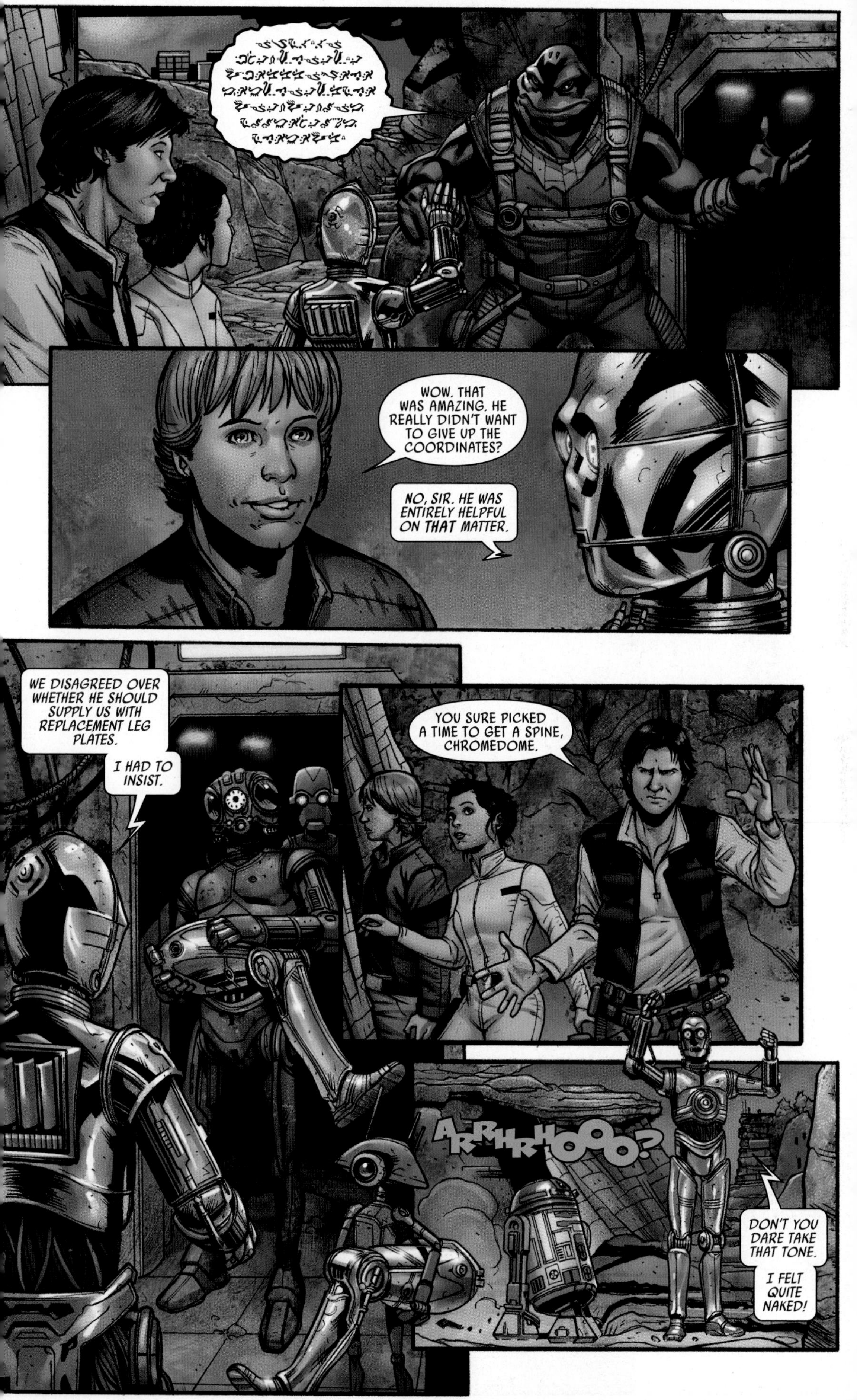

WOW. THAT WAS AMAZING. HE REALLY DIDN'T WANT TO GIVE UP THE COORDINATES?
NO, SIR. HE WAS ENTIRELY HELPFUL ON THAT MATTER.
WE DISAGREED OVER WHETHER HE SHOULD SUPPLY US WITH REPLACEMENT LEG PLATES.
I HAD TO INSIST.
YOU SURE PICKED A TIME TO GET A SPINE, CHROMEDOME.
ARRHRHOOOO?
DON'T YOU DARE TAKE THAT TONE.
I FELT QUITE NAKED!

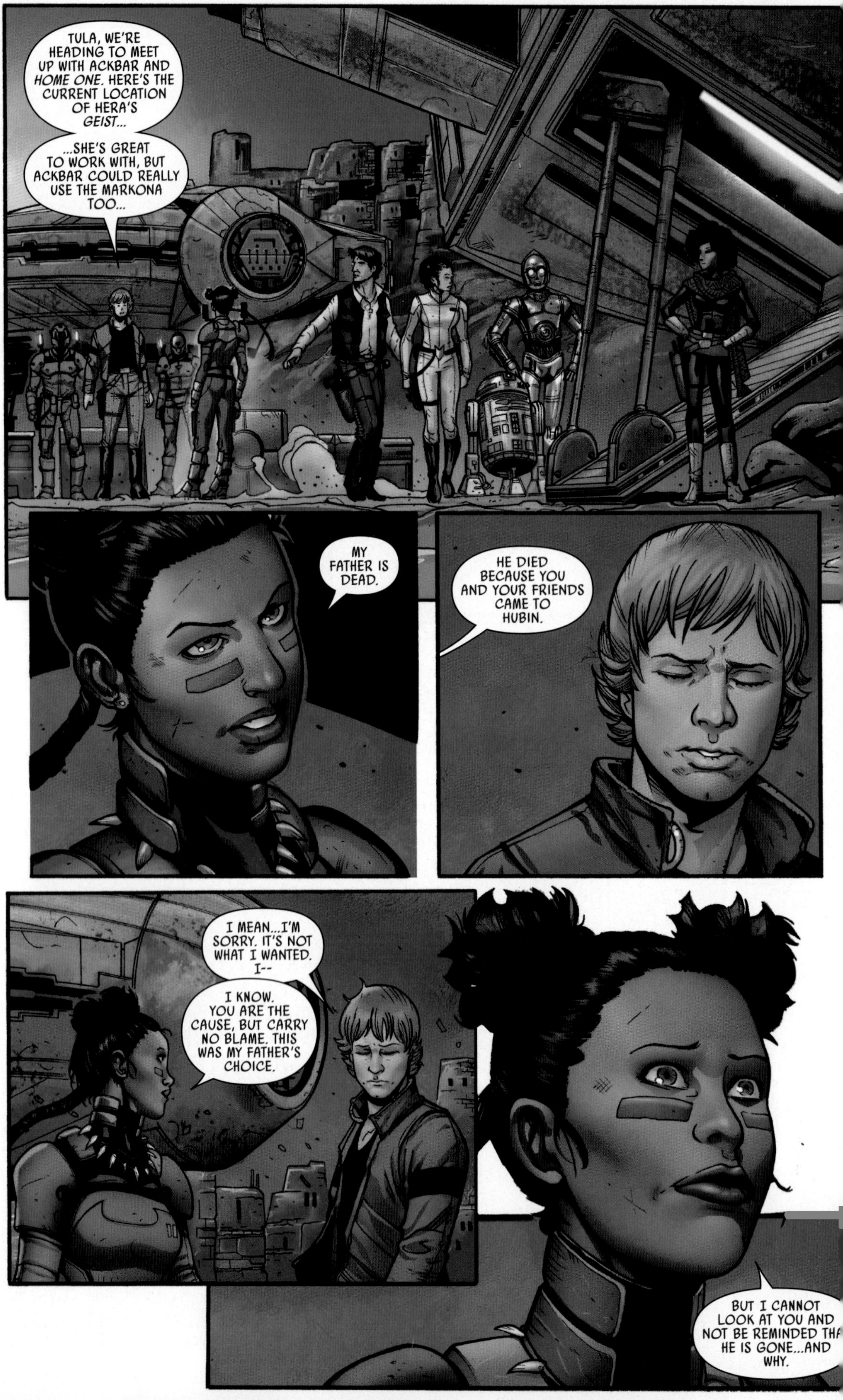
TULA, WE'RE HEADING TO MEET UP WITH ACKBAR AND *HOME ONE.* HERE'S THE CURRENT LOCATION OF HERA'S *GEIST*...
...SHE'S GREAT TO WORK WITH, BUT ACKBAR COULD REALLY USE THE MARKONA TOO...
MY FATHER IS DEAD.
HE DIED BECAUSE YOU AND YOUR FRIENDS CAME TO HUBIN.
I MEAN...I'M SORRY. IT'S NOT WHAT I WANTED. I--
I KNOW. YOU ARE THE CAUSE, BUT CARRY NO BLAME. THIS WAS MY FATHER'S CHOICE.
BUT I CANNOT LOOK AT YOU AND NOT BE REMINDED THA HE IS GONE...AND WHY.

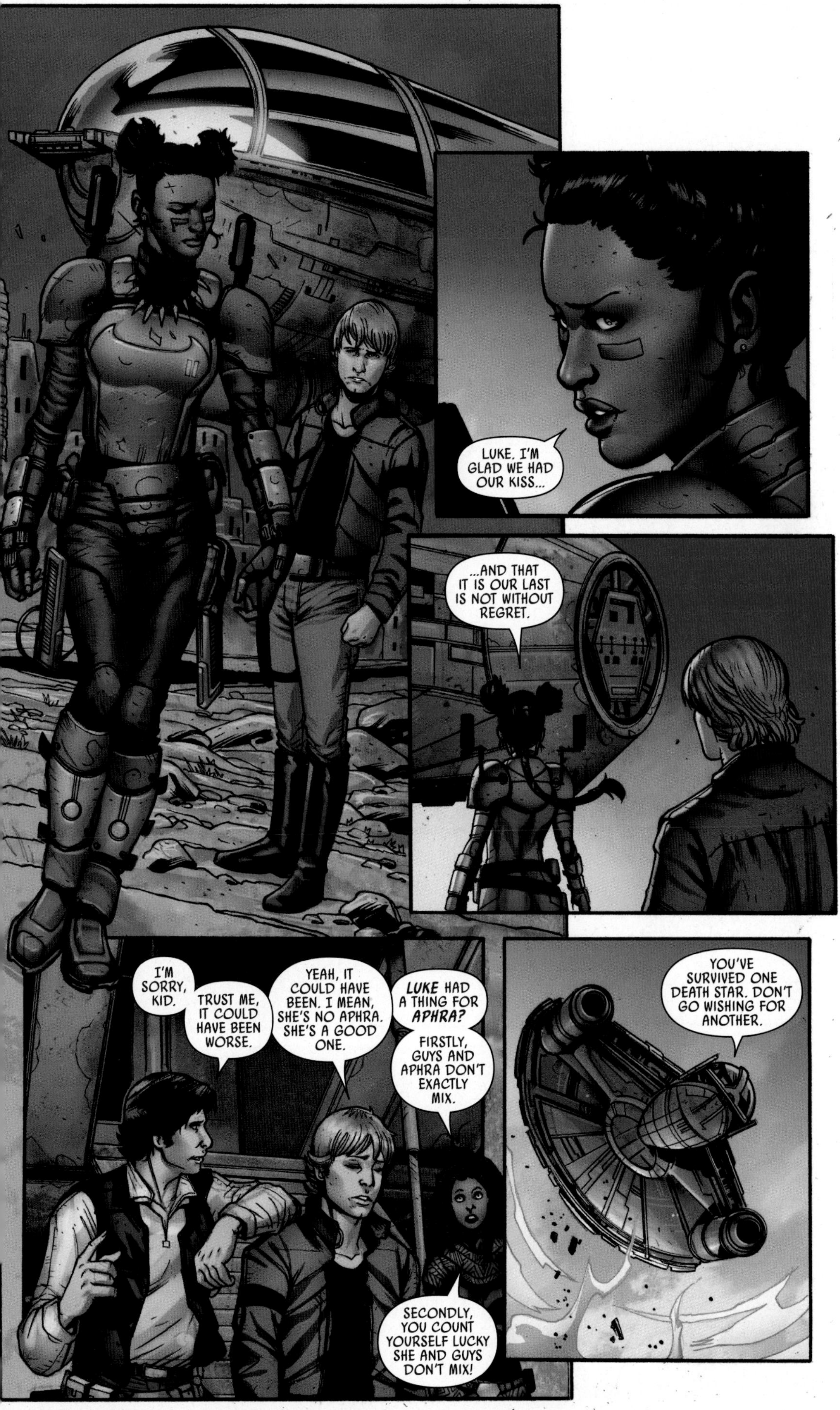
LUKE. I'M GLAD WE HAD OUR KISS...
...AND THAT IT IS OUR LAST IS NOT WITHOUT REGRET.
I'M SORRY, KID.
TRUST ME, IT COULD HAVE BEEN WORSE.
YEAH, IT COULD HAVE BEEN. I MEAN, SHE'S NO APHRA. SHE'S A GOOD ONE.
LUKE HAD A THING FOR APHRA?
FIRSTLY, GUYS AND APHRA DON'T EXACTLY MIX.
SECONDLY, YOU COUNT YOURSELF LUCKY SHE AND GUYS DON'T MIX!
YOU'VE SURVIVED ONE DEATH STAR. DON'T GO WISHING FOR ANOTHER.

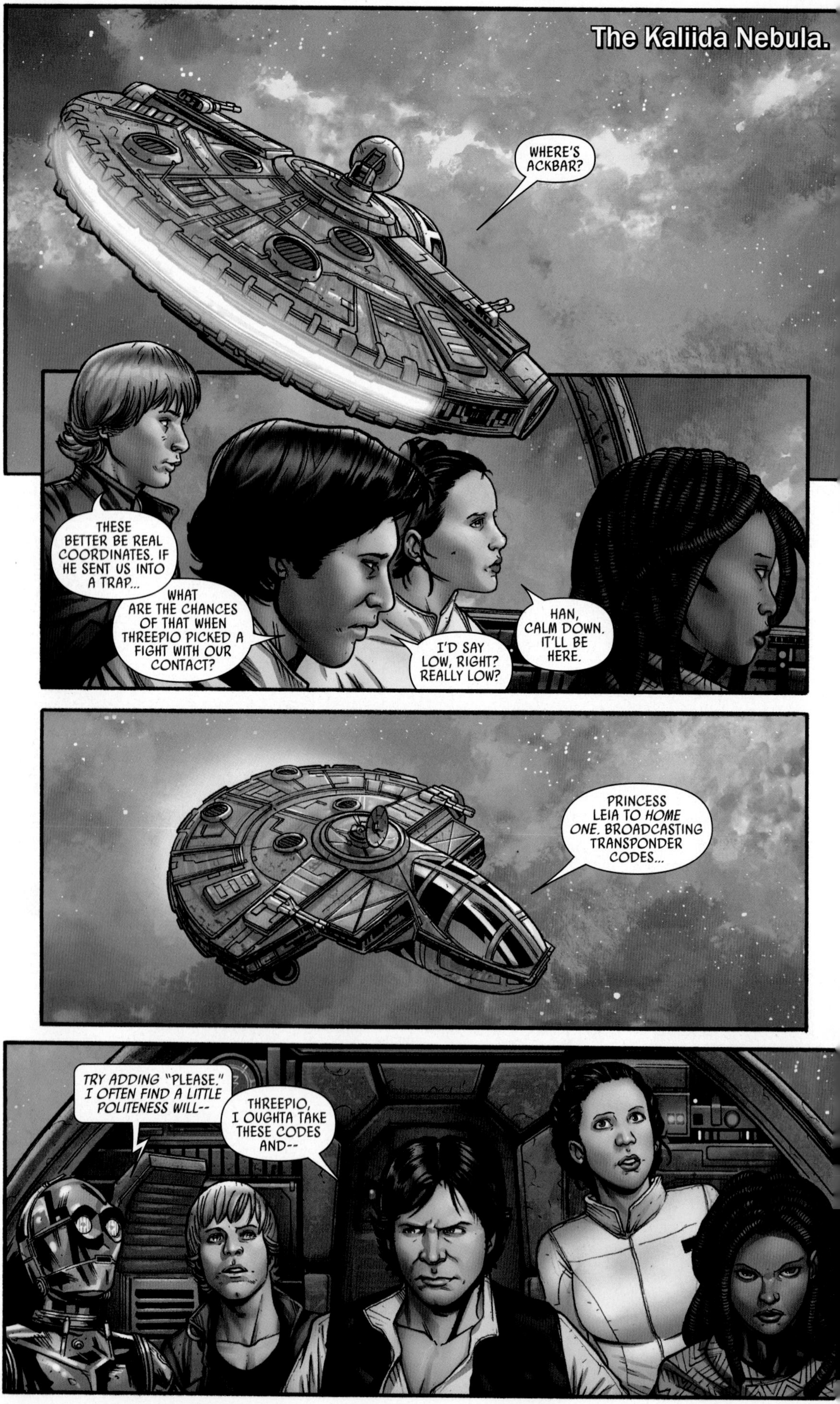
The Kaliida Nebula.
WHERE'S ACKBAR?
THESE BETTER BE REAL COORDINATES. IF HE SENT US INTO A TRAP...
WHAT ARE THE CHANCES OF THAT WHEN THREEPIO PICKED A FIGHT WITH OUR CONTACT?
I'D SAY LOW, RIGHT? REALLY LOW?
HAN, CALM DOWN. IT'LL BE HERE.
PRINCESS LEIA TO *HOME ONE*. BROADCASTING TRANSPONDER CODES...
TRY ADDING "PLEASE." I OFTEN FIND A LITTLE POLITENESS WILL--
THREEPIO, I OUGHTA TAKE THESE CODES AND--

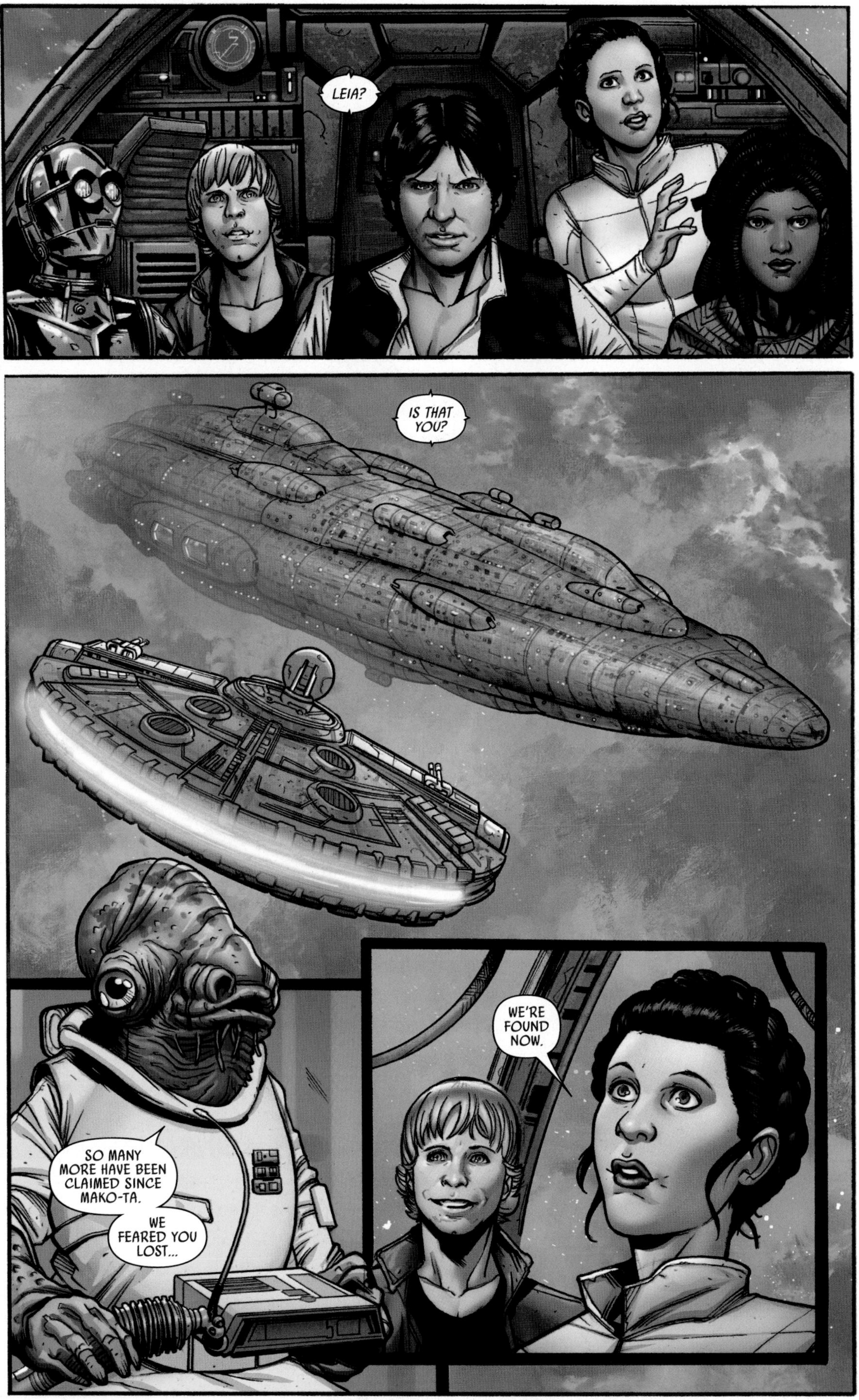
LEIA?
IS THAT YOU?
SO MANY MORE HAVE BEEN CLAIMED SINCE MAKO-TA.
WE FEARED YOU LOST...
WE'RE FOUND NOW.

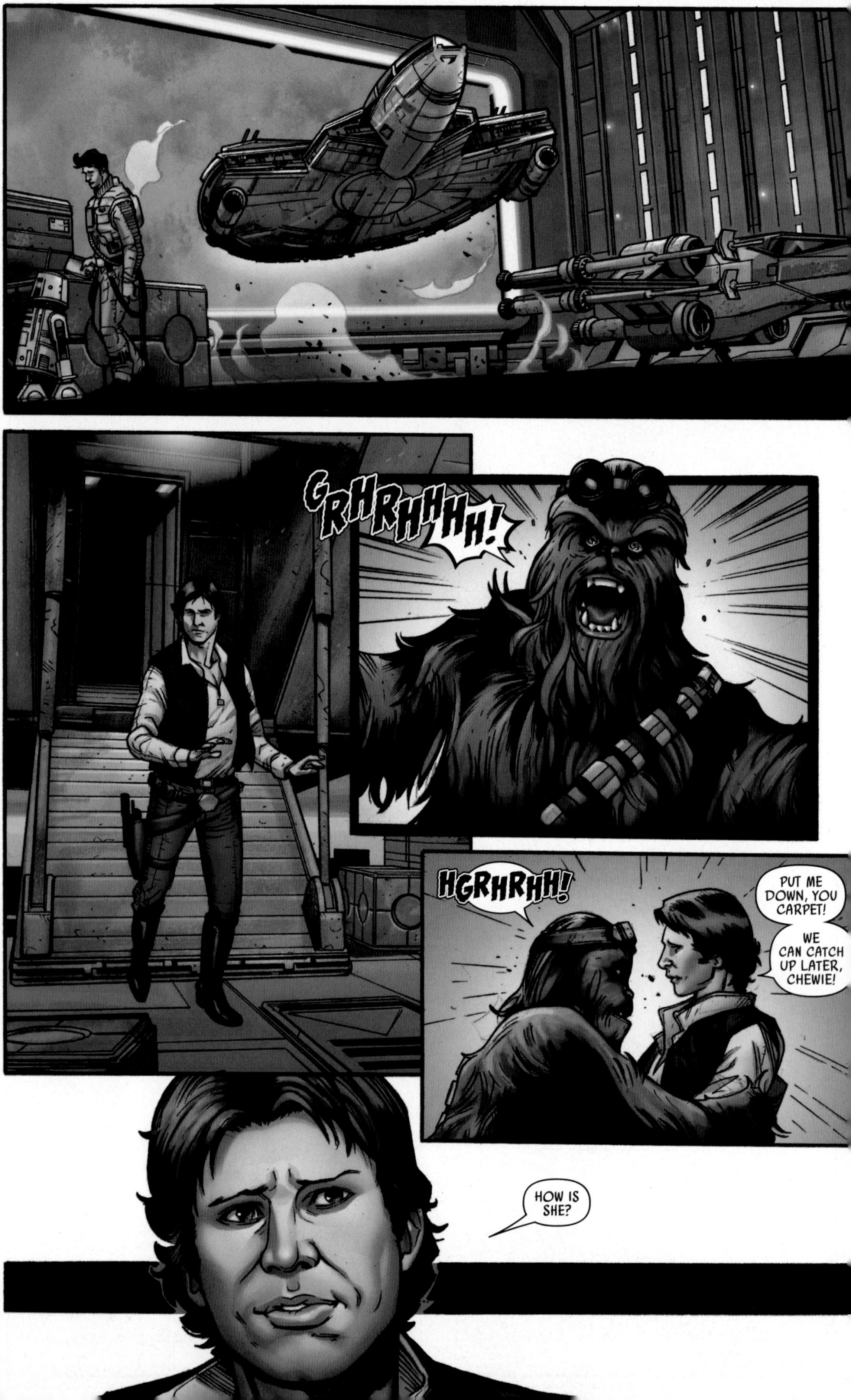
GRHRHHHH!
HGRHRHH!
PUT ME DOWN, YOU CARPET!
WE CAN CATCH UP LATER, CHEWIE!
HOW IS SHE?

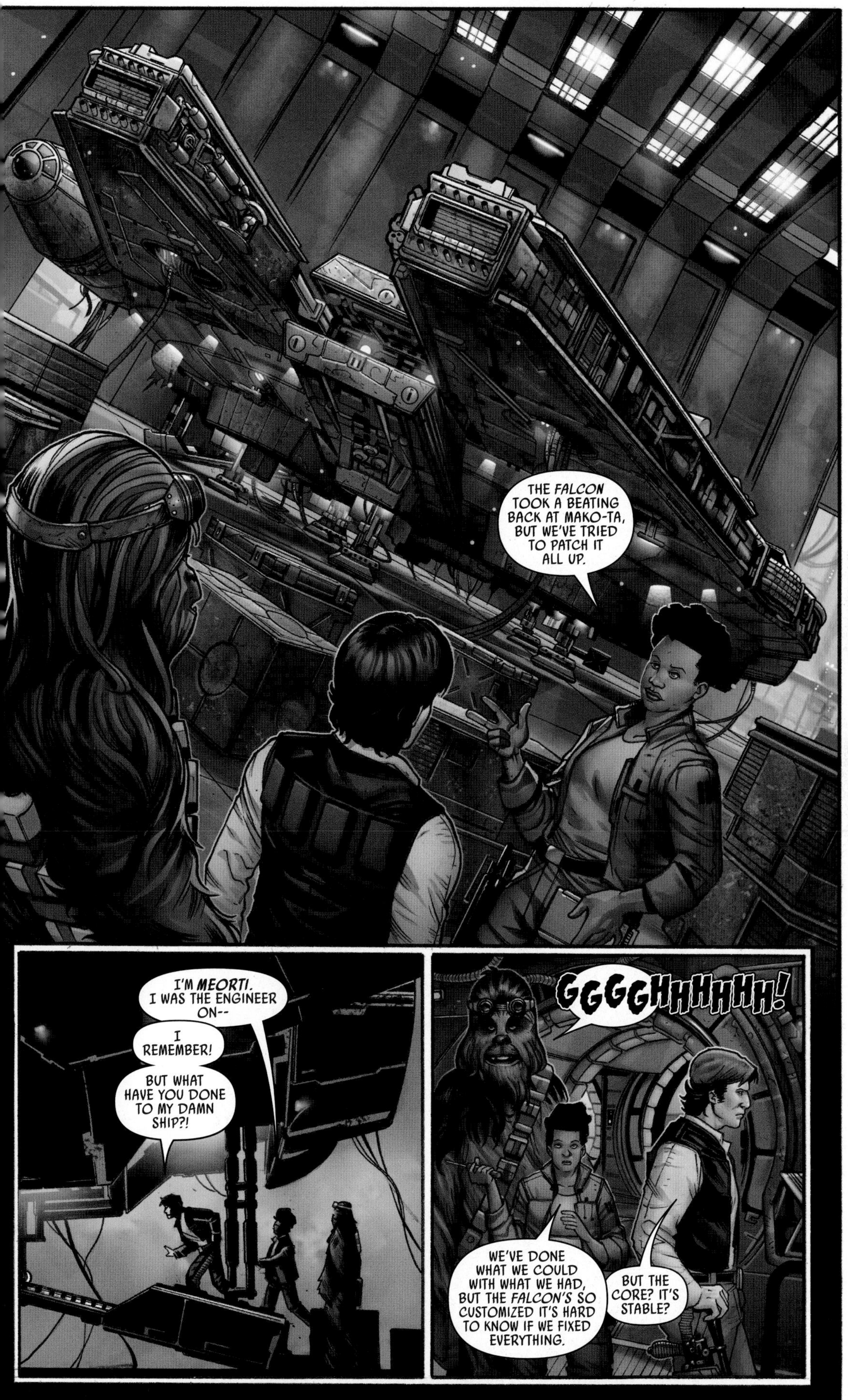
THE *FALCON* TOOK A BEATING BACK AT MAKO-TA, BUT WE'VE TRIED TO PATCH IT ALL UP.
I'M ***MEORTI.*** I WAS THE ENGINEER ON--
I REMEMBER!
BUT WHAT HAVE YOU DONE TO MY DAMN SHIP?!
GGGGHHHHHH!
WE'VE DONE WHAT WE COULD WITH WHAT WE HAD, BUT THE *FALCON'S* SO CUSTOMIZED IT'S HARD TO KNOW IF WE FIXED EVERYTHING.
BUT THE CORE? IT'S STABLE?

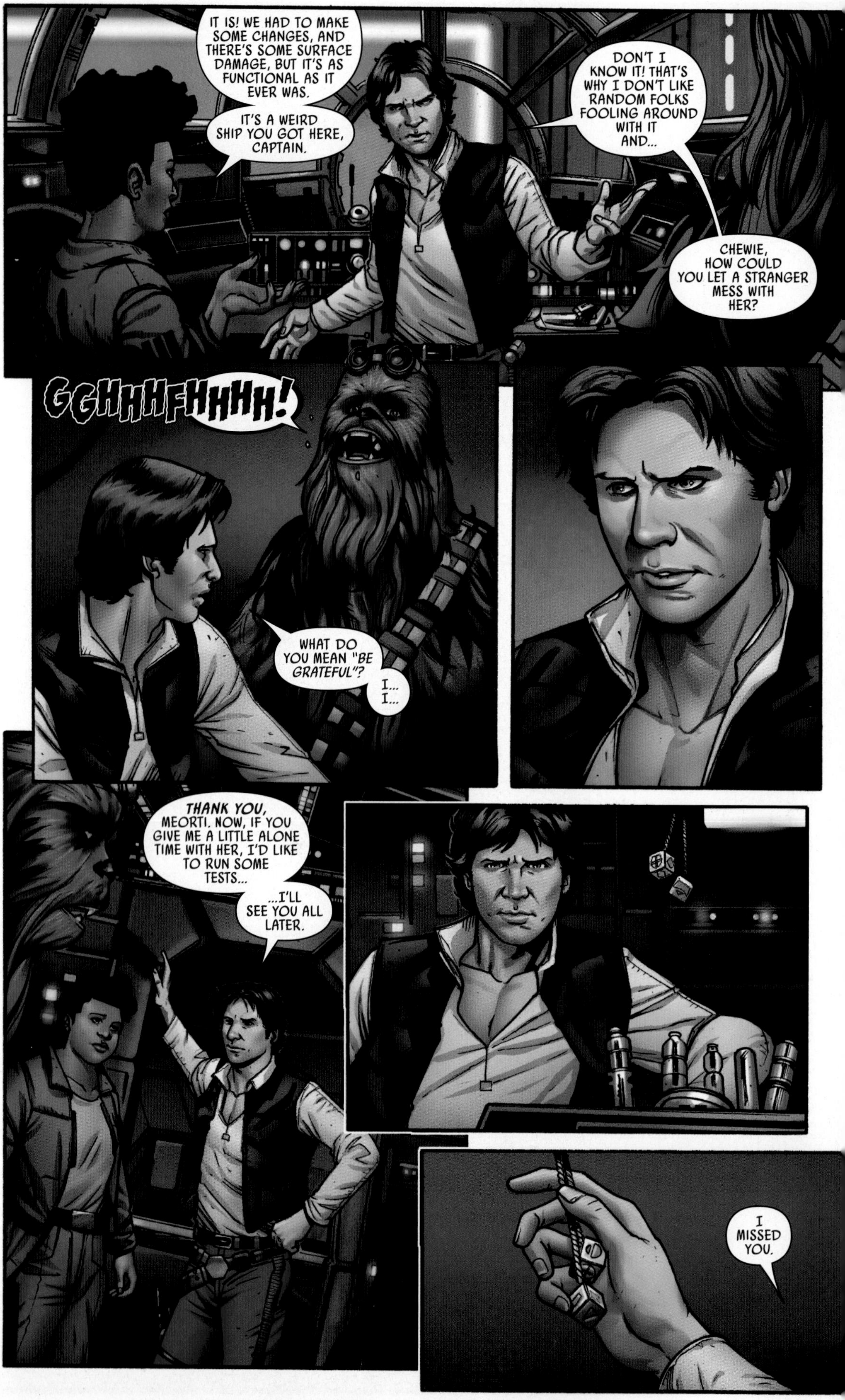
IT'S A WEIRD SHIP YOU GOT HERE, CAPTAIN.
IT IS! WE HAD TO MAKE SOME CHANGES, AND THERE'S SOME SURFACE DAMAGE, BUT IT'S AS FUNCTIONAL AS IT EVER WAS.
DON'T I KNOW IT! THAT'S WHY I DON'T LIKE RANDOM FOLKS FOOLING AROUND WITH IT AND...
CHEWIE, HOW COULD YOU LET A STRANGER MESS WITH HER?
GGHHHFHHHH!
WHAT DO YOU MEAN "BE GRATEFUL"?
I... I...
THANK YOU, MEORTI. NOW, IF YOU GIVE ME A LITTLE ALONE TIME WITH HER, I'D LIKE TO RUN SOME TESTS...
...I'LL SEE YOU ALL LATER.
I MISSED YOU.

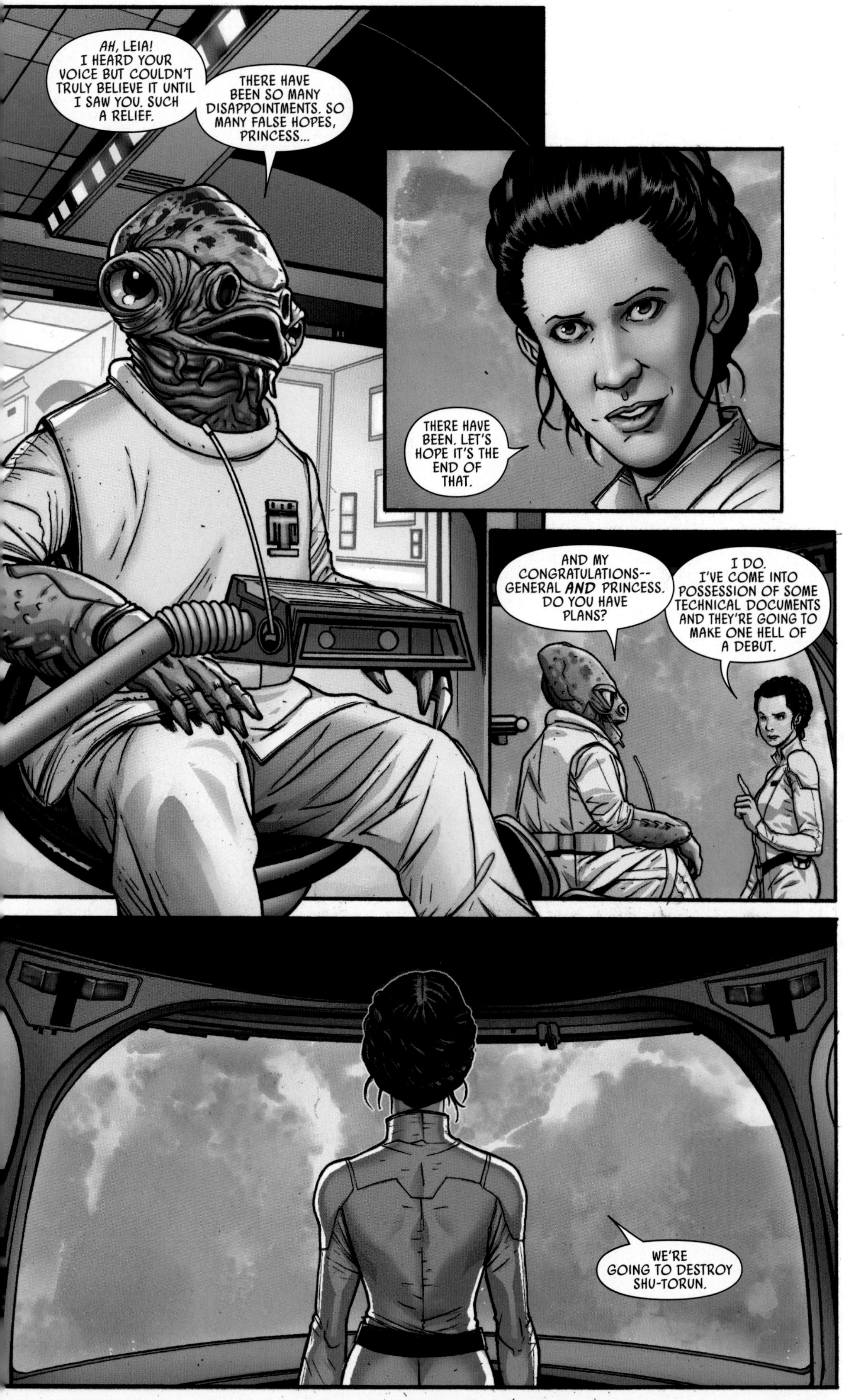
AH, LEIA! I HEARD YOUR VOICE BUT COULDN'T TRULY BELIEVE IT UNTIL I SAW YOU. SUCH A RELIEF.
THERE HAVE BEEN SO MANY DISAPPOINTMENTS. SO MANY FALSE HOPES, PRINCESS...
THERE HAVE BEEN. LET'S HOPE IT'S THE END OF THAT.
AND MY CONGRATULATIONS-- GENERAL *AND* PRINCESS. DO YOU HAVE PLANS?
I DO. I'VE COME INTO POSSESSION OF SOME TECHNICAL DOCUMENTS AND THEY'RE GOING TO MAKE ONE HELL OF A DEBUT.
WE'RE GOING TO DESTROY SHU-TORUN.

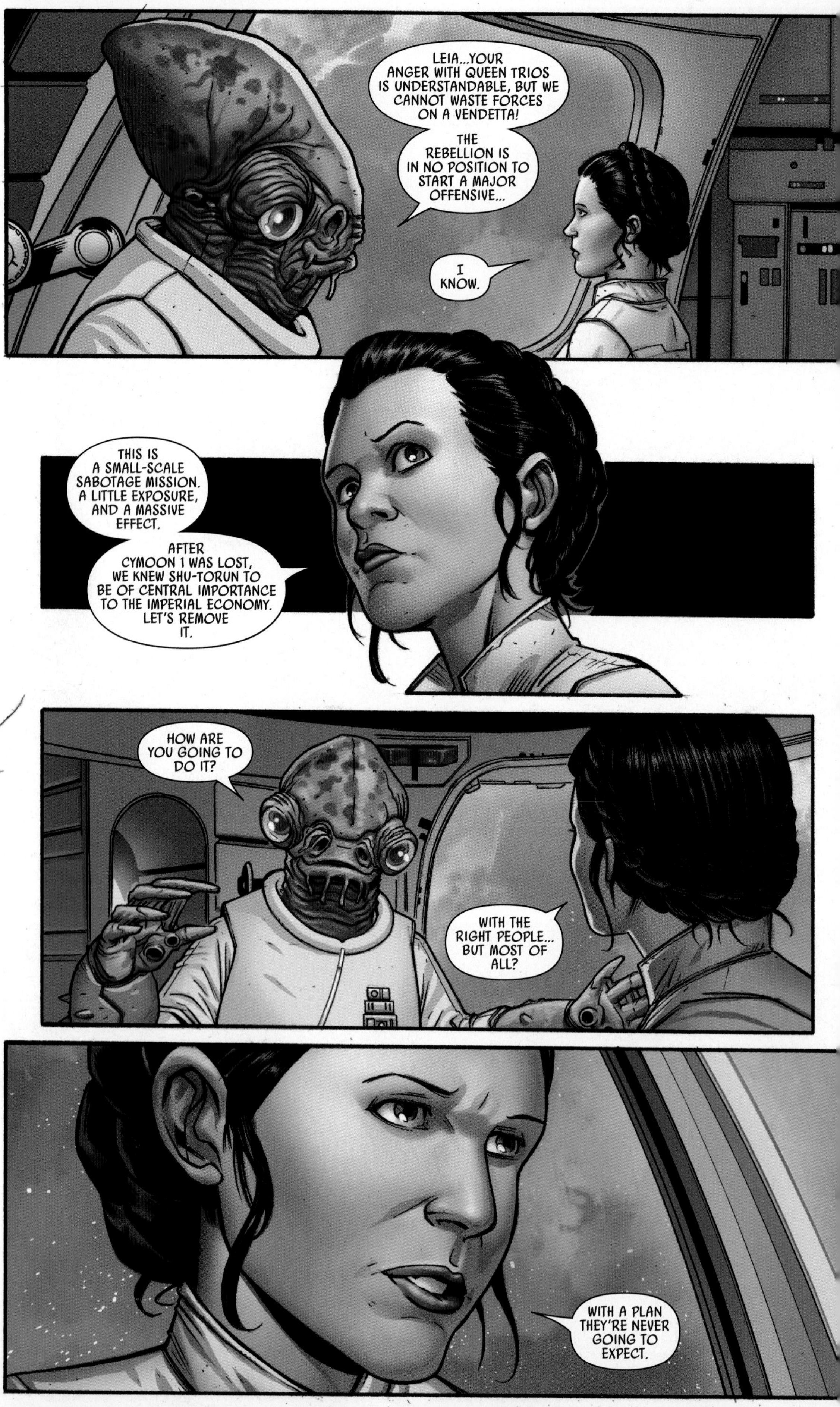
LEIA...YOUR ANGER WITH QUEEN TRIOS IS UNDERSTANDABLE, BUT WE CANNOT WASTE FORCES ON A VENDETTA!
THE REBELLION IS IN NO POSITION TO START A MAJOR OFFENSIVE...
I KNOW.
THIS IS A SMALL-SCALE SABOTAGE MISSION. A LITTLE EXPOSURE, AND A MASSIVE EFFECT.
AFTER CYMOON 1 WAS LOST, WE KNEW SHU-TORUN TO BE OF CENTRAL IMPORTANCE TO THE IMPERIAL ECONOMY. LET'S REMOVE IT.
HOW ARE YOU GOING TO DO IT?
WITH THE RIGHT PEOPLE... BUT MOST OF ALL?
WITH A PLAN THEY'RE NEVER GOING TO EXPECT.

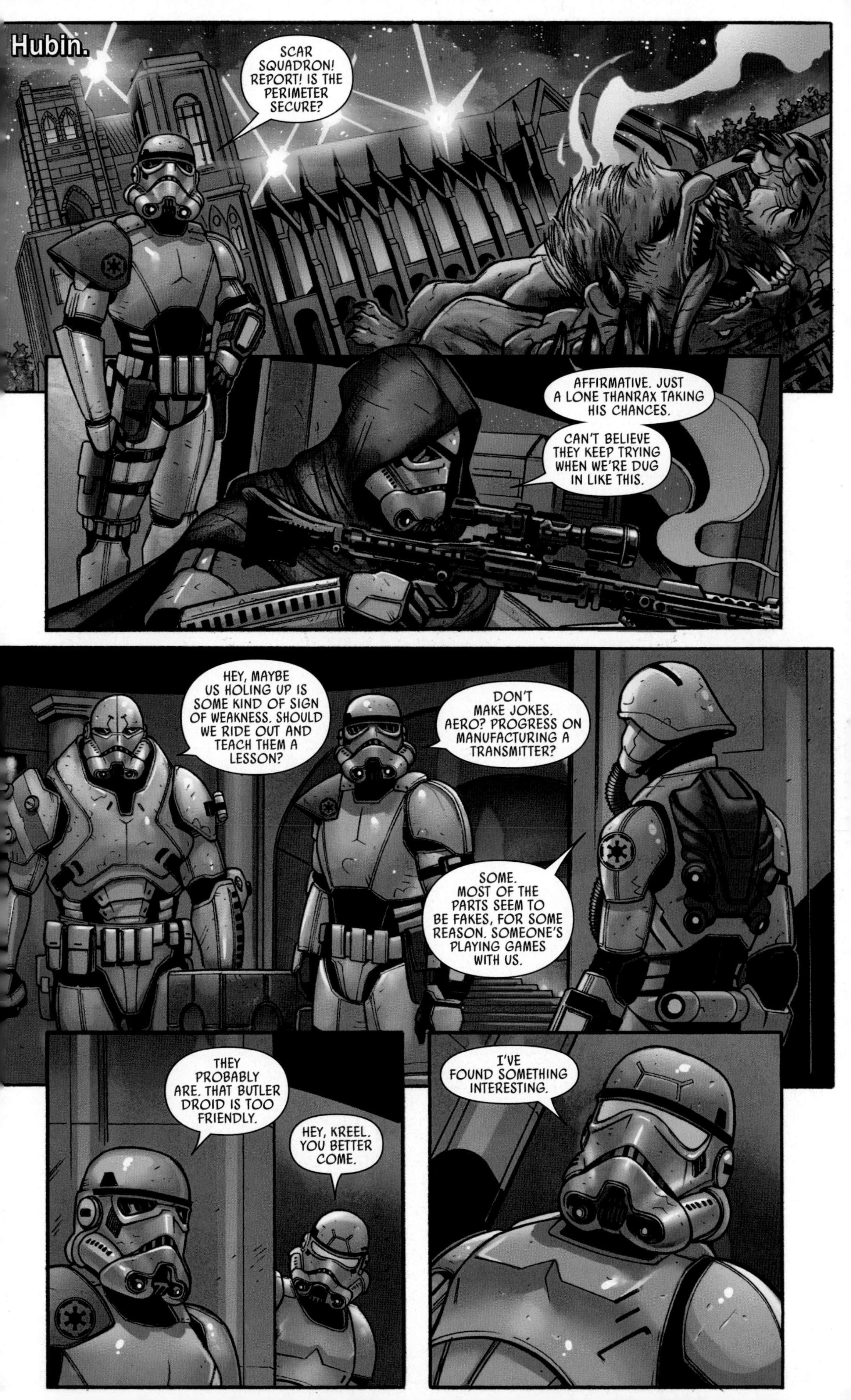
Hubin.
SCAR SQUADRON! REPORT! IS THE PERIMETER SECURE?
AFFIRMATIVE. JUST A LONE THANRAX TAKING HIS CHANCES.
CAN'T BELIEVE THEY KEEP TRYING WHEN WE'RE DUG IN LIKE THIS.
HEY, MAYBE US HOLING UP IS SOME KIND OF SIGN OF WEAKNESS. SHOULD WE RIDE OUT AND TEACH THEM A LESSON?
DON'T MAKE JOKES. AERO? PROGRESS ON MANUFACTURING A TRANSMITTER?
SOME. MOST OF THE PARTS SEEM TO BE FAKES, FOR SOME REASON. SOMEONE'S PLAYING GAMES WITH US.
THEY PROBABLY ARE. THAT BUTLER DROID IS TOO FRIENDLY.
HEY, KREEL. YOU BETTER COME.
I'VE FOUND SOMETHING INTERESTING.

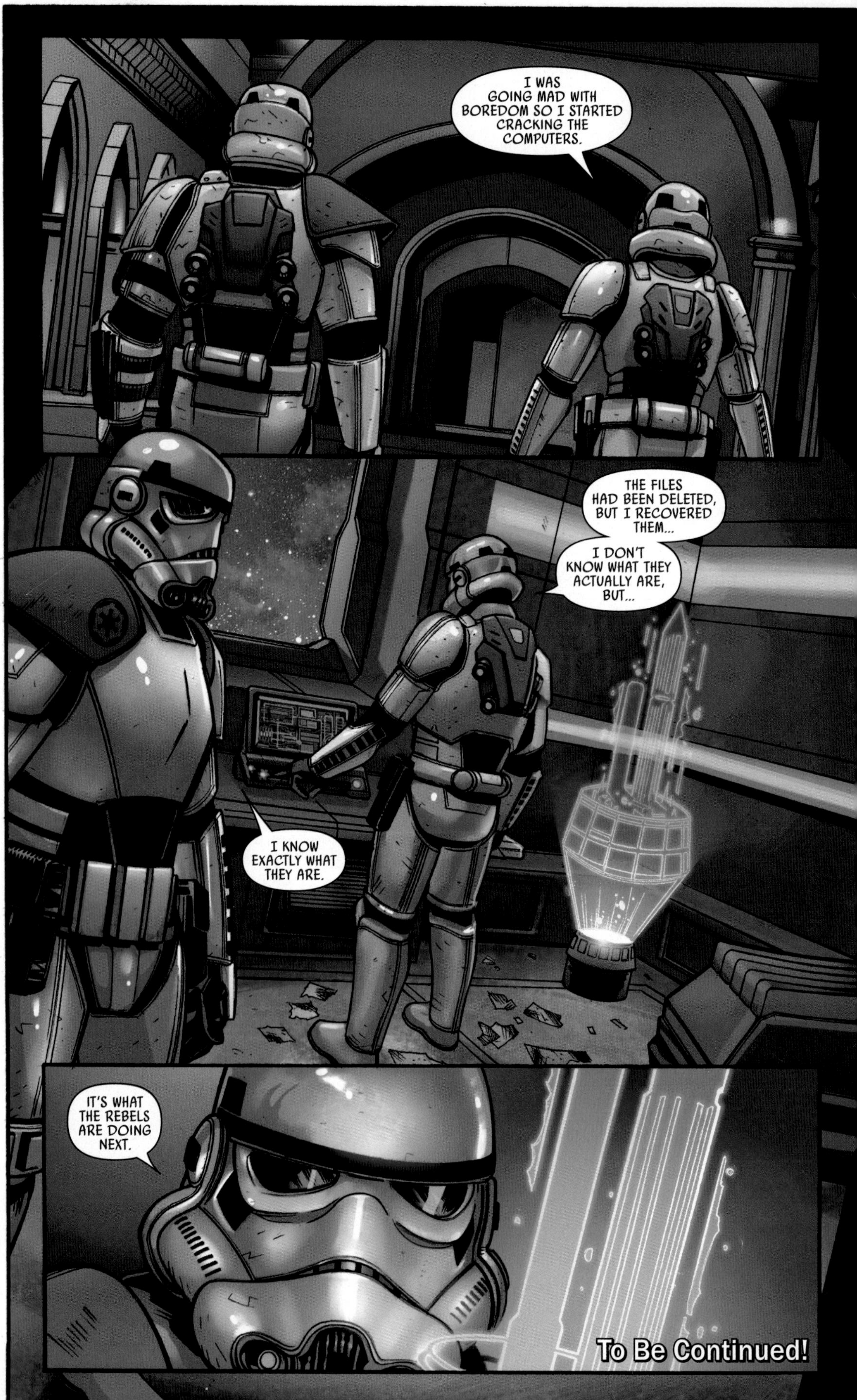
I WAS GOING MAD WITH BOREDOM SO I STARTED CRACKING THE COMPUTERS.
THE FILES HAD BEEN DELETED, BUT I RECOVERED THEM...
I DON'T KNOW WHAT THEY ACTUALLY ARE, BUT...
I KNOW EXACTLY WHAT THEY ARE.
IT'S WHAT THE REBELS ARE DOING NEXT.
To Be Continued!

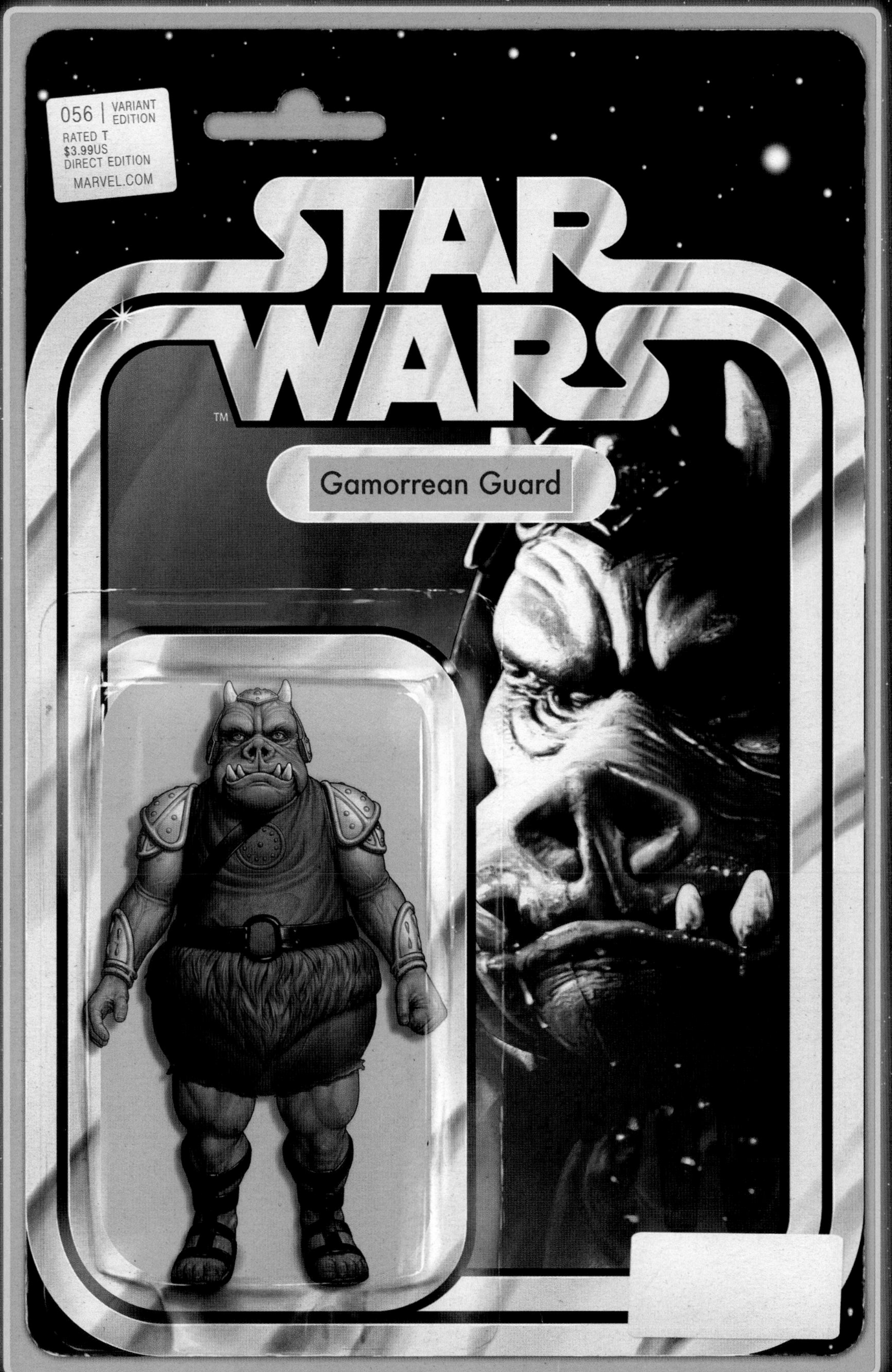
056 | VARIANT EDITION
RATED T
$3.99US
DIRECT EDITION
MARVEL.COM
STAR WARS™
Gamorrean Guard

***STAR WARS* 56 Action Figure Variant by**
JOHN TYLER CHRISTOPHER

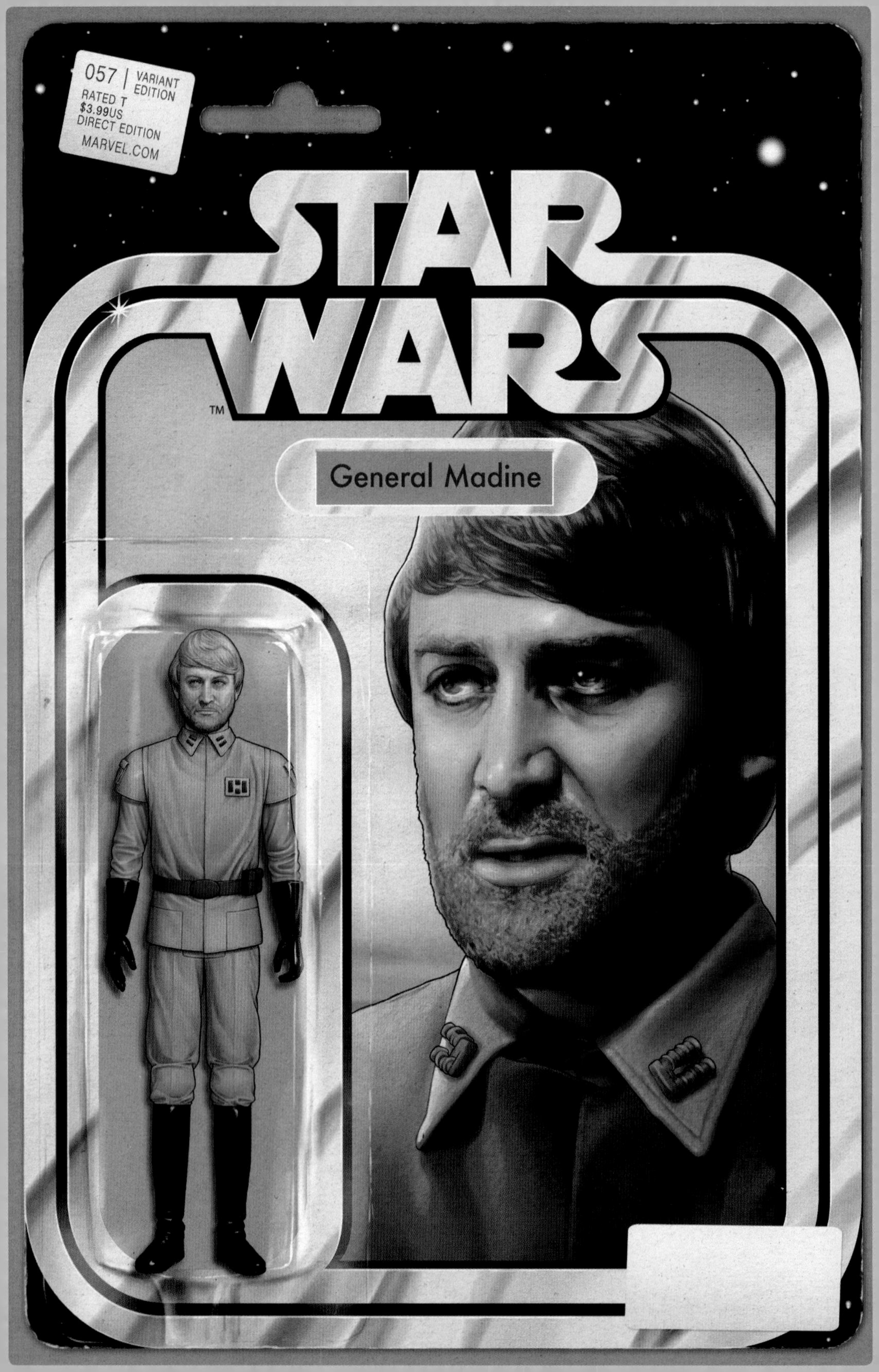

057 | VARIANT EDITION
RATED T
$3.99US
DIRECT EDITION
MARVEL.COM
STAR WARS™
General Madine

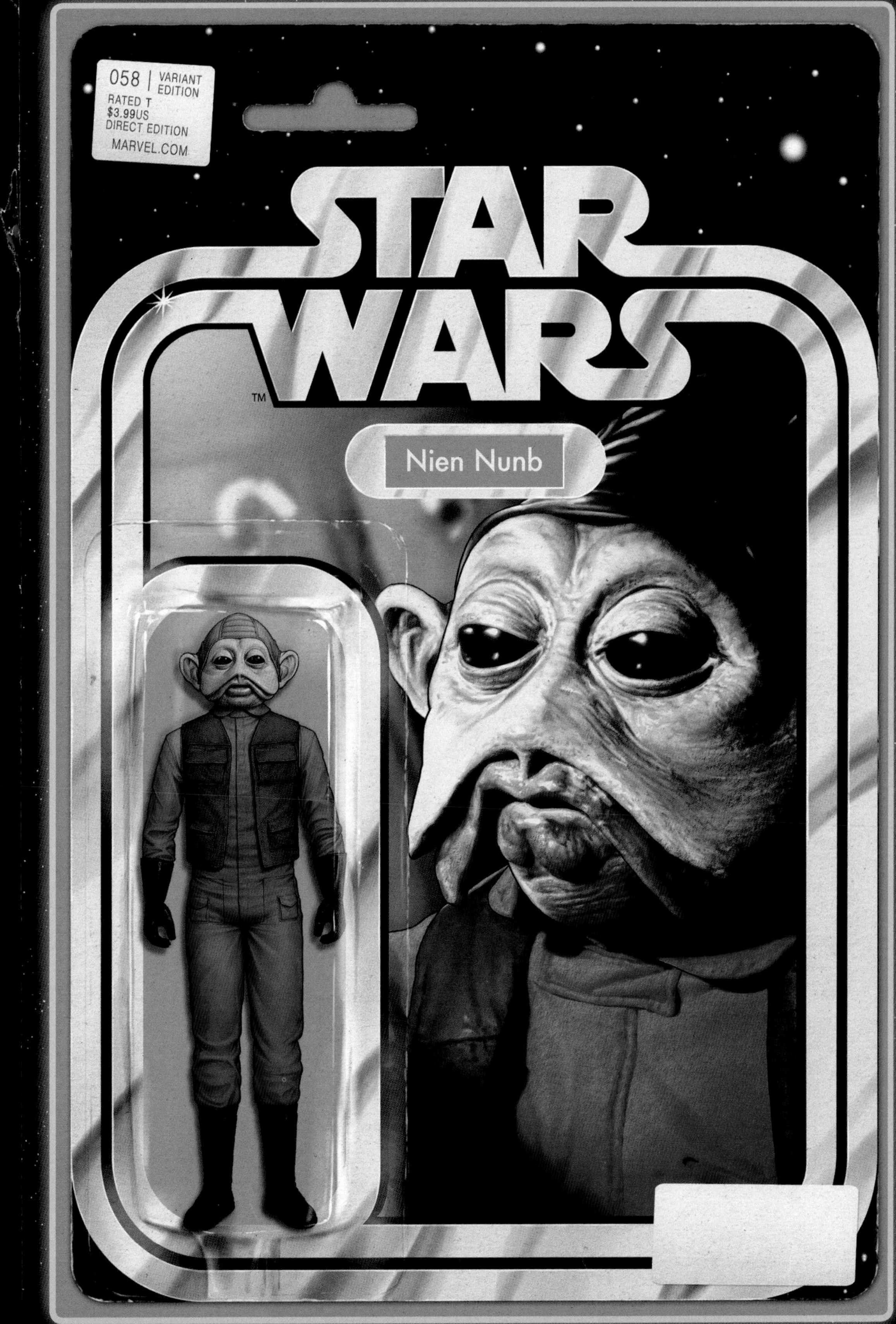
058 | VARIANT EDITION
RATED T
$3.99US
DIRECT EDITION
MARVEL.COM
STAR WARS
TM
Nien Nunb

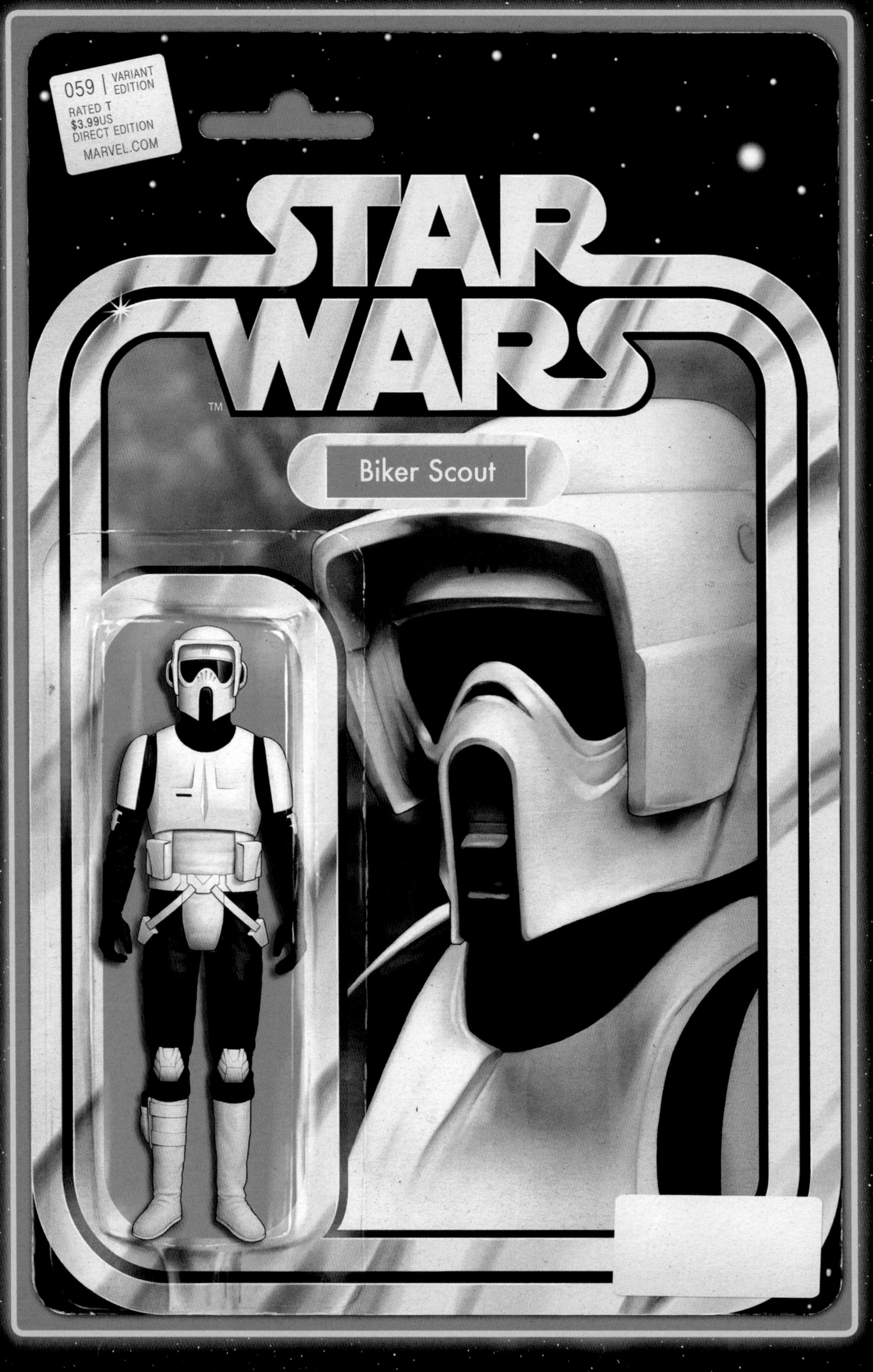
059 | VARIANT EDITION
RATED T
$3.99US
DIRECT EDITION
MARVEL.COM
STAR WARS
Biker Scout

***STAR WARS* 59 Action Figure Variant by**
JOHN TYLER CHRISTOPHER

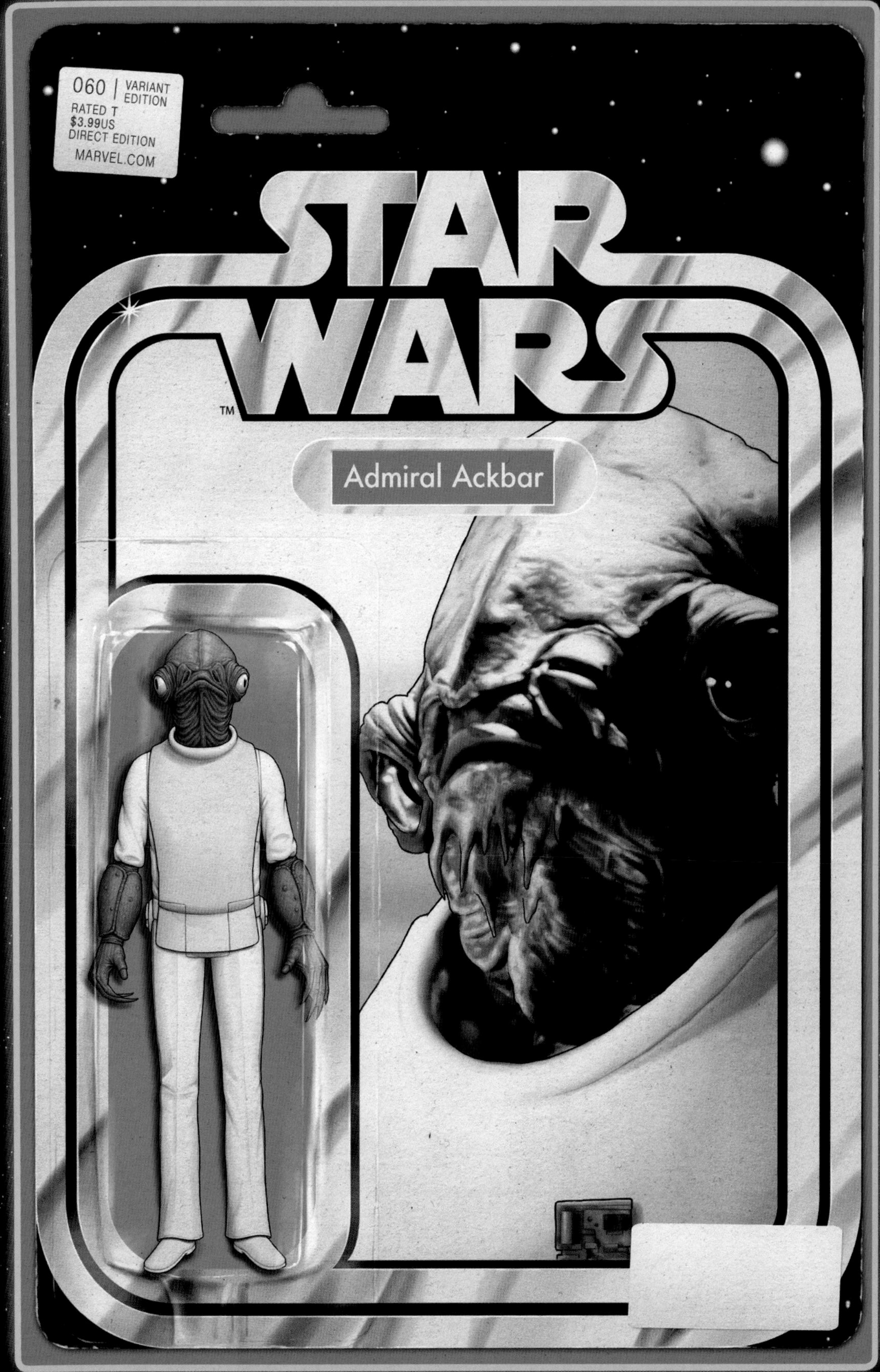
060 | VARIANT EDITION
RATED T
$3.99US
DIRECT EDITION
MARVEL.COM
STAR WARS
TM
Admiral Ackbar

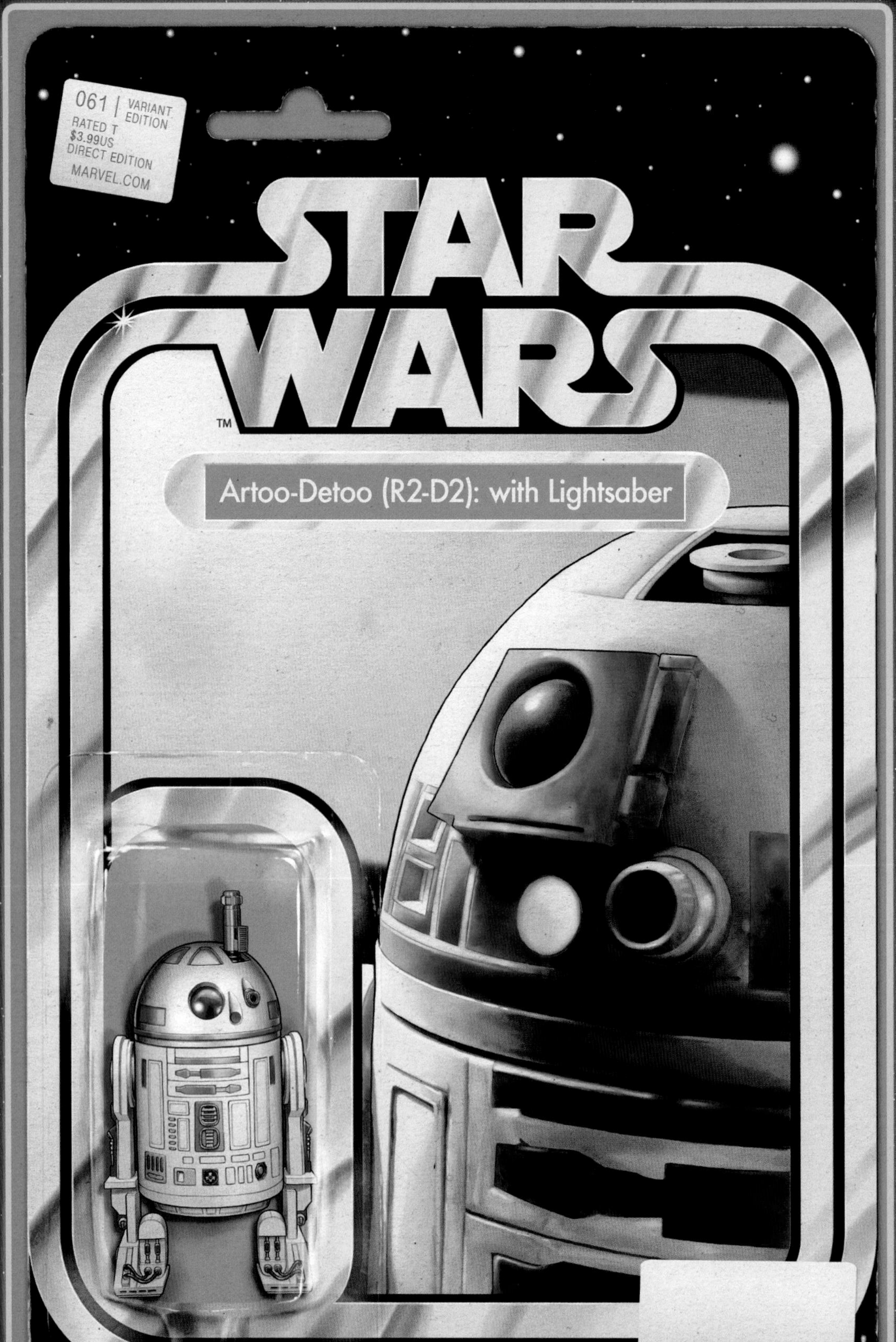

061 | VARIANT EDITION
RATED T
$3.99US
DIRECT EDITION
MARVEL.COM
STAR WARS
TM
Artoo-Detoo (R2-D2): with Lightsaber

AFTER BARELY ESCAPING DARTH VADER WITH HER LIFE, DOCTOR APHRA SETS OFF IN SEARCH OF RARE AND DEADLY ARTIFACTS!

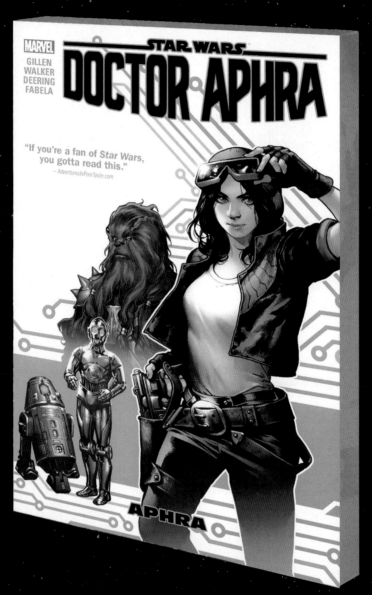

STAR WARS: DOCTOR APHRA VOL. 1 — APHRA TPB
978-1302906771

ON SALE NOW
AVAILABLE IN PRINT AND DIGITAL WHEREVER BOOKS ARE SOLD

TO FIND A COMIC SHOP NEAR YOU, VISIT COMICSHOPLOCATOR.COM

YOU LOVE COLORING.
WE KNOW.

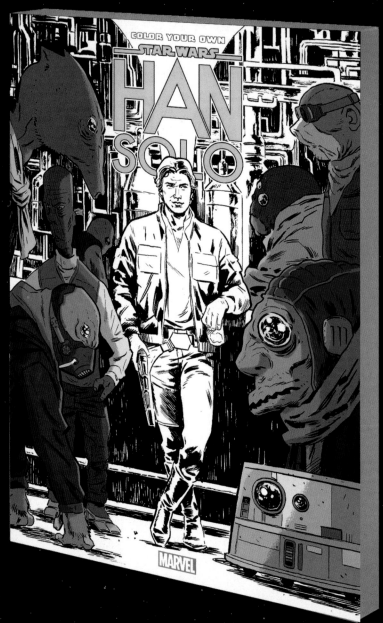

COLOR YOUR OWN *STAR WARS*: HAN SOLO
978-1302912093

ON SALE NOW
AVAILABLE IN PRINT AND DIGITAL WHEREVER BOOKS ARE SOLD

TO FIND A COMIC SHOP NEAR YOU, VISIT COMICSHOPLOCATOR.COM

HAN AND CHEWIE IN A RACE AGAINST TIME, THE EMPIRE AND THE FASTEST SHIPS IN THE GALAXY!

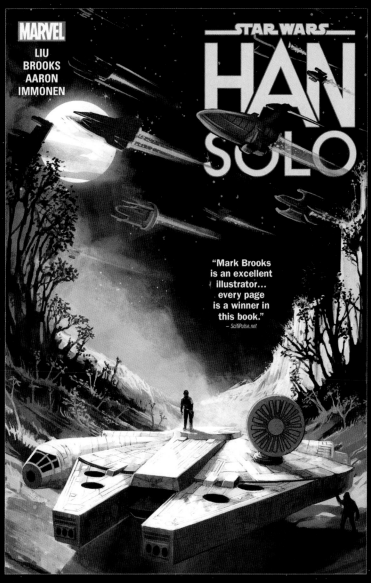

STAR WARS: HAN SOLO HC
978-1302912109

ON SALE NOW
AVAILABLE IN PRINT AND DIGITAL WHEREVER BOOKS ARE SOLD

TO FIND A COMIC SHOP NEAR YOU, VISIT COMICSHOPLOCATOR.COM

SENSATIONAL *STAR WARS* ARTWORK RETELLING THE STORY OF *A NEW HOPE!*

STAR WARS: A NEW HOPE — THE 40TH ANNIVERSARY HC
978-1302911287

ON SALE NOW
AVAILABLE IN PRINT AND DIGITAL WHEREVER BOOKS ARE SOLD

TO FIND A COMIC SHOP NEAR YOU, VISIT COMICSHOPLOCATOR.COM

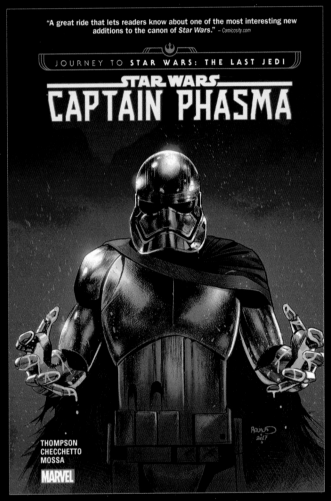

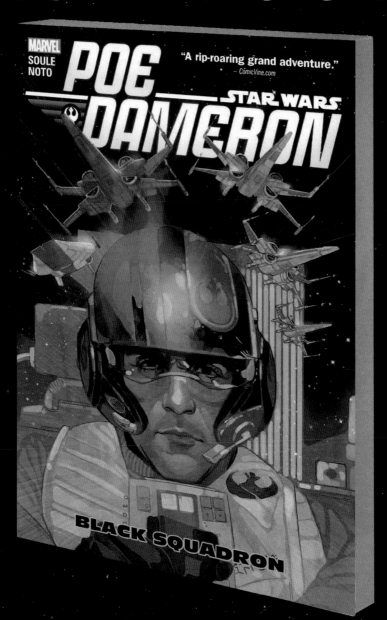

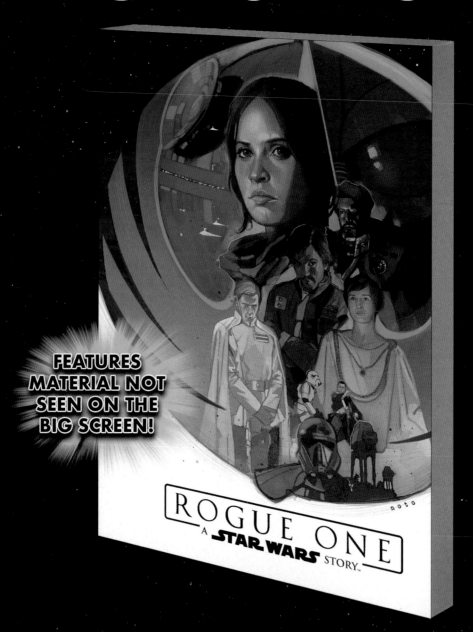